The Frankfurt Kitchen

*Forty-One Stories
about Growing Up in
Post-World War II West Germany*

Heidi Laird

Fulton Books, Inc.
Meadville, PA

Published by Fulton Books 2021

Cover art by Heidi Laird

ISBN 978-1-64952-974-9 (paperback)
ISBN 978-1-64952-975-6 (digital)

Printed in the United States of America

To Julia and Riley,

And all the other grandchildren

Of immigrants

CONTENTS

ACKNOWLEDGEMENTS

Over the years, as I told stories from my childhood to entertain family and friends during long car rides, around campfires, and at all kinds of social gatherings, I often heard: "You have got to write this down!" Finally I did. It took much longer than I ever thought it would, it left me alternately exhilarated and exhausted, and it showed me, as if I didn't already know, how sharply childhood experiences sculpt our character, and how deeply they carve themselves into our souls.

I want all who urged me to write this book to know that I would not have written it without their encouragement and enthusiasm for the project. On the technical front, I learned how to put together a proper book from my loyal and patient publication guide, Shannon Kuno.

On the home front, my husband Ted Knipe provided just the right mix of good advice, objective observations, and enduring emotional support for this sometimes harrowing venture into the realm of remembering.

My thanks to all!

1

The Jeep Driver

If I wanted to make a movie of my life, the first scene would show my mother, youthful and resolute, with soft hands and vestiges of former elegance, and me, almost eight years old and unafraid, standing in the driving rain of a cold April downpour by the side of the on-ramp to the Autobahn between Heidelberg and Frankfurt, hitchhiking. For a population of war survivors challenged daily by the extreme scarcity of basic resources, hitchhiking had become as normal as standing on a platform, waiting for an unreliable train. Eventually it would come, and you could get on.

It was 1949, and my mother, Vera Schaefer, was on one of her trips to visit my father, Harry Saarbach, in Frankfurt, about an hour's drive from Heidelberg. I was with her, as usual, because she took me along wherever she went, maybe because I was her oldest child or because I was her only daughter, an easy and familiar companion. We were drenched, teeth chattering, chilled to the bone, but Vera said that there was an advantage to our dire situation because in this weather, we had no competition from other hitchhikers on this on-ramp, of whom there would have been many on a sunny day. Of course we were extremely grateful when a U.S. Army Jeep stopped for us, and a lean, fit man in an American military uniform came running from behind his vehicle under a dripping tarp, pulled us under the tarp with him, and opened the passenger door, behind which a person was trying to get out of the way so that the back of the seat could be folded forward and we could climb into the rear of the jeep.

When the jeep was moving again, I noticed that the person who had settled back into the front passenger seat was a very pretty young German woman, who smiled at me with an air of beguiling benevolence and then turned to Vera to ask where we were going. She said that she and her boyfriend were also going to Frankfurt and that they would be happy to drop us off at the location where Harry worked. Vera and the soldier's girlfriend continued their conversation across the back of the passenger seat, in German, with occasional questions and comments—in English—by the kind and generous American who had treated us with so much personal warmth and concern for our safety.

I observed this resourceful man with his crew cut and weathered face as he navigated his jeep through the driving rain, peering through the small upside-down cone on his windshield, which the screeching and whimpering windshield wipers managed to keep clear, while he clutched the handle of the vibrating gearshift with his right hand, calming and reassuring the engine as it bucked and bolted through the deluge. I noticed that he was doing all this while apologizing for the leaks in the jeep's canvas roof and sides, through which heavy drops and rivulets freely entered the interior of this brave little warrior machine. Trying to sort out this adventure in my mind, I sensed that the soldier had spontaneously acted in good faith on his impulse to get a woman and her child out of a punishing rainstorm, disregarding the fact that, as a member of the military force occupying the country of a former enemy, he had broken the unwritten but well-understood rule that transporting unauthorized German civilians in U.S. military vehicles was prohibited.

In the course of this trip, I came to see the jeep driver with my almost eight-year-old eyes as an emissary from the America, which had led the Allies to victory over the Nazi terror. These Americans were generous, well-meaning people who were bringing peace, feeding starving populations, freeing prisoners, and liberating countries from dictatorships. This early adventure of riding in the American jeep set the idealizing tone for my numerous experiences with Americans, which would follow our eventual move to Frankfurt.

What had probably nurtured my early perception of the Americans as a generous people was the ongoing drama of the Berlin Airlift, described daily on the radio and in the movie theaters' news-reels, and followed with wonder and disbelief by the German population, including my parents. At the time of my memorable jeep ride, the Berlin Airlift was approaching the end of its improbable ten-month mission to supply the 2.2 million trapped people of West Berlin with absolutely everything they needed to survive the Soviet blockade imposed on them in June 1948. For 322 days, the newspapers and radio broadcasts chronicled the unimaginable feat of one airplane after another landing in Berlin every sixty to ninety seconds, day and night, delivering all the food, medications, dry goods, hardware for machinery repair, shoes and clothing, firewood, and coal, which the besieged population needed during the long blockade. In all, the Berlin Airlift had transported almost two million tons of provisions to the people in the encircled city by the time the blockade was lifted on May 12, 1949. After its successful conclusion, the Airlift quickly became a fabled event and joined the story of the Invasion of Normandy in the record of the defining moments of twentieth-century history. To honor the memory of the seventy-nine people who lost their lives in Airlift-related accidents, a monument greeted travelers for many years as they passed through the Berlin Tempelhof Airport before it ceased operations.

A smaller version of the Airlift was the CARE program, founded in 1945 to provide relief to survivors of World War II. CARE sent hundreds of thousands of packages to individual families, including mine, during the famine years after the war. These cardboard boxes, approximately 20" × 16" × 18", filled with survival foods like canned meats, evaporated milk, shortening, flour, powdered eggs, and deeply appreciated surprise gifts such as a bar of fragrant soap or a chocolate bar, items which, in the midst of famine, were received with a feeling of reverence, soon followed by fear that this treasure could be stolen if not quickly hidden away in a safe place. One of our CARE packages was, in fact, plundered by a thief who had climbed through a first-floor open kitchen window in broad daylight. I still hear Vera's angry cries when she discovered the theft.

A vehement discussion that a curious child could have overheard in the years after the war was about the Marshall Plan, America's iconic program to restart the ruined economies of Western Europe, including that of the hated and now destroyed Germany. The Marshall Plan was at first rejected by people in Congress who wanted to see Germany plowed under and turned into an agrarian society, which would never again start a war. This was the vision of the secretary of the treasury, Henry Morgenthau. Advocates of the Marshall Plan countered that rebuilding the German industry and helping the Germans create a new version of their first, unsuccessful attempt at democracy would enable them to build a strong economy and produce a rich return on the U.S. investment. The goal of this gigantic project was to make the war zones livable again by removing the mountains of rubble and debris in the cities, finding and defusing the thousands of undetonated bombs and live ammunition that lay beneath the ruins and putting people to work under the direction of the U.S. military government. This initial cleanup would create the environment in which the dead German economy could come back to life and form the basis for future prosperity, security, and political stability in Western Europe. It was argued that in addition to the massive return on the U.S. investment, a grateful former enemy would become an important trade partner and loyal ally in the shifting power dynamics of the emerging Cold War.

As Germany, Italy, France, and England rebuilt their economies, they could afford to start buying America's products and, along with buying its products, imported its culture. As it turned out, the Marshall Plan succeeded beyond anyone's expectations. The success of the Marshall Plan led to the unquestioned acceptance of American political and cultural leadership and moral authority in the postwar world. While I was obviously too young to participate in the conversations going on around me in my childhood, the changes I saw in my immediate environment, from ruined cityscapes to new construction everywhere, from famine and empty store shelves to a reliable food supply, shaped my perceptions and gave me guidelines for forming opinions about what was normal and what was not.

What I later read in history books was that, one month after the jeep ride, on May 23, 1949, in a giant step away from the World War II catastrophe and into an uncertain future, Germany's first postwar government was officially recognized by the U.S., France, and England, who withdrew their military governments from the three zones into which they had divided western Germany at the end of the war. The Soviet Union had opposed the formation of an autonomous West Germany, and Stalin denounced this move. If I don't remember any discussion at home about the momentous ceremony of swearing in the first chancellor of West Germany, Konrad Adenauer, it is probably because its significance remained abstract and nebulous to me and possibly also because it caused little debate in the general population, which was preoccupied by its struggles with extreme housing shortages, scarce resources, and an infrastructure still largely in ruins.

Also happening without much fanfare was the movement in the Western European countries, the new West Germany among them, to appoint the United States as the universal peacekeeper and, still traumatized by the war, to work toward a European Union, in which any future war would be unthinkable. The United States was entrusted with the power to organize the defense of Europe with the establishment of the North Atlantic Treaty Organization in 1949. The treaty included the provision that if one of its members were to be attacked, all the other parties to the treaty would come to that member's defense.

As it turned out, the only time that a NATO member was attacked was on September 11, 2001, and the NATO allies promptly stepped forward and joined the United States in its war in Afghanistan.

How all those historic events fit together was obviously something that I only understood years later, but it was easy for a child at that time to absorb a sense of alarm and pessimism amid the building boom and feverish business activity, usually from overhearing adult conversations about the atom bomb, guided missiles, Soviet aggression, and the Cold War. Making that point more directly were comments such as the one made by Harry when Vera complained to him about some punishable mischief by my younger brothers, Stefan and

René: "Let the boys have their fun. They won't have a future anyway when the Russians come."

I am sure that I did not reflect much on geopolitics as I grew up in postwar Frankfurt, where the American military continued to have high visibility, from the U.S. military personnel and their camouflaged vehicles on the streets to the large station wagons from Detroit, the PX shopping centers, the Armed Forces Network radio stations, the *Stars and Stripes* newspaper, and the American playhouse, where amateur actors, recruited from military families performed plays by Arthur Miller and Thornton Wilder's *Our Town*. And there was—unbelievably—the Seventh Army Symphony Orchestra, consisting of young American musicians who were serving their obligatory two years in the military as goodwill ambassadors in the country of their former enemies. These musicians now found themselves in the land where much of their classical repertoire had been composed, and I have often wondered how they balanced their roles as soldiers occupying the country whose culture produced so much of the music they surely loved.

What I came to sense rather early in my years of growing up in the land of the United States Seventh Army was that America meant so much more than military dominance. America meant free elections and the rule of law, scientific research and technology, popular culture, and ethnic diversity; it meant support for freedom of speech and artistic expression, it meant all the ideas which would later be called the liberal world order, and it meant being the first responders in global crises. This is what built America's enormous *soft power* and made the United States a spectacular country in the eyes of people all over the world, who had known only kings and tyrants.

This exposure to American life and the social and cultural climate of the time inevitably shaped my thinking and influenced the plans I made for my life. It also nurtured my belief that the democratic values that the United States represented were taking a firm hold all over the world and would in the future only become stronger. I believed predictions that more and more countries would be governed by the rule of law, and the rule of executive order by dictators was becoming a thing of the past.

As I write this seventy years later, in the year 2019, I recognize how distant this idealized vision of America has become, and I wonder if it will be possible to say seventy years from now that the principles and values of America's founders have survived.

2

Sebastopol

Vera's bold initiative as a hitchhiker on an Autobahn on-ramp was a small feat when compared to other arduous journeys that she had taken in the previous ten years of her life. She had met Harry, a Jew, in 1937, at a time when it was no longer possible to pretend not to be frightened by the growing Nazi hate campaigns and systematic aggression against Jews, and they fled together to Paris, expecting that this move would keep Harry safe.

When Hitler invaded France and Paris fell in June 1940, the quickly installed Vichy regime eagerly collaborated with the occupying Nazi forces and immediately detained all foreign nationals in internment camps. Vera was separated from Harry and found herself within days on a detainee transport back to Germany, where her father, Karl Schaefer, agreed to let her live in his large house in Mannheim, which she had sworn she would never set foot in again after her last angry confrontation with him. Harry, when urged many years later to tell the story of how he made his way back to Germany, said that he had found a way to escape from the internment camp by impersonating a German military driver summoned to fill in for a regular army driver who had not shown up as scheduled. Harry was assigned a truck and given the necessary travel documents to pass through all the Nazi checkpoints up to the German border, where he abandoned the truck and "went underground."

Harry never talked about his "underground" years, but members of Vera's family still tell stories about the times when he would unexpectedly show up for short visits before disappearing again, usually before dawn. Harry turned up in Mannheim several times

to visit Vera at her father's house, and there is an eyewitness ...
from Vera's niece, Rosie, that Harry even showed up in Mannheim
shortly after I was born in July 1941 to meet his first child. Rosie
remembered that Harry's visit was fairly brief and that she was very
disappointed when she found that he had disappeared again after a
few days, because, as she wistfully recalled sixty years later, she had
a teenage crush on him and had looked forward to spending more
time near him.

Vera never said whether she knew more about Harry's where-
abouts than she let on. What can be pieced together is that Harry,
later in 1941, took an action so improbable that I found it hard
to believe when I heard about it years later. He signed up for the
German *Wehrmacht* under his legal name and checked the box,
which indicated that he was of Aryan descent. Many years after the
war, unsubstantiated reports suggested that hundreds, and possibly
over a thousand, Jews had taken this wrenching step at the time in
the hope that, as the war ground on, Hitler's military would need
men to replace the soldiers who had fallen and would not have the
time or the resources to investigate false claims of Aryan descent on
enlistment papers.

Harry's enlistment landed him in a battalion which took part in
the long siege of Sebastopol in 1942. After a grueling troop transport
to the Crimean peninsula in southern Ukraine, much of it on foot,
Harry's battalion was dug in—presumably for several months—waiting for orders and training to storm Sebastopol. Harry often told the
story how he and his hungry comrades would take their minds off
their miserable circumstances by outdoing one another in describing
in minute detail the ten-course meals they had once eaten, or wished
they had eaten, or planned to eat if they ever got back home.

While Harry was fantasizing about gourmet meals in a ditch
on the periphery of Sebastopol, the methodical Nazi persecution
machine caught up with him, and he was arrested, transported back
to Germany, and scheduled to be tried for the crime of having dis-
honored the Führer's army through his false claim of being Aryan.
This arrest most likely saved Harry's life. After the war, Harry found
his old sergeant, who told him that the two were the only survivors

of their battalion, which had perished in the battle to take Sebastopol in July 1942, when I was one year old.

Although Harry never reached Sebastopol, or maybe because he had never reached Sebastopol, this city became a place in his mind, and it sculpted his identity, providing him with justification for his subsequent aversion to any form of walking and outdoor activity and lending him the aura of a witness to a legendary military campaign. Sebastopol, for Harry, meant escape from persecution at home and then escape from death on the battlefield. For me, this city with the alluring, melodious name came to stand for an aspect of Harry's persona, which I eventually accepted as unknowable, unreachable, in full view yet distant.

Harry always evaded questions about how he managed to stay alive after Sebastopol. It seems that Harry's mother, my French grandmother, Antoinette, long divorced from Harry's father, Willy, overcame her intense embarrassment and made a formal declaration before a court official that Harry was not Willy's son but the result of an extramarital affair. Antoinette was a timid, easily panicked woman who had grown up in a Catholic convent in France. The thought that she would be branded as an adulterous wife mortified her, but she bravely gave her testimony because she adored her son and only child. Her declaration was not accepted at face value but disputed by the Nazi authorities, who required that Antoinette appear at numerous hearings to repeat her claim.

It seems that Antoinette's and Harry's court dates were cancelled more than once because the increasing frequency of Allied bombing raids on German cities produced the intended results of disrupting civilian life and the functioning of the Nazi administrative state. According to one story circulating in the extended family, the jail where Harry was being held at one point and the courthouse where the legal documents of his case were stored were bombed, creating the chaotic, but fortunate, circumstances which allowed him to stay on the run.

3

Sirens

The same bombing raids on German cities, which helped Harry as a fugitive to avoid recapture, were numbing the populations of those cities into resignation that they would be spending most nights in their neighborhood air raid shelters. I still see myself sitting on one of the long wooden benches pushed hard up against the concrete walls, looking at the old woman hunched up next to me who was holding her rosary while she silently prayed. Somebody had a dim flashlight with a red lens, and in this red light, I was able to look around the dank, windowless bunker with its massive walls pressing in on the people who were seeking shelter there from the bombs falling outside. The red lenses were required to maintain a complete blackout in German cities at nighttime, intended to disorient the Allied bombers as they tried to locate their targets in the dark landscape. I don't remember seeing anyone sleep during those hours of waiting for the signal that the danger was over and that everyone could now go back home.

There were so many nights when the air raid sirens started their piercing wail just as it was time to go to bed that some people were tempted to ignore yet another siren going off, although they knew that they were required to go to their assigned bomb shelters if the alarm was sounded. For this reason, the mood in the bunkers was not always raw fear but a queasy uncertainty whether this night was just another nuisance event or if this night would bring the major destruction that other cities had already experienced.

I was much too young to grasp the danger of the situation, but I often heard Vera tell the story years later how, after one of the most extensive air raids on Mannheim, where we lived at my grandfather's house, we returned to the house, Hildastrasse 1, to find that it had taken a direct hit and was completely destroyed, along with much of the city. According to Vera's description, I took note of the fact that the house was a smoking ruin, asked about a few toys that were now gone, and then seemed ready to move on. I have often wondered if this reaction, of which I have no memory, was a very young child's first intimation of a state of consciousness which my cousin Rosie once described to me. She was twenty years old when she found herself in a refugee trek along the coast of the Baltic Sea, escaping from Berlin in the final days of the war on the only route left open, mostly on foot but with occasional lifts on various vehicles including a horse-drawn wagon. She noticed at one point that the driver sitting next to her and holding the reins was slumped over and had fallen asleep, so she took the reins and found herself, in her words, "in an indescribable state of mind, having lost everything, connected to the tired, laboring horse through the motion pulsing in the reins, the ocean to my right, the vast sky above, and the unknown ahead. The amazing thing was that I felt no fear, but a strange comforting sensation of being one with everything around me, and trusting that I would be alright."

On the day after my grandfather's house was bombed out, he and his housekeeper, Fräulein Lenkewitz, daughter of one of his loyal Dutch barge captains, moved to a country house at the end of a dirt road on the edge of a forest near a hamlet named Wahlen in the Odenwald Mountains. A little train consisting of an ancient steam locomotive and two creaking coaches from the days of the Kaiser arrived in Wahlen once a day, blew its whistle, and released an extra-large cloud of black smoke, while five or six passengers disembarked, and the local mailman retrieved the mail pouch from the locomotive's cab. The locomotive then had to maneuver itself by way of a turnout in the track to the other end of the train, and after a renewed sequence of black smoke, shrieking whistles, and hissing steam, the train would depart, retracing its course back to Weinheim, leaving Wahlen once again to its brooding remoteness, suspended between forest idyll and isolated backwater.

It was common knowledge that Mannheim's many industrial sites housed manufacturing plants whose products were critically important for the war effort, and my grandfather had made preparations for the day when his house would be bombed. He had arranged to store his large art collection of nineteenth-century Romantic landscape paintings and reproductions of classical Greek sculptures in the barn of a farmer in Wahlen. Vera's Steinway grand piano was also stored there, reportedly in a stable where the cows kept the temperature warm enough in the winter for the sensitive black lacquered behemoth.

Vera did not join her father in Wahlen. Instead, she decided that she would take on the dangers and disruptions of a journey through major industrial regions of Germany—the targets of daily bombing raids—to Berlin, where her sister Ilse lived with her husband, Richard, and their children. The family lived in a spacious house on the grounds of the Bernau Hospital on the outskirts of Berlin, where Richard was the medical director. Vera had by then given birth to my younger brother, Stefan, who was now six months old. No one ever whispered a doubt that Stefan was Harry's child, which speaks to the commonly known and accepted regularity of Harry's visits at the house of his father-in-law, with whom he got along much better than Vera did.

4

Early Distances

Vera and Ilse, the daughters of Karl and Else Schaefer, were born seven years apart. For seven years, Ilse had been an only child, a pretty girl with her mother's oval face, rich brown hair, and a beautiful singing voice. Ilse was said to have been very close to her father and knew how to soothe his irascible temperament, which had alienated the sensitive soul of his warm and kindhearted wife by the time a second child arrived.

The second child, Vera, was not breathing when she was born. Dramatic efforts by an experienced doctor were successful in reviving the newborn, who finally started the wail that her mother had prayed to hear. Vera cited reports by family members that she had been a fussy and difficult baby in her first year and required her mother's constant attention. Whether this was medically indicated or evolved as a response to the baby's persistent demand to be held remained unclear, but it seems plausible that the mother's gratitude that her child had lived and the child's expectation of uninterrupted attention created a situation in which the child's older sister could feel overlooked and no longer loved.

This early sibling dynamic shaped the sisters' relationship throughout their lives. Ilse's attachment to her father became even stronger as she watched her mother remain preoccupied with the needs of the eventually thriving little sister. The age difference between the sisters contributed to their pattern of living parallel and separate lives, with their different perceptions of their parents and, as it later turned out, of the world around them.

Ilse loved her father, who was often out of town on business, and she remained distant from her mother. Vera, by contrast, clung to her mother and feared her father. She would tell the story of how one night, while her mother was at one of the social events that her father despised, her father had determined to put an end, "once and for all," to the long nightly bedtime ritual which Else and little Vera enjoyed so much. He stepped into Vera's room, told her that it was time to go to sleep, and, with a stern "Good night," turned off the light, closed the door, and left Vera screaming and wailing so desperately that she started to choke just as Else was coming home. Vera always said that she had hated her father ever since that very early traumatizing experience.

This incident captures the essence of Karl Schaefer and Else Meincke. Karl was the oldest of six or seven children of a village schoolteacher and parishioner of the local Protestant church in Biebrich, today a part of the city of Wiesbaden. The Protestants of Biebrich were surrounded, and probably oppressed, by the diocese of the powerful bishops of Mainz, the old Roman city across the Rhine River. Karl's father died when Karl was fourteen, and Karl went to work to support his overwhelmed mother and his younger siblings. He worked his way up in the accounting department of a local river transport company and, still in his twenties, bought his first tugboat and two barges, hired a crew, and went into business on his own, transporting freight up and down the Rhine between Strassburg and Rotterdam. Frugal, untiring, and rigidly authoritarian by character, he steered his young company with a firm hand through the initial challenges, won the trust of his customers through safe and timely deliveries, acquired more tugboats and barges, and hired more crews, from whom he expected total commitment to the firm in return for his own loyalty to them in hard times. His business flourished, and he had reason to expect that he could retire by the time he was forty so that he could turn his attention to the study of the history of religion, a topic which was never far from his mind.

On one of Karl's business travels downriver to the city of Krefeld, he met Else Meincke, a graceful, well-brought-up young Catholic woman from a genteel family of somewhat frayed means. Else's par-

Pauline and Ludwig Meincke, had another daughter, Franziska, nicknamed Titi, and a son, Oscar. No one doubted that Karl genuinely loved Else, and Else seems to have enjoyed being courted by Karl, but there were also signs that Else felt intimidated by Karl's controlling manner. If Else had misgivings about a future with Karl, she kept them to herself, probably because she knew that her parents saw in Karl a son-in-law who would not only be an excellent provider for their daughter but could also hopefully be counted on for the occasional financial assistance, which the family required. Else married Karl in 1898. Their marriage lasted until 1935, when Else died as a consequence of her third suicide attempt in a little over a year.

5

Marschwitz

When Vera arrived in Berlin at Richard's and Ilse's house, Stefan was deathly ill. He had been so still during the long and arduous train ride, with its many unscheduled stops and unpredictable detours that women in the overcrowded train compartment had expressed concern for the lifeless infant and had begun sharing stories about children they knew who had died from malnutrition, exposure, and other war-related trauma. Richard diagnosed a severe systemic infection which had originated in the baby's umbilical area, and he was able to provide in his hospital a level of medical treatment that had become rare in wartime Germany. This brought about a slow but steady recovery and returned Stefan to life, leaving behind as a reminder of the ordeal only a distinctive ring of white dots scarring his navel.

Vera had no intention of staying in her sister's home for long. She was on her way to Marschwitz, a village in Silesia with a Polish population then living under German rule, and reunified with Poland after the end of the war. Vera had been invited to come to Marschwitz to escape the bombing of the cities. The person extending this generous invitation was an American woman, Mimi von Haugwitz, wife of a military officer fighting on the Russian front. Mimi was reportedly an heiress who had grown up with great wealth among the elite families of Philadelphia and had married into this distinguished, tradition-rich, but cash-poor family of East Prussian landed gentry. She was living with her three-year-old son, Dietrich, and his nanny, Edda, in the ancestral family manor house, where she headed a large household consisting mostly of Polish-speaking servants from the nearby village. She was also expected to direct the agricultural operations of the estate, but her husband had arranged for a German-speaking overseer to manage the estate, which left her free to pursue her personal interests and find that she felt isolated and miserably lonely.

Mimi was not one of Vera's childhood friends. It is possible that Mimi and Vera met through a referral by a mutual friend, or possibly through a newspaper ad. What distinguished this friendship was the absence of any kind of history, nor a subsequent chapter in their relationship in the future. Vera traveled to Silesia with her two small children not because she wanted to visit a friend but because her home in Mannheim had been bombed, and she needed a place to live where she would hopefully feel welcome and appreciated as a like-minded companion.

All the better that there was also a little boy who needed a same-age companion.

As it turned out, the two women, one from America and the other from the industrial Rhineland, got along extremely well. Both were new to the culture of the provincial East Prussian aristocracy, with its feudal social structure, in which the lord of the manor not only ruled his family household but also held the privilege of judicial and administrative control in the affairs of the village while carrying the responsibility for the well-being of the villagers. As educated women who took for granted that daily living included art and music, fashion, restaurants and movies, and shopping in fine stores, Mimi and Vera must have found life in a Silesian village amusing at first, and then intolerably boring.

There were definitely amenities in Marschwitz: servants to do the cleaning and cooking, gardeners to groom the greenery and plant the flowers, and a chauffeur, who, after the Daimler had been pressed into service to support the war effort, doubled as a coachman when the family felt like taking a ride in the horse-drawn carriage pulled by the beautiful dark-brown Petra. What the aristocratic manor house also offered was a grand piano in the salon where Vera practiced for several hours every day. Mimi enjoyed hearing the Beethoven sonatas and Schumann's *Carnaval*, and Bach's *Italian Concerto* being played in her enormous house. And if she got tired of the repetitive practicing of a dedicated musician aspiring to the highest standards of musical performance, she could find quiet in another part of the house.

What Marschwitz offered above all was a refuge from the war, at least for the moment. It was the summer of 1944, and the Allies were methodically moving toward Germany from all directions, a fact which the Nazi propaganda suppressed or distorted.

According to Berlin relatives, Vera and Mimi periodically sought relief from the monotonous life in Marschwitz by spending a few days in Berlin, leaving the children in Edda's care. Decades later, allusions were made to Vera's and Mimi's Berlin trips, which had perhaps included some socializing with "handsome young officers" on their short furloughs from the front. The conversations with these "handsome young officers" may have touched on the conditions at the front and projected outcomes of the war, but Mimi and Vera certainly did not rely on what they may have heard. They trusted the news reports of the forbidden BBC radio broadcasts, to which they listened late at night in Mimi's locked bedroom, after they had made sure that all the servants had gone to bed. The BBC nightly news reported on the troop movements of the German military and on the advances of the Allies after the invasion of, first, Italy and then Normandy, and on the slow but steady westward movement of the Red Army. The BBC broadcasts were directed at all the people in Germany and in Nazi-held territories, who knew that the official German radio news was a product of the Propaganda Ministry and not to be believed.

Edda had come to Marschwitz from a small town in Northern Germany and held a unique position in the household. As a nanny, she was obviously an employee, but her proximity to the von Haugwitz family and the fact that she had been entrusted with the family's son and heir conferred on her a certain status which separated her from the household staff. Diti loved Edda, and so did I. She was a slender young woman, cheerful and inventive, and she knew how to keep small children interested and entertained. She ate dinner and supper with the family but left the table with us children after the meals were over and spent the rest of the day with us, until she put us to bed in the evening and waited for the two mothers to come and kiss their children good night. Mimi and Vera treated Edda like a relative, but she was excluded from their conversations when they spoke English, which they did often when they felt that the servants might be listening.

Unlike our mothers, Diti and I were not bored at Marschwitz. Diti's full name was Dietrich von Haugwitz, an earnest and courtly boy, four years old, named after his father, and Mimi's only child. As a solitary child in the manor house and shielded from contact with the Polish-speaking village children, he had relied on Edda for company and diversion. His relationship with his mother seemed formal, and Edda was the person who attended to all his needs. He had reportedly looked forward to my arrival, and I have distinct memories of the two of us being good friends. When I came down with the measles once and was sequestered in a massive bed in a huge dark corner bedroom, where thick plush curtains were not allowed to be opened to prevent measles-related damage to my eyes, I remember that I missed Diti's company. What I don't remember is whether I got out of bed and opened the curtains to look at what was going on outside, which I may very well have done. In any case, several weeks after I had recovered from the measles, my left eye suddenly veered toward my nose, and I was now cross-eyed.

There were a lot of things at Marschwitz which could keep three—and four-year-olds entertained. Diti and I were busy watching how the stable hands fed and groomed the horses, how the field workers went out in the morning and came back in late afternoon on the horse-drawn wagon, and we spent a lot of time in the huge kitchen watching how Frieda and her helpers cooked the food that we later saw again as it was being served in the upstairs dining room. There were daily visits to the barn to check on the milk cows and the pigs, and the coachman took us on rides in the buggy drawn by Petra, our favorite horse, who made it look as though she found the drives through the countryside as exciting as we did.

There was also a lot to explore inside the two-hundred-year-old manor house. It was a massive, unlovely, slate-gray stone structure in which long corridors and carved wooden staircases led to double-door entrances opening to stately rooms with fireplaces, dark niches, narrow windows flanked by heavy velvet curtains, and high ceilings. The creaking floors were covered by oriental rugs, and the polished ancestral silver reflected the light from dim table lamps. At the end of a long first-floor hallway stood an imposing old grandfather clock, which announced the hours with a ponderous gong. There was everywhere a pervasive smell of old wood, musty fabric, dust, and sweet herbal perfume, which has attached itself to my memories of living in that house. It seemed to have been built for people who did not believe that life's purpose was to enjoy it, and its plain facade gave off an air of sullen devotion to duty and honor.

The warmest and most interesting part of the house was the kitchen area on the first floor with its open access to the rear courtyard. A main attraction were its many pantries and cupboards holding pastries and jams and other treats and the cooking utensils needed for making them. Frieda presided over all this with a stern presence and a kind heart. She was a stout woman with a round, often flushed face framed by wavy, graying hair, which she kept tied in a bun at the back of her neck. She spoke both Polish and German and seemed to belong to the house as though she had been there all her life.

The kitchen door to the rear courtyard was the path we all took when we heard the rumbling drone of the swarms of American-built Boeing B-17 Flying Fortresses high in the sky and ran out to try to count them as they were returning to their air bases in southern England after their bombing raids on German cities. They were flying in formations, and since it was impossible to count the individual planes because there were too many for the human eye to register one by one, the number of formations provided an estimate of how many hundreds of planes were crossing the sky toward the northwest. People said that the sky was turning black with so many planes overhead, which was their way of expressing their awe at the size of this airborne power of biblical proportions. I can still see Frieda shading her eyes with her right hand while looking up at the clouds of tiny airplane shapes in the sky and crossing herself. I was too young to wonder if she was praying for the souls of the people who had died earlier in the day because of these airplanes or perhaps also for the safe return home of the airplane crews, even if they were the enemy, or both. These B-17s would appear after the end of the war in many Hollywood movies and television series about WWII, and people learned to recognize the aircraft with the four piston-driven engines at air shows and in aviation museums. Of the approximately thirteen thousand Flying Fortresses which Boeing had built during the 1930s and '40s, sixteen remain registered in the United States in 2019.

Of all the farm animals at Marschwitz, it was the geese that terrified me. They were usually waddling around disgruntled and snorting in a fenced compound with a small pond, but they could also be found parading around the barnyard, an imperious leader and an entourage of griping and heckling followers. They were usually scrounging for food, which meant that their heads were close to the ground, and they minded their own business, but when something got their attention, their heads shot up on long stiffened necks until they were taller than me. I must have been on my way to the barn buildings when I came face-to-face with the geese, who instantly shifted to full alert, deployed their wings, and began hissing and honking at me, nipping and pinching with their mean beaks. I turned and ran in a panic, chased by the stampeding beasts, until I was saved by a compassionate person who comforted me in Polish.

Mimi loved to give parties, and when she found out that neither Stefan nor I had been baptized, she declared that a double baptism would be a wonderful occasion for a great feast, with many guests, including the village vicar, Fritz Schmidt, who would be officiating at the baptism ceremony. Two magnificent white lace baptismal gowns appeared, a floor-length creation that fit me as though it had been made for me, and a second one that fit over Stefan's infant clothes and flowed elegantly across Vera's lap and down her legs as she sat holding Stefan for the official baptism portrait. In my own baptism photo, I can be seen standing confidently in my regalia, holding the hand of my impossibly handsome four-year-old prince in his white suit, as though we were the principal actors in a Renaissance childhood betrothal ceremony arranged by two duchies, former enemies, and now allies through the union of their children. I have no memory of the grand party for which the baptism was the occasion; that is probably because it started after our own bedtime. Vera almost certainly gave a short recital in the course of the evening since the invited guests from neighboring estates would have appreciated the presence of a classically trained concert pianist and would have asked her to play. One lasting reminder of the day of the great baptism was my brand-new middle name in honor of my godmother, Mimi, whose legal name was Dagmar.

I don't remember the seasons changing in Marschwitz, but suddenly it was Christmas, and Mimi, with her love of festive occasions, presided over the holiday preparations. She knew from following the nightly BBC news that this would be her last Christmas in Marschwitz, and it is likely that those among the local population who wanted to know did know that the Russian Army was approaching, although any discussion of this was strictly forbidden by the local German government officials.

Knowing that the Red Army would be looting the great estates with their manor houses first, Mimi had the cows and pigs slaughtered and the meat distributed among the village families, along with extra-large winter rations of hay and grain so that these supplies would be consumed or hidden away and not fall into Russian hands.

The geese were also slaughtered, all sixteen of them. Vera was put in charge of cleaning out their abdominal cavities since she had been found to have the surgical skills necessary for deftly separating the gallbladder from the liver without puncturing the bladder's membrane. This was an essential skill because a punctured gallbladder would leak bitter gall fluid and make the prized goose liver inedible. Vera joked that she was merely transferring her fine motor skills from piano playing to separating goose innards.

In mid-January 1945, the BBC reported that the Red Army was approaching the outskirts of Breslau in its push toward Berlin. Vera and Mimi both knew that Vera's departure would have to happen any day now, while the trains from Breslau to Berlin were still running. They took the carriage to the railroad station in the small town of Ohlau to get the train schedule and buy the tickets. The stationmaster stamped Vera's document, which affirmed that she was not a resident of the area but a visitor, and he approved her purchase of the

necessary tickets. He warned her that train service had become sporadic and that she should be prepared for a long wait on the platform.
He spontaneously added that there would not be many more trains
coming through on this line.

That night, Vera finished her packing, and before dawn the next
morning, with Stefan in her arms and me in tow, she said goodbye
to Mimi, Diti, Edda, and Frieda as the coachman lifted her luggage
into the carriage. The heavy emotion that must have hung over this
scene did not enter my three-and-a-half-year-old consciousness, but
I do remember vividly how Petra struggled to pull the carriage out of
a snowdrift and onto the road. She had made a great effort, visibly
straining every fiber of her muscles, and when the carriage still didn't
move, she seemed to panic and reared up in a horse's scream, which
many years later I recognized with a shudder in Picasso's painting of
Guernica's destruction. The coachman instantly slipped out of his
seat, stepped up next to her neck, and calmed her with reassuring
words and a soothing touch. Petra collected herself and followed his
guiding hand on her halter, and they worked together until she and
the carriage were free of the snowdrift and on the firm roadbed.

In such moments, it is good not to have time to think about
anything other than the immediate urgency of the situation. Had
Vera had time to think that this was probably a final goodbye, she
might have lost her focus and with it the strength to go forward as
the emergency demanded. Many years later, when my memories of
Marschwitz had become fixed in the timelessness of a fairy tale, Vera
was contacted by an acquaintance who had information that Mimi
and Diti, after a harrowing escape in a refugee trek, had reached
Berlin just hours before the Red Army sealed off access to the city
and that Edda had not survived the exodus. She had walked next to
Petra on the narrow highway to shield the frightened horse from the
column of German Wehrmacht vehicles, which were roaring past the
slow-moving refugee trek in their own panicked flight from the Red
Army behind them, and she was run over by a tank. Vera's source
also reported that Mimi had been able to return to Philadelphia with
her son, but the two friends never had contact again. Fritz Schmidt,
the vicar of Marschwitz, would describe in a report to the federal

department for refugee affairs in 1949 how the conquering Russian soldiers had pillaged the village of Marschwitz and presumably the manor house as well, with "streets lined with burnt-out houses and littered with broken agricultural machinery and smashed domestic possessions, dead soldiers and rotting cadavers," which he had been forced by the Russians to remove and bury. Very recently, a search on the internet produced the information that a gentleman named Dietrich von Haugwitz, born shortly before World War II in a small village in Western Poland, scion of an old aristocratic family native to that area, had passed away in South Carolina after having devoted his life to rescuing animals and fighting for animal rights. I am left with the question if this was my friend Diti.

In Ohlau, after a final wave goodbye to Petra and the coachman, Vera gathered up her two small children and her luggage, turned toward the railroad station, and found the small railroad platform already packed with people waiting for the train from Breslau, which eventually did arrive. The train was already full, and in ordinary times, it would probably not have been permitted to take on additional passengers, but under the current circumstances, the stationmaster allowed all the waiting passengers to board the train as best they could. Babies and small children were handed through open compartment windows to helpful strangers inside, while the children's mothers pressed themselves into any available gap in the mass of bodies squeezing through the narrow doors of the train and through the packed aisles of the railroad cars.

Years later, Vera would often tell the saga of this departure from Ohlau. She said that she had asked the stationmaster if it might not be better for her to wait for the next train from Breslau. She always vividly reenacted the stationmaster's defeated posture, hollow voice, and Silesian accent as he ominously intoned, "There won't be anything more coming from Breslau after this." In the stationmaster's desolate words must have resonated the mood of the local population, who knew that the war was lost but was afraid to flee as this was considered treason by the Nazi government, punishable by immediate execution.

Once the train's exhausted passengers arrived in Berlin after several anxious, unexplained stops in open country, they were immediately swept up by the hordes of other arriving refuge seekers, and in the crush of shoving bodies, I was suddenly separated from Vera and Stefan. This heart-stopping moment could have changed the course of my tiny life forever since the chances of a frantic mother finding her child in a crowd of tens of thousands of distraught travelers streaming through a disintegrating railroad infrastructure were small. However, amid all the chaos, one *mother and child* aid station was still in operation, and a compassionate person had taken me there to be reunited with Vera and Stefan. Vera later told the story of how next to her at the counter stood another desperate woman searching for her children, speaking in a voice that sounded as if it came from the grave: "I joined a refugee trek in Eastern Prussia three weeks ago with my five children, and all I have left now are my oldest and my youngest."

6

The Good People of Lindau

Back at her sister Ilse's home, Vera found that no one was listening to the BBC News and that, in spite of the spreading devastation of the city of Berlin through nightly air raids, the family was in denial about the inevitable and rapidly approaching defeat of Nazi Germany. Ilse's husband, Richard, as medical director, had strictest orders to maintain normal functioning at the Bernau Hospital, which meant that he was to keep hospital staff at top capacity and refuse all furlough requests. Vera was aghast at her sister's and brother-in-law's refusal to acknowledge the obvious collapse of the world around them, some of which she had just witnessed herself. In later years, she always marveled how she had met people in the encircled Berlin during the final weeks of the war who still believed in their great leader: "The Führer has a plan, he is luring the Russians into Berlin, and there the Wehrmacht will encircle them and annihilate them. Mark my words, you'll see."

Vera was working on the next phase of her travel plan. She had studied the map of Germany and calculated that the most likely region to be invaded and occupied by the French army was Southwestern Germany, including the area around the Bodensee, Lake Constance. She chose the little town of Lindau, which she knew from the summer vacations of her childhood, as her next destination because she believed that it would be a good site from which to observe the arrival of the French army on the highway, which runs alongside the lake. Vera had an affinity for the French from her years of living in Paris, and she looked forward to being liberated by them. This meant, of course, another journey through regions where air and ground battles were raging. Vera was undeterred by her recent experiences with wartime train travel, packed up her children and her suitcase, and embarked on a trip which engraved itself in my memory as a mix of raw bravado, surreal imagery, wonder, sensory overload, suspension of disbelief, and ultimate survival with a return to normalcy, as though this was all just part of what happens in life.

The trip began as it had in Ohlau. Children were lifted through the open train windows into overcrowded compartments, mothers thanked complete strangers for helping them reunite with their anxious children inside the train, and weary people sat on their suitcases in the corridor outside the full compartments or stood on aching feet, held up by the tightly packed crowd rocking in the hard rhythm of the iron wheels on the scarred tracks.

As long as the train was moving, the mood of the people inside was tense but anxiously hopeful. The tension would instantly rise whenever the train stopped, and faces tightened with fear that we would at any moment be attacked by Allied airplanes, who usually bombed the locomotives and sent the passengers pouring out of doors and windows, running, rolling, and tumbling down the embankments into the open country, where they would immediately become targets in a shooting gallery for the inevitably appearing low-flying fighter planes with their machine guns. Many of our fellow passengers had experienced this nightmare before, and soon we found ourselves in this dreaded situation, just as predicted. The long, overloaded train stopped, airplanes were heard overhead, and the garbled announcement came that the locomotive had been bombed and that everybody was to get out of the train as fast as possible. We heard machine-gun fire as we ran down an embankment and through a plowed field, whose snow-encrusted ridges made running difficult, but then we realized that the low-flying screamers were no longer returning for yet another strafing pass, maybe because their skills were needed somewhere else.

In time, a fresh locomotive appeared, everybody who could got back on the train, and the journey continued. With the early darkness of a winter afternoon, there was hope that the train would now not be as easily detected as during the day, and we steadily made our way through the dark countryside until we stopped once again, this time on the outskirts of Ulm, a midsize industrial town on the Danube River.

What the locomotive driver could probably see from his perch at the controls was that the main railroad station of Ulm had just been bombed and was in flames. This late in the war, the train crew had learned to improvise emergency measures, and the passengers were instructed to get off the train with their children and belongings and form groups around quickly appointed group leaders, who were issued flashlights if they didn't have any of their own. The groups were to follow one another in a loose chain on a trek through blacked-out side streets in the direction of the river and, having reached the river, were to follow the river downstream on something that I remember as a wide, unpaved bike path. I was to firmly hold on to the hand of a sturdy man with a backpack whom I didn't know but who inspired confidence with his upbeat, robust, can-do attitude, which would have made him a popular Boy Scout leader. I assumed that Vera and Stefan were following us, but I don't remember turning around to check on them. I held on to my new uncle's left hand as I had been told to do and noticed in his right hand the important flashlight, ubiquitous in wartime Germany, which was not powered by batteries but by a miniature generator operated through the rhythmic contraction and release of a human hand. The squeezing action produced a unique sound, a symphony of rasping, wheezing, and the pulsing drone of cicadas in midsummer. I had heard that sound and seen these flashlights during many nights in air raid shelters, where they were the only light sources, their light brightening and dimming with the rhythm of the pressure in the squeezing human hand. The only other sound that I remember from this walk was the mumbled gurgling and occasional slapping of a cresting wave in the river on my left.

The river also displayed choppy, fragmented reflections of the fires, which still raged along entire streets and city blocks after the bombing raids earlier that night. It looked like the whole town was on fire on both sides of the river, with huge flames leaping out of gutted buildings, the dead windows silhouetted against the hellish-red stage props of collapsing walls behind them. The dark road we were traveling on closely hugged the riverbank and gave us safe passage through the inferno.

We silently trudged along the Danube for what seemed to be most of the night, although the distance may not have been more than three or four miles. When the last of the burning town was behind us, the trek leaders found the designated spot where we were to turn away from the river and look for the railroad tracks and a train, which would be waiting for us to continue the journey south. The rest of the trip must have been uneventful because in my next memory we are already in Lindau.

The little town of Lindau sits on a picturesque site overlooking the Bodensee, Germany's largest lake. The Rhine River enters the lake from the southeast as a rushing and tumbling alpine stream, leaves Switzerland behind, and flows through the entire length of the huge lake, until it exits, broad and muscular, at the lake's western end near the German town of Schaffhausen. It then turns north and—after one more fling of youthful excitement from a leap down a cataract near Schaffhausen—grows into its new role as the workhorse of Germany's river shipping industry, connecting major river ports between eastern France in the south and Holland in the northwest.

After the refugee trek from Marschwitz, Lindau seemed to exist on a different planet, basking in a mild, temperate climate in which flowers, vegetables, fruit trees, and grain grow in abundance. The town stretches out along the northeast shore of the lake and climbs up a steep cliff to an upper level with the famous views which decorate the postcards and souvenirs in the gift shops.

Lindau has always taken pains to present itself as a tidy and safe town, attentive to the needs of tourists who come to spend their summer vacations on the lake, while it pursues the business of providing its respectable inhabitants with a comfortable and orderly life. After the end of the war, Lindauers became known for famously venting their shock over the one errant bomb that fell on the not too distant Schaffhausen and the damage it had caused there.

Lindau welcomed its summer guests, but not the refugees. Vera had found an attic room to rent in a family's home, and I could tell that people were not happy that we had come. I had to stay in our room most of the day and play quietly, and Stefan was not allowed to cry. I know we took walks and would often take the steep street down into the lower part of town with its bakeries and grocery stores along the main highway along the lake. Later in the day, we would return to the upper town on that same steep street, which had been built on a diagonal shelf blasted out of the sheer cliff and offered a clear view of the lake below.

After rumors started circulating that the French were coming any day now, Vera casually let it be known in the neighborhood that she spoke French, and our host family suddenly changed their attitude toward us. They showered Vera with reassurances that she had always been a valued member of their household, declared that they had never been members of the Nazi party, and hinted that they would be ever so grateful to her if she could vouch for them when the French came.

And then the event happened which Vera had been waiting for, and she got to witness a sight that she would in later years describe in a tone of undiminishing amazement: the arrival of the *Grande Armee*. There had been talk in town about the chance that there would be a battle to defend Lindau, but the few local home front soldiers visible to the population were quoted as saying that they had almost no ammunition left for their few machine guns: "When we hear the French coming, we'll shoot off as many rounds as we have left, and then we'll throw the guns away and surrender, and that'll be it." And so standing on the lakeside edge of the street lining the cliff, which was Upper Lindau, and leaning over the railing to get an unobstructed view of the coastal highway below, Vera and her children, together with a sparse crowd of other curious onlookers, listened as the predicted machine gun volley went off below, just as the first French tank came into view, a *Tricolore* flying from its turret, followed by a long column of armored trucks transporting helmeted troops, then more tanks, and trucks carrying soldiers and towing cannons and all kinds of other war machinery, closed jeeps and open jeeps towing tarp-covered trailers, more tanks and more armored trucks and more armored personnel carriers winding along the curving coastal highway along the vast lake, filling the air with the sound of a sustained deep throbbing rumble, arriving and continuing to arrive, moving at a deliberate pace in an unstoppable chain, still arriving long after people had stopped counting the number of vehicles in the convoy that would not end until nightfall.

Whatever Vera told the French occupation officials when they showed up the next day to requisition the house had the desired effect: The handsome French officer bent over Vera's hand and kissed it in a courtly manner and expressed his enchantment at having met a charming German woman who had lived the happiest years of her life in Paris, his hometown. And he instructed his aide to exempt this house from the list of properties to be requisitioned that day.

7

After the End

It seems that Vera did not stay long in Lindau. The war was over, and if she had lost contact with Harry during the chaotic refugee trek from Marschwitz to Lindau, they almost certainly found each other quickly with the help of relatives who were known to have survived the war, among them Vera's father, Karl Schaefer, who was living in his forest house in Wahlen, where Ilse and her five children had found refuge after their frantic escape from Berlin. Ilse had said right up to the end that Hitler had a plan and that capitulation was unthinkable, and she was now so traumatized by what she had seen from the rear seat of the packed family car which her sixteen-year-old son Karl-Heinz had courageously steered through apocalyptic battle-fields in the disintegration of the war's final days that she could not talk about her experiences for years. What her three older children, then in their teens, told was that after the Red Army had conquered Berlin and occupied the vast city after methodical street-by-street and house-by-house fighting, the Bernau Hospital was seized, the medical personnel taken prisoner, and their father, Richard, severely injured when his car was hit by a grenade, and he was left to die on the side of a major highway, probably on the orders of a Russian commander who must have thought that having the wounded Nazi get run over by a truck was a simpler solution than the cumbersome process of picking up yet another prisoner of war.

Harry, as Vera was relieved to find out, was living in Heidelberg, where he worked as a civilian interpreter for the American military government. Before the war, one of Vera's friends had taught her how to do horoscopes, and Vera had promptly done Harry's horoscope, from which she derived the confidence that he would survive the war. This belief that they would have a life together again after the war, as suggested by the horoscope, probably sustained her during the times when she did not hear from him, and it strengthened her trust in this ancient practice, even if she was unable to defend the validity of its core principles against the scientifically oriented objections of most of her friends. She steadfastly declared that a person's character, and with it the pattern of the person's life, corresponds to the planetary configuration at the moment of a person's birth in the respective location on Earth.

Heidelberg was one of the cities which had been designated by American military strategists as a suitable site for the postwar administration of the defeated Germany, and the city was therefore never bombed. Planners for the postwar phase of American operations in the defeated Germany knew that they would be needing interpreters as they faced the enormous task of assuming the governing functions of a destroyed country, which had until recently been the enemy. Basic services like mail service, public transportation, food distribution, and law enforcement had all ceased to exist and needed to be rebuilt within the collapsed infrastructure. Interpreters were needed not only to translate oral and written communications between the occupiers and the occupied, but they also had a powerful role to play in providing the occupation forces with information on the local political hierarchy, with tips on who had been the neighborhood Nazis and who had been their victims.

How Harry got this job was unclear. What I heard over the years was that Harry had anticipated the route which the Americans would take after the Allied invasion of Normandy and that he waited somewhere near the border between Germany and France for the advancing troops while at the same time staying out of the way of the retreating Wehrmacht, found a way to get the attention of an American commanding officer, and presented himself as a trilingual Jewish survivor, with English and French for the liberators and German for the defeated. Harry made this sound simple when he later said, "I just ran into the American lines and told them I was fleeing from Nazi persecution." I always thought that this story sounded like something out of a movie script, but then it was no more improbable than many other stories about Harry which I heard as a child and which often turned out to be true.

The arrival of the American Seventh Army in Heidelberg was similar to the one that Vera witnessed in Lindau when the French arrived. As soon as the victorious troops had taken over the city, they needed to be housed somewhere, and all suitable hotels, schools, commercial buildings, and residential structures in the area were requisitioned, which meant that their owners or tenants were summarily evicted.

When Vera reached Heidelberg with her two children, Harry had been assigned living quarters in a small wooden chalet on a leafy street halfway up the hillside overlooking the city and the Neckar River Valley. Further up the hill loomed the famous Heidelberg Castle, the only ruin in this otherwise undamaged city, a reminder of an earlier war in which King Louis XIV of France had burned down not only the castle but also the entire town. Looking down on the picturesque city with its steeply gabled red-tiled roofs, narrow streets, the stately university campus, and the ancient stone bridge across the river, with its bucolic backdrop of wooded mountainsides, one would not have guessed how hard life had become there. Food was extremely scarce, and even the most basic housing had become unobtainable because in addition to the newly stationed American troops and their civilian employees, large numbers of refugees from the previously German territories in the east, now belonging to Poland and Russia, had also streamed into Heidelberg to compete with the local refugees from the large industrial cities of Mannheim and Frankfurt, which had been heavily bombed and were largely uninhabitable.

The house in which Harry and Vera now found themselves looked like it had been built for happy people enjoying fulfilled lives, but whoever those happy people might have been, they had recently been evicted by the U.S. military government and were probably suffering the same desperate food shortages as we did while living in their beautiful home. Maybe the father, like Harry, or the mother, also shouldered a backpack full of salvaged family jewelry and other treasures; found a way to travel to surrounding villages; and offered the valuables to the farmers in return for some butter, cheese, or eggs. Maybe as the winter approached, they met in nearby woods with their children's sleds, loading them up with the dead branches and pine cones they were gathering to heat the one room in which their family tried to keep warm.

I have few memories of living in the house. It was set back from the street, and the front door was reached by a long garden path. There was a patio in the back, from which one could see the river. The house seemed lively, with visitors and friends coming and going. Harry and Vera must have quickly made contact with other musicians in town and offered a small attic room to a young composer in return for babysitting. This is how it came about that as a five-year-old, I got to play children's board games with Hans Werner Henze, who became one of the most prominent composers of twentieth-century new music. When he lived with us, he was a tall, thin, fair-haired young composition student at the university, with a round, friendly face, a soft-spoken, easygoing manner, and already balding.

Vera must have resolved that now that the war was over, she would concentrate more on practicing effective parenting skills so that the children she had managed to protect well enough to survive the war would grow up to be successful adults. She made it a habit to take me on walks through the parklike neighborhood and drew my attention to the various creatures we encountered. One day, a large black beetle made its way across our path with officious deliberation, and I must have been intrigued by the way it maneuvered between the various obstacles it encountered, studiously testing the environment with its long antennae, while each of its six legs tackled a different micro-feature of the uneven terrain. I stopped while Vera continued walking. As I nervously watched how the distance between Vera and me increased, I was suddenly gripped by an irresistible impulse to raise my foot and bring it down hard on top of the innocent creature. Wanting to leave the scene of my senseless brutality behind me, I ran to catch up with Vera, and when she asked me, "Did you kill that beetle?" I said no. She turned me around without a word, and we walked back to view the crushed beetle.

As her oldest child, I had probably presented Vera for the first time with one of the great challenges in parenting. She had caught me telling a lie, and she wanted to impress on me that lying was bad and would have to be punished. With the excessive zeal of the novice who is trying to prove that she is up to the task, she announced that as a punishment, she would lock me in a pitch-black wooden shed, with the explanation that this is what happens to children who don't tell the truth. My reaction was a combination of stunned disbelief, fear, and rage. I distinctly remember being overwhelmed by the sheer power of my feelings, and the whole experience, whether it lasted five minutes or twenty-five minutes, left a mix of angry and anxious reverberations in me for some years but taught me nothing about the importance of always telling the truth. In fact, I have remained intrigued all my life by topics related to truth telling and the circumstances under which it is morally acceptable, and indeed righteous, to lie. To this day, I believe that hiding a persecuted person from a corrupt authority, and lying to protect that person from capture, is a virtue requiring admirable strength.

The punishment in the windowless shed did not teach me the virtue of unconditional truth telling, but it made the moment when my foot came down on the defenseless beetle unforgettable. This image has accompanied me throughout my life as I have tried to come to terms with the cruelty in the world around me and with my own capacity for insensitivity, ignorance, destructiveness, and disregard for living creatures. If Vera ever looked back on her parenting efforts and questioned the merits of her draconian reaction to my lying, she never mentioned this to me. If we had been able to talk about this once I had children of my own, I would have told her that I understood her motive and that she had done the best she could at the time. Hopefully, we would have ended up laughing at the ineptitude of inexperienced mothers and would have joked about the futility of her valiant efforts to turn out model citizens.

In another fearful memory from that same time, I hear a knock and open the front door of our house on a dark December evening to find a tall, fat old man with a long white beard in a boot-length, dark-brown rough woolen overcoat, his head covered by a floppy

hood, carrying in one hand a bundle of twigs and in the other a burlap sack. It is the sixth of December, and Saint Nicholas is at the door
to find out if the children in this house have been good, in which case
they would get some treats from the sack as a preview of the presents
which the Christ child will bring on Christmas Eve. If the children
have been bad, there is the bundle of twigs for a spanking.

Needless to say, this well-intentioned attempt to reintroduce
normalcy into our traumatized lives by way of restoring familiar customs of the Christmas season triggered unsuspected dormant terrors.
I recoiled in a panic at the menacing figure in the doorway, dashed
through the living room as if pursued by furies, ran mad circles
around a dining table, and couldn't stop screaming until I collapsed
into uncontrollable sobs. Vera and Harry probably guessed from my
extreme reaction that children who have come through a war, even if
they seem normal in daily life, have fewer defenses against fear-arous-
ing stimuli from so-called harmless folk traditions and fairy tales; in
any case, Saint Nicholas never showed up at our front door again.

Maybe part of the reason why I don't have a sense of consistent
daily living in the house on Wolfsbrunnenweg was that for some
weeks or months, Stefan, three years old by now, and I lived in a
Catholic orphanage in Baden-Baden, two hours south of Heidelberg
in the foothills of the Black Forest. Food shortages had become so
severe that Vera and Harry decided it would be best for us to stay
at the orphanage for as long as the nuns could keep us because their
order was known to have connections to international food aid organizations, from which they were receiving shipments of donated
Argentinian dried beef.

The dried meat chunks came in fifty pound burlap sacks deposited in a storage room off the large convent kitchen, and the daily
portions for feeding the resident children were soaked every night
and slowly cooked the next day in a large kettle, until a gravy formed,
to which potatoes and greens were added for a nutritious stew. I was
allowed into the kitchen, where I watched how the nun in charge of
cooking our food rinsed a load of freshly picked stinging nettles in
the sink. I can still see the large red welts on her swollen hands as she

pulled the nettle leaves from the tough stems before throwing them into the bubbling stew.

Stefan and I presumably gained weight at the orphanage, but we were so homesick and looked so pitiful every time Vera came to visit us that she must have questioned the benefits of the better diet. And on one occasion, when we looked especially tired, with dark rings under our eyes, she took us back home to Heidelberg. Maybe she was confirmed in this decision when I told her about hearing children's screams from the bathroom in the middle of the night, when the nuns put the bed wetters into a bathtub filled with cold water to train them to wake up when they needed to pee and not pee in their beds.

In less than a year, it was our turn to be evicted from the lovely chalet at a moment's notice because an American officer had spotted it and wanted it for himself and his newly arrived family. What I remember about our precipitous departure was the arrival of two soldiers with clipboards and tape measures who acted like they owned the place and ordered Vera to move all the furniture away from the walls so that they could press a stencil up against the back of each piece and, with a few back-and-forth swishes of a wet paintbrush, produced the words *U.S. Military Property* in a bright, penetrating authoritative blue, which I have since seen only painted in rings around the trunks of trees, which the U.S. Forest Service has permitted to be cut down.

Harry's job with the U.S. military continued to reward him with access to housing, and we were assigned a three-room apartment on the first floor of a plain three-story gray-stuccoed residential building in the Bunsenstrasse, close to downtown Heidelberg, not far from the central railroad station. The house stood out in its artless functionality from the neighboring, genteel late-nineteenth-century attached townhouses with their elaborate sandstone facades. We were allowed to have the entire apartment with all three rooms to ourselves because my grandmother, Antoinette, Harry's mother, was going to come and live with us, and Vera was having another baby.

When we moved in, I overheard some talk in a hushed tone about the history of the house. It had apparently been used during the Nazi years as a local Gestapo headquarters, and the basement cubicles had held newly arrested persons who were waiting to be interrogated. While this information meant little to me when I first heard it, its significance grew as I got older and absorbed more knowledge from my environment about what people are capable of doing to one another. The basement cells became more frightening to me the longer we lived in that building, until I could hear the screams of tortured prisoners in my head every time I passed the stairs leading down to the basement.

I didn't notice the arrival of my youngest brother, René, because for several weeks, if not months, he was placed in the care of a woman who had recently given birth to a child of her own and was able to produce enough breast milk for two babies. This was a godsend because Vera was so malnourished that she was unable to nurse her newborn. Powdered infant formula had not been invented yet, and cow's milk was tightly rationed, so the wet nurse seemed to offer a perfect solution at a time when no one was giving the possibility of a disrupted infant-mother bonding any thought.

A new person did, however, come into my life with René's birth: Anneliese Reiche. She had given birth to a son on the same day as Vera, and the two mothers shared a room in the maternity ward for an entire week, which was at that time standard medical practice for normal deliveries.

Vera and Anneliese Reiche became good friends during that week, and they remained in close contact during our Heidelberg years. Anneliese Reiche had been divorced from a midlevel civil servant and staunch follower of Nazi ideology and, like Vera, was in her midthirties when she gave birth to her second son. The child's father was an American officer with a wife and several children back home in the United States. Anneliese had not told the American of her pregnancy at their last meeting before he was reassigned to a base in Japan because she was too proud to become an embarrassment to him, as she feared was likely to happen. She was determined to raise this child on her own, even in the face of the certain criticism and rejection that she would encounter for having an "illegitimate" child. To protect her young son from this stigma, she had asked her former husband, father of her sixteen-year-old son, to give the baby his last name, with the promise that she would never approach him with requests for assistance. The former husband refused.

Anneliese found a foster family for her baby in a neighboring town, at a safe distance, to avoid chance encounters and traveling rumors. She saw a public announcement of a newly created teacher education program, applied, and was accepted immediately. One year after the end of the war, the institutions of a civil society were slowly being reconstructed, and schools had started to reopen, in spite of the lack of qualified teachers. The ranks of a whole generation of teachers had been decimated by the war, either through death on a battlefield, starvation, or detention in prisoner-of-war camps. The existing teachers, once they had passed through the obligatory "denazification" programs, were—like their students' parents—survivors of the war, with various physical and psychological scars, which compromised the quality of classroom instruction for many years, much as the war experience had affected the quality of parenting in many homes. Teachers with physical disabilities were often not up to the rigors of showing up every school day to face overcrowded classrooms, and psychological trauma caused teachers to avoid any topic that had to do with recent German history.

In a desperate move, new teachers were recruited among the general population, hastily trained in improvised night courses, and put in front of orphaned classrooms, where they could practice the skills that they had learned the night before.

Anneliese Reiche immersed herself in her teacher training courses and, after several years of enthusiastic dedication to her students and intense focus on her seminars, was a credentialed educator with a talent for teaching, which made her a role model among her colleagues. She became a mentor to subsequent graduates of her teacher training program, now a recognized department at the university in Heidelberg, and eventually joined its faculty.

I admired Anneliese Reiche more than most of the people I knew as a child, and there is no question that her example inspired me. I always wanted Vera to be like her, and I underestimated the hidden cost of Anneliese's magnificent achievement. Her son's foster parents loved the boy and did not honor their original agreement that they would act as grandparents in his life until he could be reunited with his mother. They increasingly drew the boy into their extended family and manipulated him into thinking that his mother had no time for him, although she regularly paid for his support, visited him every weekend, and talked with him about how they would be together as soon as she had finished her studies and received her academic degree.

When she was finally in a position to bring him home, he no longer wanted to live with her because he did not want to give up his life in his foster family, his school, and his friends. To spare her son the anguish of feeling torn between her and his foster parents, she let go and pretended to be content with a possible reunion in the future. There were tensions, and years later, the boy still had not come home to his mother. With her older son now grown and married and always closer to his father than to her, and her younger son bonded with a family from whom she was painfully estranged, Anneliese had quietly suffered the loss of two children for whom she must have had different hopes when they were born.

Eventually, René came home, and in my memory, we were a contented family. Harry went to work every day, and Vera was at home with us children. René was a cute baby and had a sunny disposition. He seemed to enjoy making the most of his status as the baby in the family. I must have liked playing with him since I clearly remember making little blocks for him out of cardboard boxes, which he loved to stack up and knock down over and over. Stefan, as the middle child, played the classic role of the sibling who often gets overlooked because he has neither the status of the firstborn nor the endearing vulnerability of the baby. In return for getting less attention, Stefan had the advantage of freedom from the unceasing pressure on the firstborn to reach new milestones and assume new responsibilities, age appropriate or not.

Vera had taken on the daily battle of finding food in the local markets, which were open for business but had almost nothing to sell. She would stand in long lines, food rationing stamps in hand, following a rumor that a certain store had received shipments of flour, sugar, or powdered milk, in limited quantities, to be sure, so that there was never any guarantee that she would reach the counter before the hoped-for items had sold out. Vera developed an ingenuity for stretching the basic foods she had been able to buy so that they would last for the whole month. The rationing stamps issued by the military government provided about one thousand calories per person per day. Anything beyond that had to be *organisiert*, which meant something like "using your wits to come up with what you desperately need." Meal planning was a useless endeavor as the availability of food supplies was unpredictable from day to day. Meat and dairy rations were measured in units of ten grams per person, if available at all. Store owners had no incentive for keeping their shelves stocked, even if there had been access to plentiful merchandize, because the currency was weak, and rumors were circulating that it would collapse soon and be replaced by a completely new currency.

Organisieren applied not only to food but also to clothing, shoes, fuel, tools, and other basic needs, possibly including a child's longed-for toy. I suspect that my first bicycle was *organisiert*. I had probably seen another child riding a bicycle through the neighborhood and must have asked for one because one ordinary day—it wasn't my birthday, and it wasn't Christmas—a beautiful small red bicycle appeared on the landing in front of our apartment door, and Vera said that it was for me and that I could practice riding it in the garden behind the apartment building. Once I felt secure enough to ride the bicycle on the garden path, and then on the sidewalk in front of our apartment, I was even allowed to ride it to my one-pupil school. I did this with great pride for several weeks until one day, on the way home, I found myself suddenly surrounded by a group of jeering ten—or eleven-year-olds. They shouted threats and grabbed the handlebar, yanking and shaking it to knock me off the bike, and pulled it away from me once I had let go of it. I was stunned and probably crying when I saw one of them ride off with it, with the others following. When I got home to tell the story of what had just happened, Vera reacted in a way that made no sense to me. Instead of voicing outrage and saying that we were immediately going to the police to report this robbery, she looked sad and discouraged and deeply uncomfortable. She consoled me and looked relieved that I seemed to recover from this incident rather quickly. I have obviously never forgotten this moment, in which I understood that Vera had wanted so much to give me a bicycle that she used her wits to somehow find a way to come up with a bicycle, never mind how questionable its provenance.

Vera had made friends in the neighborhood (she would call them acquaintances since the word *friend* was reserved for much deeper relationships), and she would get from them the latest imaginative recipes for dishes which combined whatever ingredients happened to be on hand with fillers that stretched the yield and resulted in larger portions. The topic of sawdust as a possible filler was seriously discussed at one point since sawdust was rumored to actually be digestible. Fresh meat and cheese were dreams from a past era. A favorite approach to this kind of cooking was to finely chop whatever you had, such as a couple of boiled potatoes, leftover cooked barley, dandelion greens, suet, bread crumbs, and on a good day, an egg, or even two; add water to moisten the mass; and knead it into a melon-sized dumpling, which would be immersed in simmering water until it showed signs of wanting to levitate to the surface, at which point it was drained and served sliced, like a roast, maybe with some gray, creamy-textured liquid substance that could pass for gravy. When someone in the neighborhood discovered that using carbonated seltzer water made for a lighter texture of the dumpling, the innovation was circulated quickly and eagerly adopted.

There were times when we did have small pieces of meat in our Sunday dinner. I did not make the connection between this luxury and the recent departure of our pet bunny, Hansi, who went home with Erika, a young farm girl who came to the city once a week to help Vera with the cleaning. Erika had so convinced me that Hansi would be much happier living in the rabbit hutch with the other bunnies on her father's farm that I found it impossible to imagine that the bites of meat that had been part of my dinner had once been Hansi. I am certain that Vera had given her consent to Hansi's sacrifice with a heavy heart, and I never mentioned my suspicion once it had occurred to me. I suppose I hoped that not talking about it made it not true.

Looking back, I am surprised how little I perceived of the hardships during the immediate postwar years. I don't remember being hungry, nor did I miss toys. I had some clothes and a pair of shoes, and I probably had a coat or a jacket and a sweater for the winter. Nobody cared what our clothes looked like or questioned where they came from; all that mattered was that they kept us covered and warm in cold weather. The deprivation was experienced by everyone, and there was no shame attached to living in impoverished circumstances. It merely showed that you obviously had no connections to the illegal black market dealers, who were operating in a thriving shadow economy fueled by American cigarettes as a substitute currency, while store shelves remained empty.

Even though time very quickly erased the sensory memory of feeling acute hunger, which I and all those around me obviously endured, our attitude toward food was shaped by these experiences. To this day, my generation abhors the wasting of food, and all my life, I have recoiled from throwing food into the trash. To me, food is a wondrous thing to behold. Having enough to eat stirs in me a deep gratitude, and the fear of not having enough to eat still distorts my judgment when I buy too many groceries for a household of two or cook meals in quantities that could serve twelve people.

While the severe food shortages of the postwar years dominated the thoughts and actions of people in the world around me, we did have in our sparsely furnished living room a large, stately, dark lacquered wood Grundig radio. It sat on a table against the wall, flanked by two upholstered chairs for intent listeners, and was obviously the most important object in the room. On the illuminated glass display, which had a soothing, almost hypnotic effect when the room was dark, the Western world's great cities—Paris, London, Madrid, Rome, Berlin—were listed in staggered diagonal columns along with intriguing names like Brno, Hilversum, Yerevan, Uppsala, Thessaloniki, and Gijón. The ghostly bluish dial moved silently through these exotic places as if they were way stations on the Silk Road to Samarqand.

This wonderful radio brought us the news, and it brought us music. Within a year of the German capitulation, there was an improbable resurgence of classical music concerts in Heidelberg and many other cities, and these performances were broadcast over the radio. On certain weekday evenings, and always on Sundays, these broadcasts turned our plain living room into a virtual concert hall, where Vera and Harry relived their prewar days as young musicians studying, practicing, rehearsing, while envisioning a career as professional concert artists. Now in the midst of famine, they observed how symphony orchestras were making early efforts to reunite their musicians and schedule concerts in makeshift venues, and as they were listening to the broadcasts and commenting on the quality of the playing, they probably began to dream that such a resurgence might be possible for them too.

In Heidelberg, the pink sandstone Kunsthalle was intact and ready for performances by orchestras, which were welcoming back their musicians and conductors who had escaped the Nazi persecution and been scattered all over the world. Harry bought tickets to one of the first concerts at the Kunsthalle since the end of the war. He and Vera wanted me to have an early introduction into the world of music performance, so he bought a third ticket for me, and Vera "organized" a beautiful apricot-colored embroidered silk dress with a scalloped neckline and hem for me. When we arrived at the completely sold-out hall in plenty of time to take in the festive preconcert atmosphere, the ticket taker would not admit me. He explained unapologetically that the hall management policy favored adult listeners, of whom there were many standing in a line outside the box office, hoping for last-minute seats for this much anticipated event. The message was clear: the management did not want to "waste" such highly sought-after tickets on a seven-year-old child, who was in any case "too young to understand the music."

8

Family Photos

Accepting our living circumstances as normal, and incapable of imagining that parents had a life before their children arrived, I had no sense that Harry and Vera were struggling to adjust to an extremely challenging postwar existence for which they, like the general population around them, were completely unprepared. Nor did it occur to me that their lives had once been much easier, at least financially, revolving mostly around music, and I gave no thought to their relationship with each other. At seven, I saw them simply in their roles as my mother and my father. I had heard stories of how they had met as promising young musicians who were just starting to perform in public at chamber music recitals, where they played sonatas for piano and violin. Vera made her debut as the soloist in the Schumann piano concerto, conducted by the famous Carl Schuricht, who had agreed to give the young pianist Vera Schaefer an opportunity to perform for an audience which included a noted music critic. The warm and congratulatory review by the music critic was accompanied by a photo of Vera during her performance, and Vera kept this newspaper clipping among her most treasured possessions, which somehow even survived the war.

I also knew that these early performing experiences were cut short by Harry's and Vera's escape to Paris, and by the time I got to see the newspaper clipping with Vera's photo, those early successes had become a distant memory and were bringing, along with the warm glow of relived joy, a mix of regrets, recriminations, and silent resignation. Throughout the war and the early postwar years, there still must have been a strong emotional connection between Vera and Harry, maybe nurtured by their shared memories of their life in Paris, because they managed to stay together and give their children the feeling that they were living in a normal family. In doing this, they struggled with tasks and responsibilities which periodically overwhelmed them.

From photos more than from daily life with him, I could see that Harry was a very handsome man, with a courtly manner and distinguished bearing in the style of the Hollywood movie actors of the forties and fifties often referred to as matinee idols. Harry was tall and lean, with thick straight black hair; a narrow face with strong, even features; a prominent curved nose; and bushy eyebrows shading his dark-brown eyes, which were quick to burn with intensity but could also pierce in cold dismissal, summoning up an emotional force that could annihilate. Similarly, he could caress but also crush a person with a few deceptively casual words. Suits and ties were his natural attire, even in times of famine, when the securing of basic subsistence was a full-time job and left little time and energy for matters of personal appearance. In a photo of a family gathering taken when he was a much older man, his shoulders are hunched, he is not as tall as he once was but none of this diminishes his dominant presence, and in his last years, during a visit on a cold winter day in Paris, he cut a formidable figure in his long black overcoat, even as he struggled with shortness of breath. No photos were taken on that day, but the image of this compelling old man, soul mate of the great musicians of the nineteenth-century Romantic era, is etched in my memory with perfect clarity.

Even if in the early years of their life as a couple Harry and Vera were attuned to each other, they related to other people in very different ways. In contrast to Harry, whose charismatic persona attracted people but could also be intimidating, Vera won people over with her warmth, spontaneity, and empathy, and her exuberant enjoyment of beauty in music, art, and landscapes was contagious. With all the photos of her adolescence and young adulthood, mostly taken on vacations at beach resorts or on trips to Paris or London—first with her parents and later with her friends—the one portrait that fully captures her beauty shows her in her midthirties, seated in a photographer's studio surrounded by her three young children: René, less than a year old, on her right arm, and Stefan and I leaning against her on her left side. She is thin, not from dieting to look fashionably lean but as a consequence of not having enough to eat. The skin of her narrow oval face looks taut yet luminous, accentuating her cheekbones, strong nose, and pointed chin. There is a tenderness and confidence in her eyes, which is surprising, given the hardships of life in the year 1947. A hairdresser must have been consulted to style Vera's hair into an intricate composition on top of her head, and we all look well taken care of and dressed appropriately in summer clothing.

No matter how hard psychology tries to explain the attraction which binds couples together, the dynamics of such an attraction remain a mystery. It is said that opposites attract each other. Harry loathed confrontation and controversy and tended to solve conflicts by telling the people on both sides of a dispute what he thought they wanted to hear and then found himself accused of manipulating, dissembling, or worse. By contrast, Vera saw herself as a deeply intuitive person, who would often take bold action on an impulse and fail to see its potential for unhappy consequences. I remember many instances when Vera complained bitterly about people, including me, who did not freely say what was on their mind but instead held back and calculated the effect on others of what they were going to say and adjusted their statements accordingly. Facing these kinds of personality differences requires—even under the best of circumstances—superior communication skills to identify and resolve them, or at least to recognize them for what they are. But if nothing in Harry's and Vera's life had prepared them for the hardships of the postwar period, they were even less prepared to talk openly and courageously with each other when conflicts erupted; instead, they resorted to what we know from psychology as the classic defense mechanisms: he retreated into avoidance and left the scene, and she developed an extensive repertoire of passive-aggressive maneuvers to punish him.

Whenever I sensed tension between them, I tried to think of diversionary tactics or mollifying interventions in the hope that a looming crisis could be averted, and I was relieved when they seemed on good terms again. What I saw during moments of conflict was that Vera would be angry at Harry and that he would react to Vera's anger by becoming distant, either sitting through her complaints and reproaches in silence or leaving the apartment without saying a word. When he returned, she refused to acknowledge him and ignored his conciliatory gestures for days. There is an art to systematically ignoring a person in a small crowded apartment, and Vera had mastered that art.

In time, I came to understand that Vera's anger was triggered by Harry's affairs with other women. Once, on an early evening walk with Vera through neighborhood streets, I noticed that she seemed to be listening for sounds from apartment windows opened to the warm summer breeze, and eventually we passed an open second-floor window draped in white gauze curtains, behind which someone was playing the violin. Vera recognized the violin and the music, and she stopped to listen, visibly pained. I sensed her unhappiness without knowing the tortured emotions which must have raged inside her at that moment, and I watched as she seemed to be making a decision, took a step forward, and began walking home. I followed a few paces behind her, trying to guess why she was too upset to talk to me, but I intuitively knew that Harry's performance on his violin for someone else had hurt her deeply.

While Harry and Vera were unable to hide their complicated and conflicted relationship from us, they did their best to shield us from the physical reality of the postwar famine. They always managed to have food for us, even if it was just a soup of bread and clabbered milk, and if they felt exhausted, frustrated, or dejected, they did not show it, or I did not notice it. Early in the morning on Easter Sundays, they must have hidden the eggs, which they had presumably colored the night before, so that we could have an Easter egg hunt and have our picture taken with our Easter baskets, and early in the day of every Christmas Eve, the living room was locked with the explanation that it had to be made ready for the arrival of the *Christkind*. Soon after it got dark, when we could no longer stand the suspense, a little bell would ring inside the living room, the door would be opened wide, and there was the Christmas tree, mounted on a table with plates of cookies and nuts and oranges and a gift for everyone, illuminating the otherwise dark room with the warm glow of its dozen or more white beeswax candles. Family photos in black and white show Harry and Vera and their three children gathered around the spindly skeleton of an anemic pine tree, its branches decorated with homemade paper garlands and assorted repurposed ornaments, radiant in the light of the candles in their tin candleholders, which were clipped to the tree's outer branches. The candles would burn down completely in the course of about an hour, during which time the family remained near the tree, opening humble presents that were deeply touching in their simplicity, singing Christmas songs, and watching that the candles would not come in contact with anything flammable. I think of the modesty of those early postwar Christmases whenever I hear the familiar comments on how the meaning of Christmas today seems to have been drowned in the sea of consumerism, and I sense that there is more to that complaint than easy sentimentality.

Our radio played Christmas music, of course, but the dial would be quickly reset to the sounds of classical music broadcast by the newly established state-run radio stations. Within an amazingly short time of a year or two after the capitulation in 1945, revered orchestras like the Berlin Philharmonic were giving their first performances, and the Salzburg music festival in Austria started to show signs that it could be brought back to life. Broadcasts of political commentary or intense debates on current events alternated with music broadcasts, and children were expected to sit still and listen or leave the room and play in the kitchen.

Years later, I was able to piece together the fragments of anguish, irrational outbursts, grief, rage, rejection, and abandonment which littered the emotional landscape around me. I came to wonder if Harry had been raised by parents who may not have had experienced much love from their own parents and who, in turn, had been unable to give him the nurturance, security of attachment, and recognition that children need in order to thrive emotionally and develop the feeling that they are worthy of being loved. As a consequence, Harry, throughout his adult life, may have compensated for the love he didn't receive as a child by seeking it in the women around him. He found it in Vera when they felt united in their music making but missed it in her when, in her hurt and anger over yet another infidelity, she rejected him and acted as though he wasn't in the room. Their common absorption with music continued to be a powerful bond, but there were also strong crosswinds pushing them apart.

The image of Vera and Harry sitting next to the radio, critically listening to performances of which they either enthusiastically approved or which they hotly rejected, followed by nuanced discussions on the merits of playing a piece in a certain tempo, lends a nostalgic glow to the way in which I think of that time in history when an entire population suffered from chronic malnutrition, which had caused many thousands of people to die of starvation and had so weakened Antoinette that she was close to death. We children were told that Omi was sick and needed the room in which we all slept for herself. The door to her room was kept closed for a long time, and at one point, a priest came to administer last rites, but eventually, she started to get better, maybe because extra food rations had somehow been obtained for her.

Had Antoinette died, it would have been the quiet passing of a gentle soul who had gone through life without ever finding her voice. She had grown up on the periphery of the romance and elegance of the Gilded Age and lived her early adult life assuming, as did everyone else she knew, that her world would continue as she knew it. She was born in 1883, when being born "out of wedlock" meant being stigmatized by illegitimacy and barred from inheriting family name and property. Her parents were the Marechal de Beaudricourt and his mistress, Madame Gauthier, whose beauty was captured on many photographs. She was also thought to possibly be Jewish, but this was never substantiated. The Marechal and his lady, or so the story goes, were at sea on their long journey to Peking, where he had been posted as the next ambassador, when her pregnancy could no longer be concealed, and the decision had to be made that she would return on the same ship to France to give birth to the child there. A healthy daughter, Antoinette, was born, and it was decided that a Catholic convent school would be a suitable home, where the little girl would be cared for and educated according to the standards of the time.

Not a single photo exists of Antoinette's childhood or adolescence. It seems that her parents separated in her early childhood because she had no memory of ever having seen them together. After the separation of her parents, she obtained a second father, Papa Nouvel, her mother's new lover, who usually arrived alone to visit Antoinette at the convent and remained a loyal friend and adviser to her for the rest of his life.

The Marechal was an honorable man and met his financial obligations toward his young daughter, whose existence was not hidden from his much older, legitimate children, because Antoinette enjoyed a lifelong loving relationship with a motherly half sister, Jeanne, and her husband, Henri, who lived in Besançon, a provincial city in southeastern France. Jeanne probably provided some of the maternal affection which Antoinette never received from her mother, and even though both world wars disrupted the communication between the half sisters, contact was reestablished at the end of each war, and in 1955, Antoinette undertook a journey by train to Besançon and visited Jeanne and Henri for several weeks. The photos of the trip, which Jeanne later sent to Antoinette, showed a happiness in my grandmother's face and an élan in her posture that I had not seen before, and which did not last long after she had returned.

The convent education had prepared Antoinette for becoming the wife of an upper-class gentleman who would be willing to overlook the issue of her illegitimate birth. A young German by the name of Wilhelm Eduard Saarbach, son of a well-to-do Jewish wine merchant in Mainz, met Antoinette in London, where she had impressed her local circle of acquaintances with her charm, grace, beauty, increasing fluency in English, and the ease with which she won bridge games. Willy had just been put in charge of his family's new venture in England, and the handsome couple married and settled down in comfortable lodgings in keeping with the living standards of upper-class Edwardian London. It was the year 1908. Sepia-tinted photos of the time show Willy and Antoinette in elegant travel attire reclining in the back seat of an elaborate convertible automobile or waving from the deck of a ship, Antoinette's lovely profile flattered by the sweeping curves of a broad-rimmed hat. With such scenes of wealth and stability all around, it was still possible to ignore ominous signs that this privilege for the few at the expense of the masses of the world's exploited poor could not possibly last much longer.

It seems that within a few years, the London assignment was either completed or passed into the hands of a successor because Willy and his elegant French wife returned to Mainz, where their son Harry was born on July 23, 1911. Little is known about Harry's infancy in Mainz, and whoever cared for him during the first year of his life did not take any photos, maybe out of indifference. The young family had a socially prominent presence in town, and soon their household included Alla, Harry's long-term nanny, who would become a de facto family member and more of a sister to Antoinette than an employee. She remained a lifelong friend to Antoinette and Harry, and I remember meeting her when I was about twelve years old, and Alla and Antoinette were close to seventy. Alla was a warm and kindhearted person, with a practical, down-to-earth approach to life, from an urban Rhineland civil service family, strict when it came to things like bedtimes and homework but with a great sense of humor. She raised Harry to be comfortable with friends from working-class families in public school while supervising his daily practice sessions required by his private violin teacher. Willy traveled frequently on business, Antoinette had become a sought-after bridge player in Mainz society, and both parents found it only natural to leave the raising of their son in the hands of this capable and completely trustworthy nanny. Alla saw to it that Harry was exposed to people of diverse social classes and cultures. This may have given him his remarkable natural ease in a wide spectrum of environments as throughout his life, his friends ranged from communists to aristocrats, small shopkeepers and craftsmen to world-famous musicians and conductors, and even included at least one ultimately incarcerated con man and various other problematic characters. All this made for unceasing drama in Harry's life and gave rise to stories that could not be told without at times straining the limits of plausibility.

Soon after Harry reached school age, Willy found that he loved his secretary, Fredel, more than his wife, and he and Antoinette separated without much protest from Antoinette, as long as he was agreeable to a financial arrangement that would allow her to raise their son in the style to which she was accustomed.

Antoinette was known to have had a special bond with August Saarbach, the stern and distinguished patriarch whose official portrait made him look like one of the great founders after whom the era was named, and who was reportedly quite taken with his French daughter-in-law. This may have strained Antoinette's relationship with other family members, although no details have ever been recorded. After August's untimely death in 1912, Antoinette's rank in the family hierarchy seems to have gradually slipped, and once Jenny Saarbach was recovering from the loss of her husband and started to grow into her new role as the head of her large family in the imposing villa on Heidesheimer Strasse 45 in Gonsenheim near Mainz, Antoinette no longer appears in any family photos. Willy's new bride, Fredel, was welcomed by the extended family, which was looking forward to the prompt arrival of offspring, but after Fredel suffered a series of miscarriages, it became clear that Willy and Fredel would remain childless, and Harry would be Willy's only heir.

It appears that there was someone in the family who liked to take photos because there are striking portraits of Jenny and her six children, as well as pictures of lovely moments in Jenny's garden, with Jenny seated in front of a thick hedge holding two of her young grandchildren on her knees and beaming straight into the camera. She looks healthy and resolute, her rich white hair brushed loosely away from her face and gathered at the back of her neck, with a strong forehead and clear smooth skin that seems accustomed to being outdoors in the sun, kind and generous eyes, a well-proportioned nose, and a confident mouth. There is also a photo of Jenny's villa, with its first floor mostly hidden by the trees and shrubs which fill the garden, while the second and third floors rise above the dense vegetation. Blooming geraniums spill out of the flower boxes hanging from the second-story windows and the balcony, where three figures, the one with the white hair probably being Jenny, are looking out across the garden to the distant camera. There are three young women standing at the open windows on the third floor, balancing the composition of this architectural still life.

Harry never talked about the family history. He never mentioned that his father, Willy, had served in the Kaiser's army in World War I; that his father had two brothers and three sisters; that the oldest sister, the striking and strong-willed Hedwig, had caused a scandal in her day by running off with an orchestra conductor; that a younger brother, Max, died of meningitis at the age of fifteen; and that the youngest brother, Ernst, had been wounded so severely in World War I that he remained in pain until his suicide in 1923. Nor did Harry ever refer to Jenny's younger daughters, Anna and Elisabeth. Anna had been able to escape to England in time to avoid deportation to a concentration camp, and Elisabeth, who had lived her entire married life in the small eastern town of Bernburg on the Saale River (where in 1940 a section of a large state hospital for the mentally ill had been converted into an extermination camp), died in 1944 in Bernburg under mysterious circumstances at the age of fifty-three, "under house arrest pending her deportation," as one document indicates.

What Harry did mention more than once was that Jenny, living alone for twenty-eight years after her husband's death but having frequent visitors, including her daughters and a growing number of grandchildren, could not sleep at night and was known to sit up in her bed, propped up on large cushions, alone with her thoughts, knitting until dawn. Harry must have known but couldn't bring himself to tell us that Jenny's life was destroyed in 1940, when she was disowned by Nazi decree and ordered to leave her house. She was forced to move into a Jewish nursing home for the elderly, and she died in the local Jewish hospital a few days before the other residents of her nursing home were deported to Auschwitz and murdered there.

9

Hydrangeas

Famine or no famine, I turned six in 1947 and started school. Since I was cross-eyed and wore glasses, I qualified for an exemption from the rule that all six-year-olds had to attend the pitifully overcrowded and poorly equipped elementary schools in town. Vera had found a private teacher, Fräulein von Pittoni, who would invite me into her world and spread out before me such a rich tapestry of wonderful things to learn that from then on, throughout my life, the experience of learning something new has served me as a deep source of consolation when all else around me seemed uncertain and painful.

I know nothing of Fräulein von Pittoni's life. She was an apparition from an earlier era, seemingly ageless, with the ethereal grace of a being which hovered between earthly existence and the spirit world. She was a tiny figure, always dressed in black satin ankle-length, long-sleeve gowns, the collars trimmed with white lace. Instead of a necklace, she wore a wide black velvet band around her neck, closed with two tiny hooks in the back, and a small glittering medallion in front, directly below her soft, round chin. Her smiling face and inquisitive blue eyes radiated kindness, and her silvery hair, carefully fashioned into silken ringlets, added to the aura of timelessness which surrounded her and gave her a magical appearance, conjuring for the visitor a sense of being transported into an earlier century, whose stories this lovely person would tell all those who wanted to learn.

My school day with Fräulein von Pittoni began with a ten-minute walk down the Bunsenstrasse, past a row of stately, attached four-story townhouses, each with a different facade marked by balconies, bay windows, niches and corbels and recesses, in different shades of ochre, gray, pink, and beige, set back about eight feet and separated from the sidewalk by wrought-iron fences and gates of intricate design, behind which moss-covered fieldstones paved small leafy font gardens dominated by the perpetually blooming hydrangeas. These hydrangeas—the chameleons of the plant world—used their uncanny ability to change the muted hues of their large globular blooms to complement the colors of whatever facade they were to adorn, and they struck me as opportunistic and pretentious, flaunting a distinguished pedigree, much like servants in aristocratic houses have been known to look down on the servants of less illustrious households. I have over the years kept alive my whimsical antipathy against hydrangeas with the same reluctant emotional attachment that we feel toward an unloved object which has managed to hold on to its place in our lives and in the end deserves some respect simply for still being there in spite of not being wanted.

Arriving at the busy intersection with the Rohrbacher Strasse, I carefully looked to my right and to my left, as I had been taught, then crossed the street quickly and headed uphill to the Gaisbergstrasse, where I turned right and passed another series of three-story townhouses of lesser stature, their front doors right up against the often cracked sidewalk, and their first-floor curtained windows at eye level with an adult passing by. Other houses were entered through tall, wide, heavy wooden gates leading into courtyards with small industrial workshops and residential quarters in the back.

Once I reached the house where Fräulein von Pittoni lived, I entered through the front door, walked down a dim hallway, and climbed two flights of a wooden staircase to a landing and an apartment door that opened before I had even rung the bell. Fräulein von Pittoni would be at the door, greeting me with a smile which hinted that she had something marvelous in store for me again.

The room in which we worked was a combination of dining room and study. The furniture—heavy, darkly varnished pieces from a patriarchal era, such as a massive, highly polished round table with clawed feet gripping the floor; a tall and wide bookshelf with glass doors; various chairs lined up against the walls with side tables between them—looked as though it had once been part of a much more expansive household, before circumstances demanded that the pieces were to be moved to much smaller quarters. Two tall, narrow windows looked out at the street below; their fine lace curtains gilded the light streaming in from a sunny day and turned the light to pewter when it was cloudy and rainy outside.

Fräulein von Pittoni did not have the air of retired teachers, who often seem scarred and weary from decades of doing battle with their school bureaucracies and steering their classrooms like ships full of distracted, unmotivated, and often rebellious sailors. If she was a former classroom teacher, she had miraculously kept alive her joyful enthusiasm for connecting with children and making each learning moment an unforgettable event. As a reward at the end of a particularly successful school day, she would pull out a folder with sheets of pictures the size of playing cards, each with a lovely design of flower bouquets or songbirds, precursors to today's sheets of stickers; invite me to choose a favorite design; and then carefully cut it out for me with exquisite antique scissors in her gentle hands.

During the two years in which Fräulein von Pittoni was a large part of my life, she taught me how to write words and to read sentences and to string written sentences together so that I could express the thoughts she had helped me to form in my mind. She taught me addition and subtraction, multiplication and division in such a natural way that each new skill seemed to arise from the preceding one without effort. She would ask questions that led to conversations in which we explored new ideas as though we were a team of researchers. I don't remember if she had me do homework or if we accomplished the day's learning objective in the course of the daily four hours, but I am fairly certain that my lifelong habit of reading every day whenever possible goes all the way back to the Heidelberg years.

It was no surprise that in those two years of intensive study, Fräulein von Pittoni managed to prepare me for the entrance exams to the *Gymnasium*, which children normally took after four years of elementary school. This would lead to more unique school experiences once we moved to Frankfurt.

Sometime during my daily walks to and from Fräulein von Pittoni's house, I witnessed an event that touched me so deeply that

I see it to this day as the awakening of my capacity for feeling powerful emotion. It was a cold and windy afternoon, and I was walking home from my unique one-student school when I saw a man, really more of a stumbling bundle of rags, slowly and unsteadily limping up the Gaisbergstrasse toward me, and just as I realized that I needed to make a decision whether to look at him or look away as he passed me in his desperate condition, he turned into the open gateway just ahead of me to my left. I stopped because I couldn't think of what else to do and watched as he lurched a few more steps forward into an open courtyard, from where I then heard a woman's piercing scream and saw her running down a flight of stairs in the rear and cover in an instant the short distance to where the man had now stopped, enclosed him in her arms, both now sobbing and shaking in this moment of their reunion.

The man who had found his way home was a *Heimkehrer*, a returnee, one of the many hundreds of thousands of people who had not been heard from since the war ended in 1945. Their names were listed on endlessly long public notices of missing persons, which were displayed on large bulletin boards outside government offices and read on the radio daily, in the hope that someone seeing the poster or hearing the radio would have some information about the persons whose families were so desperately searching for them.

Watching this couple now clinging to each other, I felt my detached curiosity give way to a dim understanding that their sobs were eruptions of immense joy and pain, and then I noticed that I was choking with my own emotion and welling up with tears for them. I pulled myself together and went on my way, but when I got home, I was unable to talk about the scene I had witnessed. It would be many years before I was able to mention this experience to someone, and then only in passing.

10

Inherited Stories

Vera had such a vivid way of talking about her childhood that I look back and feel as though I had grown up with her in the elegant apartment on the distinguished *bel étage* at Beethovenstrasse 10, in Mannheim; had adored her mother the way she did; had known her childhood friends; and had been at her birthday parties, where some of the children wrecked her toys but were invited year after year because their father was the pastor of her mother's church. I felt as though I had spent time in the kitchen with Rose, who came from a nearby village after she had finished school at fourteen and worked for ten years or more in my grandparents' household, tirelessly cooking and cleaning, until she found a husband and started her own family. I would have been able to explain that the *bel étage* was the second floor in the stately, attached townhouses that lined the leafy streets in the wealthy part of town, while the first floor was called the *partèrre,* French for "ground level, and less prestigious than the bel étage," which was elevated above the street traffic and reached by a sweeping staircase. The third and fourth floors were less desirable because these houses had been built before elevators made reaching the upper floors effortless. On the top floor were the attic rooms for the maids, with low ceilings and small dormer windows.

I never stopped to think that I had no sense of what Harry's childhood might have been like. He did not talk about his relationship with his parents, nor about the home he grew up in, and never reminisced about milestones in his early life, which family members were present, or what event was celebrated. In fact, Harry did not weave stories out of his own experiences; instead, his stories were about other people and their lives, dramatic but also detached, in the style of journalists who report interesting events to audiences who can now imagine that they had been there themselves. It is the story that matters, and the journalist stays on the periphery. It was this style that made it easy to think of Harry as a person who had always been the man whom we knew as our father, unimaginable as a child or adolescent, and when he did tell a story of a particularly harrowing experience, such as the time when he sat alone on the driver's bench of a horse-drawn beer wagon parked at the curb while the driver was making a delivery, and the horses ran amok because of the screech of a passing tram, there was such a cinematic quality to his description of the event that it came across less as a unique personal experience and more like a commercial for Anheuser-Busch.

This reference to a specific brand of beer is not entirely arbitrary. Among Harry's school friends were the grandchildren of Adolphus Busch from Mainz, who had emigrated to America in 1857. Adolphus had sailed to New Orleans and from there up the Mississippi River to St. Louis, where he took a job as a beer salesman for the *Bavarian Beer Company*, owned by an earlier German immigrant, the soap and candlemaker Eberhard Anheuser. Adolphus met Anheuser's beautiful daughter, Lilly, and the couple fell in love and married in 1861, and Adolphus merged his recently started beer business with his new father-in-law's brewery and named their new company *Anheuser-Busch*. Adolphus was an innovator with a prodigious capacity for work, and within a few years, he had established a pasteurizing process in the brewery for heat-treating his beers to prevent spoilage, and he had developed refrigerated railroad cars so that he could sell the brewery's legendary top seller, Budweiser, a product name invented by Adolphus himself, from coast to coast.

Adolphus died as an immensely rich man in 1913, and his widow, Mama Busch, as Lilly was affectionately called, spent all her remaining summers in Mainz, traveling in grand style on trans-Atlantic luxury liners, accompanied by a maid and a butler and a dozen steamer trunks. Harry described Mama Busch as a kind, down-to-earth person, heavyset and not as tall as she was on her wedding portrait, who remained approachable in spite of her vast wealth and her formidable appearance, always dressed in long black gowns, with five long strands of rare pearls loosely draped around her neck and cascading over her bosom. Harry said that she joked—or maybe it was whispered behind her back—that after her death, each of her five granddaughters would inherit one strand, each long enough to go around a slender neck several times.

There was one youthful exploit which Harry did enjoy talking about when his childhood in Mainz came up in conversation. It seems that a favorite summer pastime of Harry and his school friends was swimming in the Rhine River, at a spot where floating beams had been anchored in the riverbed to designate a safe swimming area. The boys would dive under the safety beams and swim out into the shipping lanes where they latched on to heavily loaded, low-riding rear decks of passing river barges being towed upstream. After a couple of miles of traveling upstream in this way, the boys would let go of the barges and leisurely float back to Mainz. Safety regulations were obviously not a high priority in the 1920s, but then no injuries or deaths were ever reported, at least not to Harry's knowledge.

The rest of Harry's life as a child and adolescent has to be pieced together from incidental documents and memories of relatives and is subject to conjecture. As Willy's and Antoinette's only child, Harry's one true parent figure seems to have been his nanny, Alla. Willy had moved to Cologne with his second wife, Fredel, and Antoinette, now no longer a part of the Saarbach family, followed the advice of her friends to maintain her life in Mainz society and was sought out for her charming way of teaching even the most untalented students how to play bridge. There had to have been quite a bit of flirting going on at the afternoon teas and evening dinner parties, which Antoinette alluded to on the rare occasions when she talked about her life in Mainz during and after the First World War, and I even remember comments about a friendship with a French military officer in the post-WWI years, but the fact remains that she never remarried. How all this affected Harry as a young boy is not clear, but it is likely that the experience of growing up as the only child of a mother who had been raised in an orphanage, where she had no role models for someday parenting a child of her own, and an emotionally distant father like Willy whom he seldom saw, resulted in a degree of emotional deprivation, which can give rise to feelings of being excluded, unloved, and plagued by self-doubt. There must have been noteworthy school experiences, friendships, successes, and disappointments, as well as years of violin lessons, with teachers who influenced his intellectual and emotional development, but Harry did not speak of them, and I never thought to ask him. He was probably known as a gifted violin student, but academically less distinguished, and after passing the obligatory Abitur exam, he moved to Berlin in 1933, when he was twenty-two years old. At his father's urging, he took a job in a bank to support himself while continuing his violin practice and seeking out the performances of some of the world's greatest musicians and orchestras who regularly appeared in Berlin in this first year of the Nazi era. Without ever dwelling on these things, I have always had the feeling that Harry did not want to remember his childhood because it had been painful in ways that he probably could not articulate even to himself.

Maybe Harry confided in Vera and talked to her about his childhood memories, but if he did, she never referred to any of them in casual family conversations. It was always understood that Vera's family dynamics were driven by passion and drama, while people on Harry's side of the family were inexplicably distant, maybe as a consequence of some wrenching events anchored in the past. There was, for example, the story of how August Saarbach, Willy's father, had said after the death from meningitis of his fifteen-year-old son, Max, that "the wrong son died." It is not known if Willy heard his father say that or whether Willy even knew that his father had said such a thing, but the relationship between this father and his oldest son was clearly not a warm and nurturing one.

The Saarbachs were nonobservant, secular Jews. Some family members had converted to Christianity at different times in the family's history and attended Protestant or Catholic churches. There must have been a strong desire to leave Jewish rituals and traditions behind and to take on the customs of the dominant culture because Christmas was celebrated in grand style in several branches of the family, and there were Sunday dinners instead of Sabbath seders. The rules of keeping kosher were treated with benign neglect or outright dismissal, and Harry's father, Willy, took pride in his friendship with the Catholic cardinal in Cologne. An earlier generation, including Willy, had fought in the Kaiser's military in World War I, and before that in the Franco-Prussian War of 1871, and there were even stories of certain family members having said things that were outright anti-Semitic. The extended family had obviously chosen assimilation into the dominant culture of whatever country they lived in as a safeguard against the periodic acts of persecution and violence which had been visited on them over the centuries. Since Harry had absorbed the family's culture of avoiding difficult subjects, he never talked about what, if anything, it meant to him that he came from a Jewish family, nor did he recognize that this could conceivably be a topic of some interest to his children. Had he been open in later years to frank discussions of the topic of assimilation, and the role it played in the Jewish diaspora, there might have been lively conversations about the cost of denying one's innermost identity for the purpose of winning acceptance from the traditionally hostile dominant culture. We might have even talked about the delusional belief held by so many Jews that their assimilated identity would protect them and how, when Hitler came to power, they thought that they would be safe, until it was too late.

11

Frankfurt

Early in 1949, the year which saw the founding of the Federal Republic of Germany, Harry transferred to a new job with the American military government, which would take him to Frankfurt. He would move there first, and we were to follow as soon as he had been able to find a place for us to live. Although life had been difficult during the Heidelberg years, I think we were sad to move away. In spite of the famine, life in Heidelberg had seemed not so bad when compared to the previous war years. The reassuring stability of peace, with a place to live, and the continuity of going to school and coming home to a family with a mother, a father, two brothers, and a grandmother, even in a time of hardship, seemed comforting when compared to the wartime uncertainty of what each day and night might bring, with air raid sirens, bomb shelters, burning houses, streets in flames, and advancing enemy armies creating an emotional landscape of anxiety and foreboding.

When Harry started his new job in Frankfurt, the city was still in a very early stage of reconstruction, and there was no housing available for families. He was assigned to one of two rooms in a cramped apartment shared with two single women who also worked for the military government. This meant that the rest of us stayed behind in Heidelberg, an arrangement which greatly alarmed Vera, and understandably so, given Harry's history of entanglements with women, who, from my perspective, were always falling in love with him, intruding in our family, and causing Vera a lot of turmoil. Of course, I did not understand that Harry brought these dramas on himself, and I resented the lovelorn damsels in distress who complicated our life with their foolish yearnings.

Harry's new lodgings were located in a large housing development on the northern outskirts of Frankfurt, called the Römerstadt, which had been built in the 1920s and had been spared in the massive Allied bombing raids on Frankfurt. The Allies had calculated that they would be winning the war and had planned to use this housing tract as barracks for their occupation forces. By 1949, in the four years of ruling the American sector of Germany, the military government had built large new barracks for its single enlisted men and officers, and they vacated the converted Römerstadt apartment buildings, while married soldiers and their families remained for another year or two in the row houses, until housing had been built for them as well. As a sign that the Americans were going to have a prolonged military presence in Germany, plans were drawn up to build a vast housing area with schools, chapels, a giant post exchange, and even a radio station in a different part of Frankfurt. While Harry was still an occupant of an officially designated U.S. Army-requisitioned room in the apartment building Im Burgfeld 143, he was lucky enough to observe that in the apartment building next door, Im Burgfeld 145, soldiers were moving out, and he applied for one of the newly vacant apartments. With his wife and three children and his frail mother, he qualified for four rooms, and when a suitable apartment became available, he received a permit to move in. We were given a chance to briefly inspect our new home, where all the rooms were still painted in the characteristic drab Army green, and the scrapes on the walls showed where the soldiers' sleeping bunks had stood. We were given a move-in date, and Vera still talked years later about her sense of disbelief that we had been lucky enough to be chosen to live in this four-room apartment at a time of extreme housing shortages in German cities, where entire families were assigned by the *Office of Housing* to single rooms in overcrowded, substandard, war-damaged structures.

12

The Frankfurt Kitchen

It would have never occurred to me as a child that the cramped and cluttered kitchen in which Vera cooked dinner every day, and was clearly overwhelmed by the task of cleaning up afterward, would one day become a famous museum exhibit. But half a lifetime and six kitchens later, I found the kitchen of my childhood depicted in a newspaper article extolling the revolutionary design elements of this kitchen as it was exhibited in an architecture museum in England. I was speechless and felt a mixture of uncomfortable exposure and hilarious disbelief that the site of my family's deeply personal and intensely painful struggles had become a public space studied by museum visitors and architecture students.

It was the famous *Frankfurt Kitchen*, created in 1926 by the Austrian architect Margarete Schütte-Lihotzky for a massive progressive housing project in Frankfurt. Little did I realize that our kitchen with its daily messes and mini-dramas, the core of the household in which I grew up, was inspired by the streamlined kitchens on board luxury railroad dining cars of the 1920s, nor would I have been impressed by this because I came to detest that kitchen, and still cringe when I think of it.

Making the most of very little space, the *Frankfurt Kitchen* design called for a compact room six feet wide by twelve feet long. One entered the kitchen at one end from a small hallway and saw at the other end a 4-foot-wide window, flanked on the right by wall hung, glass sliding-door cabinets above a sink, a swiveling faucet mounted above the sink on the tiled backsplash, a drainboard to the left of the sink below the window, a hinged dropleaf work surface in front of the window that could be folded away for access to the window, and more cabinets and utensil drawers below the counter. To the left of the window, and across from the drainboard and sink, was an additional built-in waist-high cabinet for storing potatoes, onions, and canned goods. This cabinet later came to serve as a base for the small refrigerators of the future.

A signature design element of the *Frankfurt Kitchen* was the array of fourteen rectangular, 6-inch wide by 8-inch tall aluminum bins, in two rows of seven each, with large, curved vertical handles on the front plates for a firm grip and chute-like spouts at the rear for easy pouring. With these bins and their embossed labels—*Flour, Sugar, Rice, Oatmeal, Lentils, Peas*, etc.—the cycle of consuming, depleting, and replenishing the basic foods in the kitchen was to be managed in a well-organized flow. For years, these bins drew me into an internal conflict between my appreciation of organization and my irresistible urge to defy conventional norms and to mischievously sow confusion by filling the sugar bin with lentils, the flour bin with oatmeal, and the coffee bin with salt. I am fairly certain that I did not do this to annoy Vera but to make some kind of statement about freedom, individuality, compliance with convention, and opposition to the tyranny of public opinion on how things should be done.

Immediately to the left as one entered the kitchen, and directly across the narrow kitchen floor from the signature bins, stood a four-burner electric stove with a built-in oven for cooking and baking the meals whose ingredients were stored within arm's length behind the cook's right shoulder.

The kitchen had a second door on the left, beyond the stove, which led into the immediately adjoining combined living and dining room. The modern cook, after expending a minimum of energy on accessing and processing the meal's ingredients, could now carry the finished meal to the dining table, which was only steps away.

The designers of the *Frankfurt Kitchen* did not have Vera in mind when they thought of ways to improve women's lives. Vera had spent very little time in kitchens and had grown up with the expectation that one day, when she married and formed her own elegantly appointed household, her mother would train a maid specifically with her needs and preferences in mind.

Vera would not have been impressed to know that her new kitchen was one of fifteen thousand identical copies of the *Frankfurt Kitchen* design installed in the apartments and row houses of the sprawling *Römerstadt* development project, built by the city of Frankfurt between 1926 and 1932 to provide affordable housing for its underpaid civil service employees and to relieve the housing shortage that existed after the end of World War I. Nor was she an admirer of the architectural ideas of the Bauhaus School* with its progressive agenda of liberating women from domestic drudgery and proclaiming the need for egalitarian living standards applicable to all segments of society.

Vera had been raised in a household where the women's suffrage movement was scoffed at as hysterical theatrics by her father and dismissed as unneeded by her mother, and she had been too absorbed in her music studies to give much thought to distractions like political and social issues. She had grown up in large rooms with high ceilings and two rows of paintings on every wall, her private bathroom, and a maid to tend to the various fireplaces, which kept the rooms warm during the cold seasons. She would not have felt drawn to a design aesthetic, which dictated that the apartments and row houses would be built unadorned, strictly for efficiency, with modern amenities, to be sure, such as electricity, hot and cold running water, a bathroom in each housing unit, central heating, and cable radio, but no unnecessary features promising comfort and indulgence.

---

* The Bauhaus School was founded in 1919 by the architect Walter Gropius. During the Weimar era of upheaval, disillusionment, and a surge of unrelenting experimentation in all the arts, the Bauhaus movement pursued design principles such as radically simplified forms, strict rejection of ornamentation, and the harmony between the function of an object or a building, and its design. The basic idea was to replace history with modernity. The Bauhaus School closed in 1933 under pressure from the newly installed Nazi regime, which had accused Bauhaus teachers of "Communist intellectualism," after some of its leading architects had accepted an invitation by Stalin to design and build megacities in the Soviet Union.

The city of Frankfurt had chosen as the site for its experiment in publicly funded housing construction a stretch of farmland on its northern edge between the villages of Heddernheim and Praunheim, on the banks of the Nidda River.* The pastoral Nidda Valley gave no indication that 14 feet below its surface lay the remains of the large Roman city of Nida, with its forum, houses with tiled floors and roofs, frescoes on the walls and pots and dishes in the kitchens, shops with workbenches and tools, streets, markets, academies, temples to the various gods, a public library, and public baths, where an ethnically diverse population of legionaries, craftsmen, slaves and freed slaves, men and women, and children of the Roman province of Germania led their busy lives as local citizens of the far-flung Roman Empire, whose capital, the legendary city of Rome, was so far away that they would most likely never see it in their lifetime. Their Roman governor oversaw the judicial system, the building and maintenance of the infrastructure, the collection of taxes, and the periodic taking of the census, but left local political and cultural issues to be resolved largely by the local population. Readers of the New Testament recognize this system, in which the governor of Judaea, Pontius Pilatus, administers the law of the empire but leaves the ultimate determination of Jesus's guilt and punishment to the local interest groups.

Nida had been a busy commercial hub on the supply line for the massive construction project on the nearby Imperial Roman border, where in the early years of the second century AD, legionaries, the forerunners of today's Army Corps of Engineers, were building a massive palisade wall, the "Limes." This one-hundred-kilometer-long wall, with its fortified gates at one-half-mile intervals, closed

---

* Without any regard for the antiquities in the ground, the city council of Frankfurt had appointed the architect Ernst May in 1925 to develop the overall design and supervise the construction of the huge housing development. Its name, Römerstadt ("City of the Romans"), was to honor its ancient history, and street names like Hadrianstrasse, Am Forum, Titusstrasse, etc. echoed the culture of Roman times. Other street names, such as Im Heidenfeld ("Field of the Pagans"), and Mithrasstrasse, commemorating the cult of Mithras, a Persian deity accepted into the Roman Pantheon as evidence of Rome's tolerance of foreign religions as long as they acknowledged the supremacy of Jupiter, celebrated Rome's early multiculturalism.

the gap in the empire's natural boundary formed by the Rhine and the Danube Rivers and marked the farthest reach of Roman expansion, as decreed by the Emperor Hadrian in AD 120.

The Roman occupying forces, who 1,900 years ago had lived with their families on the same riverbank where I grew up, had been stationed there to secure the "Limes," much as a later occupation force, the American military, after the end of the Second World War, stationed a contingent of their soldiers on the banks of the Nidda so that they could provide support services for the troops who secured the West German side of the nearby Iron Curtain, which protected the free world and the communist world from each other. It occurred to me many years later that I may have at an early age absorbed the deep-seated existential condition of living on the periphery, in a border region, where one's identity is constantly tested by the proximity of a foreign culture and shaped by the constant adjusting to frequently shifting alignments. Looking back over the crucial choices I have made in my life, I see a discernible pattern of feeling most at home where one environment ends and another one begins.

The Römerstadt has a clearly defined northern boundary in the form of its main traffic artery, the Römerstadtstrasse, which follows the original Roman road. The Römerstadtstrasse is lined by a looming rampart of flat-roofed, attached three-story apartment buildings facing north toward the distant Taunus mountain range with its extant Limes ruins. The Römerstadt's southern boundary is defined by the Nidda River. The fields surrounding the village of Praunheim are the western boundary, while the cemetery of Heddernheim forms the eastern edge.

The look of the new city contained no hint of what lay buried below. With every design feature, the Römerstadt architecture proclaimed its determination to erase historical heritage and overthrow all ornamentation, especially the decorative excess of the recent *Gründerjahre* style. History was to be replaced by modernity. All facades were kept free of any hint of the embellishments and sumptuous displays of earlier affluent urban architecture. The new building aesthetic called for flat roofs, bleak stucco facades, hard edges, and brutishly uninviting windows, which—maybe because of their ungainly heavy frames—added a harsh, industrial effect to the cold linearity of this architecture. Growing up with these windows in the urban landscape all around me, I always thought of them as apertures, which could at any moment be thrown open to rain reprimands on soccer-playing boys or scoldings on noisy neighbors and then be slammed shut again with an angry thud.

Compact flat-roofed, two-story row houses (kitchen and living room with dining area on the first floor, two small or three even smaller bedrooms and the bathroom on the second floor) formed straight, long, narrow streets with two lanes, one lane for moving traffic and the other for the parked cars of the inhabitants. The row houses on the north side of the narrow one-way streets were set back from the street by twelve feet, which meant that there was room for a tiny lawn and three rosebushes in front of each house. On the south side of the streets, the row houses were shielded from the street traffic by seven-foot-high concrete walls, which reached almost up to the concrete overhangs shading the front doors and created dank and often moss-covered, cave-like entrances. These forbidding walls had regularly spaced gaps to accommodate wrought iron entry gates, each shared by a pair of houses. Whether the tenants perceived these concrete walls as welcome privacy screens or as oppressive ramparts probably depended on their momentary mood and general outlook on life.

The monotonous streets of little row houses were given some visual relief by intermittent three-story apartment buildings set at a right angle to the streets, which forced the flow of one-lane traffic to navigate in a dogleg curve around the edge of the apartment building and resume its path down the street in a slightly different orientation. This configuration created a sudden wide spot in the street, with an adjoining miniature park in the form of a round bastion looking out over the pastoral Nidda River Valley, and just enough room for eight stately mulberry trees in a half-circle and four benches to benefit from their shade in the summer.

As a special architectural design feature, the massive square shapes of the apartment buildings bulged at the far end to create round, flat-roofed towers, evoking a blend of fortress and ship's bridge. Bands of continuous windows on each of the three floors of the towers strengthened the impression that the inhabitants, especially those living on the first floor, had a mission to use their strategic positions as enforcers of community rules and regulations.

While the tenants in the three-story apartments buildings could enjoy leafy views of the river's greenbelt, the row houses between the apartments buildings had individual gardens in the form of long, thin strips of earth, each as narrow as the house it belonged to, and separated from its neighbor by a three-foot-tall, twelve-inch-wide privet hedge. The uniformity of these meticulously maintained dimensions created the effect, when viewed from a third-floor apartment window above, of a giant green comb. In these gardens, paths of every imaginable configuration, from arrow straight to gently curved, from zigzag to hopscotch, led from the tiny terraces at the rear of the houses to small gates at the garden's end. The little garden gates allowed access to a footpath, which ran along the backs of all the gardens and provided strolling neighbors an opportunity to judge the gardening skills of their horticultural rivals and, if psychologically inclined, to speculate on their rivals' personality types as evidenced by their choice of garden design.

The streamlined functionality in the architecture of this new city, and the small floor space and ingenious efficiency of each dwelling, conveyed impatience with clutter, both material as well as ideological and aesthetic. There was just enough space available for what the designers had deemed the essentials of modern living, with no room for unwieldy, dust-collecting treasures inherited from an earlier era. Modern living demanded clear visual lines, efficient use of time and resources, clarity of purpose, and transparent reasoning; it abhorred obscure thinking, unexamined beliefs, tribal impulses, and turgid emotionality.

When the first phase of construction of the Römerstadt was completed, Vera was a twenty-year-old student at a small private women's liberal arts institute in the exclusive Nerotal section of Wiesbaden, near Frankfurt, and two hours away from Mannheim by train. Vera was focusing on her music studies with the prominent piano teacher Alice Goldschmidt, who prepared her most talented students for the master classes of the internationally recognized authority on Beethoven's piano music, Arthur Schnabel in Berlin. It was Vera's dream to study with Schnabel in Berlin, and with that goal in mind, she spent her days practicing the piano and studying for the art history and literature classes, which were part of the institute's curriculum. The Nazi nightmare was still three years away, and it is unlikely that Vera followed the news of the day, with the daily reports of government crises, strikes, suicides, and violent street demonstrations which plagued the Weimar Republic.

For the families chosen in the early thirties to be among the first to live in the brand-new Römerstadt, moving day into one of the apartments or row houses must have been a momentous event. Since families of civil service employees received special consideration in their applications for the publicly funded housing, the original Römerstadt population was demographically rather uniform: municipal clerks lived next door to streetcar conductors and firemen, railroad workers, grade school teachers, postal workers, and bookkeepers, all united in their common purpose of keeping the city of Frankfurt functioning effectively.

In a typical Römerstadt family, the parents had been born in the last decades of the nineteenth century in Imperial Germany, had grown up as subjects of the Emperor Wilhelm II, celebrated the emperor's birthday each year with a parade and nationalistic speeches, had wondered what the new century would bring, and had felt more patriotic enthusiasm than existential dread when the Great War came in 1914.

If the men had survived the war, they and their families would then have lived through a deadly influenza epidemic in 1918, food shortages and chronic scarcity of essential resources, the ruinous hyperinflation of 1923, followed by years of political instability, the worldwide stock market crash in 1929, a number of attempted political coups, turmoil and unrest in the streets, and a series of short-lived governments failing in quick succession. Along with a pervasive feeling of being unjustly and too harshly punished for Germany's role in the Great War, these survivors had to wonder what kind of a world was waiting for their children.

Many of these survivors of the early twentieth century may have found the harshness of the Römerstadt aesthetic difficult to accept, while others probably applauded the eradication of tradition and convention and resonated with the ideas and gestures of the new architectural movement. People who had begun to despair of ever seeing stability return to their lives might have felt some optimism as they moved into their new, streamlined homes, in which every detail announced the modern way of life. While there was no clear definition of what *modern living* meant, it is likely that for many of the new residents, spare design with clear lines promised a way of shutting out traumatic memories and moving forward into a more manageable life.

The completion of the Römerstadt occurred in stages, as did its occupancy. While the new residents had their civil service status in common, there were religious and political differences among them. Reflecting the demographic of the city of Frankfurt and the surrounding state of Hessen, there was a majority of Protestants, a minority of Catholics, and a much smaller Jewish community. Politically progressive people were likely to have joined the Social Democratic Party, while more conservative people aligned with the centrist parties affiliated with the church. It is also likely that the population included members of the Communist party on the far left and the National Socialist German Workers' Party, the infamous NSDAP, on the far right.

By 1932, the Römerstadt was an established city, with stores, businesses, schools, and voting locations where the residents could cast their ballots in the fall elections of that same year, which led to President Paul von Hindenburg's fateful decision to name Adolf Hitler as Germany's new chancellor on January 30, 1933.

If there had been any hope that people living in egalitarian housing and belonging to a similar demographic would form cohesive, mutually supportive communities, the events following Hitler's rise to power were a harsh disappointment. As a microcosm of German society, the Römerstadt saw its population deeply and bitterly split between regime followers and their opponents who rightly feared the regime and became mute in order to survive. Neighborhood Nazi party functionaries kept a vigilant eye on the local street life, and they were notorious for documenting and reporting any suspicious activities and visible lack of patriotic enthusiasm by the residents.

And as it turned out, the inhabitants of this brand-new city, built in the course of only five years on top of the remains of a much earlier Roman city, came to experience firsthand the transition of their government from a republic to a dictatorship, just as their Roman ancestors had some two thousand years earlier, and they played out their small part, each in their own way according to their beliefs, fears, and temperament, in the catastrophe which was to come soon. If these inhabitants had somehow managed to survive the end of this dictatorship, they could observe through a traumatized haze that the defeated Germany was divided into the four sectors, governed by the victorious Allies. What had during the war seemed on the ground like indiscriminate carpet bombing turned out to have been strategic in its intent to leave certain sections of some German cities, Frankfurt included, intact as future sites for housing the military personnel which would occupy what looked like a landscape of rubble and ruin. The Allied forces routinely evicted the inhabitants of the urban structures that had been deliberately left intact. It was commonly understood that resisting such eviction orders was futile because any appeals would fall on deaf ears. People who at the end of the war had found themselves fortunate enough to still have a roof over their head may have even seen the wisdom of complying silently with the evictions, either because they had a sense that there was justice in their defeat or because they had a glimmer of hope that this eviction would be temporary, and they would be able to return to their homes once the initial chaos was over.

The vast American military forces, which had chosen Frankfurt and nearby Wiesbaden as their headquarters, issued summary evictions for the entire Römerstadt. Thousands of single-family dwellings were converted into barracks for the troops, the tidy hedges between the miniature gardens in the rear of the row houses were torn out to create open space for improvised baseball games, and tanks were driven through the massive walls around the bastions down to the lower-lying terrain where a motor pool with the dimensions of a football field was established for the purpose of repairing and maintaining an immense fleet of jeeps and trucks.

Eventually, the Römerstadt returned to its original purpose of housing a largely working-class population, although this time of much greater cultural and ethnic diversity than the designers had imagined, and memorials of the catastrophe, and the Holocaust it brought with it, are being installed in several Römerstadt streets as they have been in the streets of many large and small German cities. These memorials are very small, yet powerful and deeply moving. Called *Stolpersteine* ("stones to trip over"), they are brass-covered pavers, no more than four or five inches squared, placed flush with the sidewalk pavement in front of each house where a Jewish family had lived before their arrest, with the name of each family member and the date of their deportation to the death camps inscribed on their own *Stolperstein*.

13

The Wing

When we moved into the Römerstadt apartment, Vera was thirty-nine years old, at the exact halfway point in her life. The first half of her life had most certainly not included the housekeeping chores and kitchen drudgery from which the smart kitchen design wanted to liberate her. As she unpacked her dishes and pots and pans from Heidelberg and stowed them away in their new cupboards, there must have been an unsettling moment when she realized that this apartment was most likely going to be her permanent home. If she had ever imagined that, once the war was over, the genteel world of her youth would somehow reemerge, the reality of this utterly sober, functional, but charmless apartment surely must have convinced her that she was now going to be living in unfamiliar territory, and there was no return to the world that her mother had promised her.

I, on the other hand, was now eight and, having marched in refugee treks through destroyed cities and lived through the prolonged postwar famine, thinking that these experiences were part of normal living, took the move in stride and naturally assumed that my opinion of the new apartment was the only one that anyone could possibly have; it did not occur to me that others might feel differently about the move. I walked through the vacant rooms, which looked large without furniture, and I tried to imagine our new life there, with very vague expectations. I was used to sharing a room with my two younger brothers, six and three years old, and our grandmother, and I found nothing wrong with continuing to do so; in fact, I would have been astounded to find out that in some parts of the world, children each have a room of their own. I liked the bathroom, a long narrow tiled space with a washbasin, wall-mounted hot water heater, and a built-in bathtub running parallel to the long narrow kitchen, with its plumbing tied in with the kitchen plumbing through a thin wall for maximum construction economy. The toilet was an object of some curiosity since it was bashfully hidden from view, tucked into a small alcove at the far end of the bathroom, with a long pull chain dangling from the ceiling-mounted tank. The apartment was on the top floor of a three-story building, which meant climbing six stone steps, from the entry vestibule, where every tenant family had their mailbox mounted on the wall, up to the first floor, and from there, two flights of solidly built wooden stairs to the top landing. The other novelty in our new home was that the living room had a complicated shape, as though a lighthouse had collided with the rectangular building; a massive column in the middle of the room added to the odd appearance of this space.

Part of what made the move to the Frankfurt apartment a critical event for Vera was that she now had room for her Steinway grand piano. She had been separated from her magnificent instrument since it was placed in a farmer's stable for safekeeping during the war, and now she would finally be reunited with it.

This Steinway was not the full-size grand piano starring in concert hall performances but the somewhat shorter version built for the music salons of affluent families. The German word for grand piano is *Flügel,* which means "Wing," and refers to the majestic sweep of its lid when it hovers at an angle above the open instrument.

Vera had been given this piano on her sixteenth birthday by her father, probably at the urging of her mother, in recognition of her accomplishments as an outstanding young music student. Since then, she had played her piano several hours every day, practicing the sonatas, etudes, and impromptus assigned by her stern and demanding teacher Alice Goldschmidt in Mannheim, who, after years of intensive study, referred Vera to the well-known orchestra conductor and teacher, Arthur Rother in Wiesbaden, where she began to study the solo parts of the piano concerto repertoire. The Wing traveled with Vera not only to Wiesbaden but ultimately to Berlin, where Vera had been accepted into the master classes of the pianist Arthur Schnabel,

who was, in the 1930s, widely considered to be the world's preemi-
nent interpreter of Beethoven's piano sonatas. On her Steinway, Vera
had learned how to play the standard pieces of the classical repertory,
had developed a strong technique, had competed and won prizes
in local and regional competitions, had grown in her understanding
of the deeper layers of meaning in the music which she was studying, had found a medium through which she could express her own
emotions, and had matured into a promising young performer who
was beginning to test herself in solo recitals and in appearances as a
soloist in regional orchestras.

The Steinway stayed behind in Mannheim, when Vera and
Harry went to Paris to escape the intensifying Nazi harassment and
persecution. After Hitler's invasion of France in June 1940, Vera
was briefly interned in a camp outside of Paris and then expelled.
She returned to her father's house, where she was reunited with her
piano, and since she was pregnant with me, I was exposed to the
powerful piano music that poured from its unseen source no more
than twelve inches away from my developing brain. The many hours
each day during which I absorbed the vibrations and sound waves
of Bach's *Italian Concerto*, or Schumann's *Carnaval*, surely formed
pathways in my as yet unborn brain and trained me to respond—to
this day—to the sound of piano music with a deep, consoling sense
of being home.

Vera was once again separated from the Steinway when her
father wisely arranged for its storage in the farmer's barn in Wahlen
before the massive bombing attacks on Mannheim. With the exception of the times when Vera played the piano in Marschwitz, she had
lived through the refugee months and the Heidelberg years without
any opportunity to play the music, which was always alive in her
head. And now she was waiting for her Steinway as it was making its
way to her new home.

It arrived in an unmarked delivery truck, but as soon as the
vehicle maneuvered back and forth to park as close as possible to the
apartment building entrance and four men got out with wide, heavy
leather straps draped over their shoulders, it was clear that there was
something mysterious about to be unloaded. The rear doors opened

to reveal a very large, prone, glossy black curved object, to which the deliverymen attached themselves with their straps, testing for balance and resilience until they had distributed the estimated weight of the leaden behemoth evenly among themselves. Then they gingerly slid the still legless piano out of the truck bed; let its weight settle into their straining shoulders; inched toward the entrance; disappeared into the building, miraculously managed, with no room in the stair-case for spectators, to lift the piano up the six stone steps to the first landing; shift their load to the right and up the first flight of wooden stairs, shifting right again on the small landing for the next flight of stairs; arrive on the second-floor landing; repeat this feat one more time to reach the third-floor landing, clear the doorway into the apartment by mere centimeters; and move along the short hallway, past the bathroom door and the kitchen door, and into the living room with its column and curved band of twelve windows. The Steinway had reached its destination, known from that moment on as the music room. The men, exhausted and sweating from their extreme exertion but also exhilarated by their success, tackled the final step of mounting the piano on its beautifully carved wheeled legs, two beneath the keyboard and one supporting the tip of the wing, now folded flat, and coaxed it into the position where it would remain for the next forty years.

At first, the Steinway was mute. Fortunately, Vera had been pre-pared for the possibility that her piano might have lost its voice in the years during which the cows kept it warm with their body heat, but no human visitor came to rouse it from its stupor. She had heard of cases where pianos had been given up for dead, only to come back to life under the loving hands of devoted musicians willing to fight off the despair and play the numb keyboards anyway, until the first muffled sounds gave rise to cautious hope. If at that point the untiring work with the hammers and strings continued, and the still resistant keys were treated as though they were functioning normally, they would, in the end, remember how to function normally, and the music returned.

Vera played her mute wing with unwavering devotion and was rewarded for her faith. It may have been days or weeks, or maybe even months, before this distressed instrument had recuperated, but eventually, the famous Steinway sound returned with its full radiant resonance.

Before the dramatic arrival of the Steinway, I had no idea that Vera owned such a piano, nor did I have the capacity to imagine what this reunion with her instrument must have meant to her. What I did notice was that she was now happy in a way I had not seen before, and that confused me because I thought that I knew her and knew what kinds of things made her happy. I sensed now that there was a side of her that I had not known before, and I think in my confusion I also felt some resentment because I decided not to pay any more attention to the piano and accepted that if Vera wanted to spend her days—except for the obligatory midday two-hour quiet period stipulated in the house rules—playing her piano, then that was how it was going to be, and I thought no more about it.

14

The Weir

What Stefan and René and I had in common was our interest in the things that could be observed from our bedroom window. Below us, in a long row of attached flat-roofed houses, lived about fifty American military families, all with one or more children who looked to be between three and eight years old, just like us. The small gardens behind the houses had been consolidated into a large playground and a ballpark, which we thought was a terrific idea, and this is where the American children swung sticks at balls, rode tricycles or bicycles with training wheels, and carted one another around in sturdy red wagons with white wheels. We watched these children with unending fascination, but we knew that their world was inaccessible to us. They were living there because their country had won the war and their fathers had freed the Jews from the concentration camps and liberated the political prisoners, but they were not there to become friends and neighbors. I am sure that I had no secret desire to join in their ball games, and I was too old for the wagon pulling and the playground slides, but I knew that I wanted to live like these families, eat for dinner what they ate for dinner, and eat dinner in the evening like they did and not in the middle of the day, which is what we did, and which made no sense. I wanted to wear the kinds of clothes and shoes that I saw them wearing, I wanted to ride in a yellow school bus like they did, and I wanted to be able to speak English.

These American families would eventually move to their new U.S. military housing areas in another part of Frankfurt, but to our delight, they lived in close proximity to us for at least the first couple of years.

Our days were spent at home in the apartment or, if a willing adult was available, on adventure walks in the fields and woodlands along the Nidda River.

This modest-sized river, which in Roman times had the same name written with only one *D*, flowed through the city of Nida—now buried fourteen feet beneath the surface that we were walking on—toward its confluence with the Main River in the Frankfurt suburb of Höchst. The Nida River was navigable for the large rowboats that carried merchandize and supplies on the last leg of their long trips through the intricate river transportation system, whose main trunk line was the Rhine River with its principal tributaries, the Main River among them.

The Nidda River of modern times would still be navigable for rowboats and canoes were it not for the weirs that have been installed intermittently up and down the river to speed up its sluggish current. The engineered river was also tampered with in other ways. If you knew where to look, you could see here and there the ends of large clay pipes just above the water's edge, discharging liquids that you didn't want to examine more closely before they blended with the river water and made it easy for you not to think about them anymore. If you walked along the river long enough to reach one of the weirs, you had to think about the pipes and their contents again because the turbulent gray water roiling and blistering at the foot of the weir sent up tufts of white foam sailing through the air in playful clumps when there was a breeze. Had we given any thought to Roman times on our nature walks, we would have probably figured out for ourselves that the use of the river as a sewer was nothing new.

Another way in which the speed of the Nidda's current had been increased was by straightening its curving river bed until it took on the appearance of a canal. This straightening process had left several oxbows cut off from the Nidda's efficient new course, and in their new isolation as elongated ponds, these stagnant bodies of water evolved into new ecosystems, attracting squadrons of dragonflies as the most eye-catching of the multitudes of species which arrived in swarms on fluttering or buzzing wings, or on foot, like the bugs that walked, crawled, and burrowed in the thick leaf mold and snorkeled in the puddles forming in the soggy soil between the root systems of the leafy tree canopy. An adult with an interest in biology could have pointed out that the clouds of insects and legions of bugs were part of the great food chain that nurtured the frogs and the songbirds and the small mammals in this unofficial nature preserve, all of which were, in turn, the potential prey of the creatures higher up on the same food chain.

I am not sure that I would have found such information interesting at the time. I was busy absorbing the feel of the overgrown, untended natural space; the freedom from straight lines and imposed design; the randomness of the fallen trees that were decomposing; and in their decay housing and feeding insects while enriching the soil around them for the thriving saplings. Meandering footpaths were maintained simply by their repeated use and sometimes led nowhere because shrubs and vines had taken over, knitted together into a thick, pliable, but impassible barrier. This overgrown refuge was commonly referred as the *Altarm,* a word which sounded archaic and mysterious until I figured out that all it means is "old arm [of the river]." I was drawn to this *Altarm* environment, where I experienced for the first time the powerful feeling of being related to everything around me and having a place in the profusion of life-forms that quietly existed on the periphery of the larger world of order and control. I have tried throughout my life to find this feeling in many different natural environments, and I experience it now most intensely in the canyon worlds of the Colorado Plateau.

By contrast, the straightened river nearby was lined by dikes topped with graded and paved bicycle paths. Slender poplar trees marked its course, and their foliage offered a pleasing sequence of color displays appropriate for the changing seasons—delicate light green in the spring, shimmering mature emerald in the summer, and golden yellow in the fall. In the winter, the leafless branches sketched stark geometric compositions into the cold, overcast sky. In the early years of my life along the Nidda, the tidy look of the river misled some of the local inhabitants into thinking that the water was clean, and on warm summer days, I would watch them with skepticism as they took the few steps down the sloping riverbank in their bathing suits and took a swim, followed by a thorough bathing treatment with a scrub brush and a bar of soap. In later years, as awareness of environmental pollution grew in the population, this practice was abandoned, and the river served primarily as the centerpiece for a recreational corridor of bicycle and jogging paths serving the needs of a more health-conscious population.

Wherever a weir had been installed in the river, it became a welcome distraction from the monotonous course of the engineered Nidda. I never got tired of watching how leaves and sticks floating on the glassy water picked up speed as they approached our local weir, jostling one another as they prepared to ride the broad tongue of falling water across the steel barrier into the deep and getting swallowed by the turbulence below before shooting back up to the surface and resuming their course at their new, lower level toward the big city with its traffic-choked bridges and its confluence with the Main River on the other side of Frankfurt, in Höchst. There was something sinister about that weir, something threatening and unholy about the way it would pull you forward and throw you into the maelstrom if you were in a canoe and had gotten too close to the suction of the accelerating water. The weir pursued me into my dreams, and I remember to this day a particular dream in which I saw Stefan hanging by his hands from a rope strung across the churning water, screaming for help. I was frantically trying to find a way to help him but could not figure out how, and the dream ended before I had to witness his fall.

If I felt drawn to the *Altarm*, it wasn't because I had an idyllic notion of wilderness. It had more to do with my experience that there was always something unplanned and unforeseeable going on in that undisturbed world. There were mallards paddling about where I had never seen any before and herons balancing on one of their impossibly long stick legs, frozen in their garden ornament poses. Interesting treasures could be found in the grasses, such as tiny eggshells from which songbirds had hatched, or small animal skulls, some intact and others bearing marks of fatal injury. Being born and dying seemed to be happening side by side, these mysterious transitions that touch on the sacred in all of life, while they are at the same time nothing but ordinary events in the reproductive process, leaving traces of innumerable small dramas that had lasted no longer than a single season, or maybe just a day.

15

The Tattoo

After a summer of settling into our new apartment and watching from our bedroom window what the Americans were doing, it was time to think about what schools my brothers and I should go to. Stefan was enrolled in the first grade just as the Römerstadt Elementary School, conveniently just down the street, was starting to function again as a school instead of a military barracks. René, at three, would still be at home with Vera. In the two years spent in my fairy-tale schoolroom in Heidelberg, with Fräulein von Pittoni's undivided attention and loving instruction, I had been able to advance through the grade-school curriculum at a much faster rate and was doing fifth-grade work without realizing it. This turned out to be a problem. German schools at that time required from parents that they make a fateful decision for their children during the fourth grade. If parents saw their ten-year-old as a future university student, they steered their child toward the Gymnasium, which required a fairly strict entrance exam. At age eight, I was too young to be admitted to this exam, and Vera resisted the school officials' suggestion to place me in a lower, more age-appropriate grade, where I would be bored but learn socialization skills and make friends. Fortunately, I was still cross-eyed and wore my ungainly wire-rimmed round glasses, a sure target for mean-spirited classmates, and so I was once again exempted from the mandatory school attendance.

For a second time, a fairy godmother sent me an exceptional teacher in the person of Annie Hamann. Frau Hamann was a serious and determined woman, maybe around fifty years old, of average height and sturdy build, with frizzy salt-and-pepper hair casually brushed back just enough to be out of her resolute face. She seemed to enjoy being known as a person who had no patience for foolishness and who was driven by a relentless impulse to avoid wasting time, to succeed, and to teach her students how to succeed. However, once the students understood that in her classroom tomfoolery and pranks were out of place, they found in her a teacher who was completely committed to their progress and treated each child with great kindness and generosity of heart. Frau Hamann was a native of Frankfurt, mentioned once in passing that she had lived elsewhere during the war years, and had returned to find that the apartment building in the Mendelsohnstrasse in which she had grown up was still standing. She had managed to find a way to move back into her family's apartment, where she started a school with the help of her soft-spoken husband, Kurt, who took charge of the practical and administrative aspects of running a small private school, while she took over the teaching.

The Hamanns had transformed one of their rooms into a classroom for six children, with student desks, a large blackboard on one wall, bookshelves along the other walls, and a massive teacher's desk in front of the blackboard. The students, a mix of boys and girls, were of different ages and were expected to study together but at different academic levels, each guided by Frau Hamann according to their individual needs. She would start a lesson by introducing a topic designed to make us think independently and ask questions freely, without fear of being treated dismissively by an older classmate. She encouraged open discussion and expression of doubt, challenged us rigorously, made her high expectations known, and pushed us to excel, not in competition with one another but for the joy of discovering that we could do more than we had thought. She drew in all the students regardless of their grade level, introduced a topic, invited comments from everyone in the class, and then assigned work on the topic to each student tailored to that student's capabilities. Frau Hamann did this so skillfully that I always had the feeling that I was her only student, and I imagine the other students felt the same way.

To my delight, Frau Hamann's school did not offer physical education classes because there was no playground or public park available in the vicinity. What I loved even more was that one of the subjects we studied was English. With the intensive pace of our studies, there was little opportunity for socializing among the students. We were usually done by one o'clock, and each of the students went home in a different direction, on a different streetcar, which is why I have only faint memories of my classmates and did not form any lasting friendships there.

Since Frau Hamann's teaching method consisted of a lecture followed by work with each individual student, there were many times when she would stand behind my chair, leaning over me to make a quick correction to something I had written or pointing to a passage in a book which she wanted me to pay attention to. All her dresses and jackets had long sleeves, and when she leaned over me in her familiar manner, what I would see was the fabric pattern of her sleeves, but on one particular day, her sleeves were not full-length, and as she stretched her curved arm around me, I saw the underside of her forearm uncovered, revealing a series of blurry numbers tattooed into her soft pale skin. I stared at the dark-blue numbers, searching my memory where I had seen such numbers before, then felt a rush of recognition, and for the first time in my life, I had the sensation that my heart stood still. I had seen photos of people's arms with tattooed numbers on them in newspaper articles about concentration camp prisoners liberated at the end of the war, and now I was inches away from the embracing arm of my teacher, a Jewish woman who had survived unimaginable evil.

Every time I recall this scene, I relive the piercing realization of that moment: I was growing up amid the ruins of the country which just a few years earlier had developed monstrous methods to commit mass murder at an industrial scale, and a few of those who had survived were living among us. I never learned how the Hamanns had managed to stay alive in the Nazi death machine, but here, every day, they quietly bore witness to what they had seen and demonstrated with their quiet actions that they intended to go on living and teaching the children of a new generation to think for themselves.

I went home that day, still in a fog, and told Vera what I had seen. She stopped her piano practice, recognized my agitation, and gave me the time I needed to talk about what I had seen. She voiced her own revulsion against the defeated Nazi regime, but she obviously could not bring herself to use this opportunity to tell me about my own Jewish roots because she never said a word about it. I have no memory of talking with Harry about this, although I can't imagine not telling him what I had seen in school that day, unless he came home so late again that night that I was already asleep. In the following days, the visceral force in my reaction to the tattooed numbers on Frau Hamann's arm diminished, and I was able to focus on my schoolwork again, but my awareness of the guilt, shame, and unresolved questions that hung over the postwar German population never lost its intensity. To this day, every documentary about the actions of Hitler's armies stirs up shame in me, and I wonder about the people in younger generations who are tired of feeling shame and are testing their appetite for patriotic slogans, rallies, and songs.

The privilege of a private education by unforgettable teachers in my early school years prepared me for a lifetime of reading, thinking, solitude seeking, and the joy of learning. What I carried away as gifts from my teachers confirmed me in my natural inclinations, such as my aversion to competitive team sports and my complete lack of interest in winning a game. I did not notice until many years later that there were important skills which I did not have a chance to learn in the sheltered educational environment of my childhood.

I must have been an insufferable older sister. Stefan and René formed a pact of mutual support and presented a united front—in spite of the three-year difference in their ages—whenever they felt unfairly treated by me in my frequent role as their temporary supervisor. As the older sister, I was assigned, by the prevailing culture of the time even more so than by Vera herself, the role of mother's helper, and I accepted this responsibility unquestioningly because I saw it played out all around me as a normal feature of family life. I helped Stefan with his homework and entertained René so he wouldn't distract Stefan, and I fulfilled the poorly defined task of seeing to it that the boys were staying out of trouble.

Stefan was a serious, intense boy who always seemed to be preoccupied by some suspicion or fear, which made him seem, at least to me, hard to get along with. I remember how guarded he always was and how angry he could get over what I thought were little things. As the older of the two brothers, he could lift heavier things and reach higher shelves earlier than René, but most importantly, he had already learned to read, which gave him access to precious information, such as the names of the popular soccer teams and their players and the speech bubbles in the comic books that they both loved and which Stefan collected with fanatic zeal. As a natural-born collector, Stefan was an anxious protector of his treasures, who could fly into a rage when he thought he had evidence that someone had violated the sanctity of his space, where everything he owned was kept in various boxes on the shelves at the foot of his bed.

René, three years younger, was cute, with a winning grin, and usually in a lighthearted mood. He was nimble, clever, and wily, and he was quick to grasp the nature of a challenge and come up with a solution. He was the idea man in the team of brothers. For several years, one of their favorite antics was to impersonate a well-known politician at the time, Herr Doerpinghaus, and his chauffeur, Herr Matern. René was Herr Doerpinghaus, smoking a cigar while riding in his official limousine, and Stefan would be driving him to all his important meetings. Whenever the team of brothers got in trouble over one of their memorable pranks, René would win over an irate adult with a soothing phrase or defuse a tense situation with a witty retort, which usually had the desired effect of averting unpleasant consequences. If that failed, he used his uncanny ability to extricate himself from the difficulty at hand by slipping beneath the radar, leaving Stefan to face accusations that he had been the one responsible for the joint misdeed because he was, after all, the older of the two brothers.

Stefan, René, and I were seldom interested in the same activity and had our separate lives, except when it came to going to the movies on Saturday afternoon at the Römer Lichtspiele, the local movie house. We walked together about a mile into the adjoining village of Praunheim, which had a humble theater in an old corner building so close to the winding village road that the big city bus which maneuvered around the tight corner every fifteen minutes and honked its horn to warn the traffic became part of the movie soundtrack inside the theater, blending in with the sounds of gunfire and railroad whistles in the American Wild West. The audience consisted almost entirely of children of various ages, seldom accompanied by adults. We watched the same movies that Americans of my generation remember watching as children in their American hometowns, starring Audie Murphy, Roy Rogers, and Hopalong Cassidy. Sheriffs were pursuing bad guys, whinnying horses were galloping out of burning barns, and Indians were either noble chiefs or perpetrators of heinous deeds. The dialogue was dubbed and sometimes slightly out of sync so that the German words came out of the actors' faces before their mouths had moved to speak. We got carried away by the unbearable suspense of a daring escape, or when we saw an ambush coming, we shouted in unison with a hundred other kids, "Pass auf!" which means "Watch out!" Through an improbable convergence of circumstances, I find myself today living in a house diagonally across the street from the expansive home which the actor William Boyd built for himself after his financial success as Hopalong Cassidy.

Vera had advanced in her parenting skills since the Heidelberg days. On my eighth birthday, the first family celebration in the new apartment, I received the gift which I had been yearning for—a wristwatch. In those days, having your own watch conveyed status and provided ubiquitous access to important information—the time of day, very much comparable to getting your first cell phone in today's world. Wrapping the watchband around my wrist, I felt that I was performing something like a rite of passage because not only would I now be able to know at a glance what time it was, but I could organize my day and keep track of time without needing reminders from adults. Vera invented a third function for this watch. She said that wearing the watch was a measure of my growing maturity and that if I suffered lapses of behavior, she would expect me to voluntarily relinquish possession of the watch for a number of hours or days, depending on the severity of my misdeeds. I swallowed hard, but I agreed, and there were quite a few instances when I had done something I wasn't supposed to, and I took off the watch with a heavy heart and handed it over as an agreed-upon consequence.

Asserting her parental authority over her sons, however, seemed beyond Vera's reach. She had grown up without brothers or cousins, had only attended girls' schools, and had conflicted relationships with her father, her brother-in-law, boyfriends that we never heard about, and Harry. And she seemed utterly at a loss of how to relate to males of all ages, starting with her youngest son. Both boys, and probably all three of us, were unplanned babies, conceived at a time when pregnancies were not the result of a choice but were accepted with varying levels of resignation. For Vera's world, a baby girl was probably a better fit than two little boys, who brought with them a foreign presence which left her uneasy. I am certain that Vera loved her sons, and many events in later years prove this, but the practical and emotional needs of boys, and their energy level, visibly overwhelmed her. She turned matters of discipline over to Harry, who had grown up himself without an interested and engaged father and was just as unprepared to play an active and nurturing father role in the lives of his sons. Indoor entertainment such as board and card games, or outdoor fun like playing ball, hiking, fishing, or going to the zoo, did not exist in Harry's world, and we would have been astounded to see him in casual clothing such as shorts and short-sleeve shirts, which he considered an abomination; swimming trunks would have left us speechless. As a result, Stefan and René consolidated their resources and formed a team, in spite of the striking differences in their personalities and temperament.

16

Käte

Harry could have taken some hints from the Americans if he had stood at our window looking down and seeing fathers come home from work, get out of their uniforms, and come through the back door of their living rooms to the ball field beneath our perch, where they pitched balls to their sons and taught them how to swing a bat. But Harry never came to our window, and within a year or two, the Americans were starting to move out, and the German families, many of them reclaiming their old homes, moved in. They replanted the hedges, which separated the tiny garden parcels, tilled their soil, and planted bushes and trees for shade and privacy. Observing all this activity provided material for amusement of a different sort as one could observe different personality types at work creating welcoming micro-environments, with their outdoor lives in full view, or protecting themselves against the curious glances of the apartment dwellers with umbrellas, curtains, and screens.

Among the original inhabitants of the Römerstadt who returned to claim their homes after the Americans left was Käte Martin. It was her two-room apartment to which Harry and the two secretaries had been assigned the year before, and now that we lived in the adjoining apartment building, Käte and Vera were neighbors. This was a momentous reunion for the two women who had met in an earlier, now unfathomably distant life.

Käte came from Cottbus, a small city in eastern Germany. She was born there in 1882 as her parents' only child. At a time when girls and boys attended separate schools with different educational agendas designed to prepare them for separate roles in society, Käte's father, a high school principal, used his influence to secure a place for his daughter in a local boys' high school. Käte excelled in the classes, which prepared the students for science courses at the university, and when she passed the Abitur exams with honors, her father devoted himself to helping her gain admission to the University of Jena. She became a science educator and taught for a number of years in both girls' and boys' high schools, seeing with dismay the differences in curriculum and expectations that shaped the academic performance of the male and female students.

In her late thirties, at the same time when American women finally won the vote, Käte, with the support of her parents and especially her father, took a giant leap of faith and applied for a sizable bank loan to open a women's residential institute for higher learning in Wiesbaden, an elegant resort town on the Rhine River in western Germany. At a time when the university was still an almost exclusively male institution and women were steered away from rigorous academic studies and instead encouraged to learn the skills admired in a wife of whom a successful man could be proud, Käte wanted to provide her women students with the same high-quality academic courses which she had encountered in her own hard-won university education but without the pressure of having to constantly prove that they, too, had a place in the academic world.

Käte's institute, which she named the *Pensionat Bernhard*, was housed in an elaborate twenty-room villa from the mid-nineteenth-century *Founders' Era*, with a parklike garden, ornate wrought iron balconies in front of the dormitory rooms, French double doors connecting the classrooms on the first floor with the terrace, and a gravel driveway on which the arriving cars with their fashionably crunching tires delivered the newly enrolled students and their parents to the stately main entrance and palm tree-shaded reception counter. Vera and her mother, Else, had arrived in this same way at the Pensionat Bernhard for a visit to determine if this was a suitable place for Vera to continue her education while she pursued her advanced music studies in Wiesbaden. Vera had been strongly drawn to the modern concept of educating young women in science and the humanities instead of the domestic and social skills taught in the traditional girls' finishing schools, and Else was intrigued and cautiously supportive of her daughter's ambitions.

Vera was coming to Wiesbaden primarily to study with Arthur Rother, a sought-after piano teacher and the conductor of the Wiesbaden symphony orchestra. She and Else were made to feel at home on their first visit to the Pensionat Bernhard, and after the school agreed that Vera could bring her grand piano with her, the decision was made that Vera would apply for admission, and she was promptly accepted.

Vera's years at the Pensionat Bernhard were rich in educational experiences, and she made great strides in her development as a musician. She seems to have adjusted quickly to the communal routines of the Pensionat, and her new friends liked her laughter and enjoyed her stories of pranks and mischief that she had inflicted on earlier teachers. Käte surely recognized Vera's antics as the superficial veneer of an insecure young person and sensed a vulnerability which was never far beneath the surface. Vera was a very pretty young woman, slender and chic, carefree, and perhaps a bit too flirtatious when she went dancing, with her brown hair in a stylish cut, and a choice of clothes that expressed her enjoyment of life. What Käte probably found endearing and at the same time troubling was Vera's deep yearning to be taken care of, her trusting nature and open heart, and a temperament given to dreaming about a happy future that would surely arrive once all obstacles had been moved out of the way. If this future was slow in arriving, Vera was given to dwelling on what others had that she didn't have; this opened a path for the poisonous tentacles of envy to creep in and make themselves at home in her heart.

In any case, Vera stood up to the rigorous academic demands of her new environment and became, during her four years there, an accomplished pianist, who was testing herself in local recitals as a soloist and performing in small ensembles. Many of Vera's fellow students were young women who had come from all over Europe and especially the Americas, sent by parents or grandparents who had emigrated from Germany, been financially successful, and now wanted their young heirs to spend some of their formative years in the country of their family's origin. The young women all spoke German with varying levels of fluency and in an exotic mix of accents, which Vera would recall years later with fascination and nostalgia. Vera lost contact with her international friends through the war years, but one friendship was restored after the war through a set of lucky circumstances, and Vera was able to resume her correspondence with her friend Ruth Kopp from Curitiba, Brazil. Forty years after they were roommates at the Pensionat Bernhard in the Freseniusstrasse, the two friends were reunited in Los Angeles, where Ruth had moved with her American husband and where Vera was visiting me.

Käte Martin was a person of towering authority in her school, and all who knew her there—faculty and students—deferred to her with admiration and a hint of fear. She set the tone for her small staff of dedicated teachers and reminded them at every opportunity that the three or four years which their students spent at the Pensionat Bernhard would most likely be the last time in their lives that they could focus exclusively on learning strictly for the joy of it before the responsibilities and necessities of adulthood would steer them into more pragmatic occupations. Käte insisted on high standards in the work that she accepted from her students, and knew how to challenge them to do their best without discouraging them when their best fell short. Vera, with her special emphasis on her music studies, nevertheless was expected to attend the history, literature, natural history, art history, and introductory science lectures, and do the required classwork. She must have found many of her classes inspiring because decades later, she was able to recall the discussions led by Käte about what is an ethical action or how we recognize meaningful art. The literature classes must have been compelling because Vera was able to talk about the characters in the novels and dramas she read with such familiarity that she sounded as though she had known them personally.

Very little was known about Käte's private life. She seldom spoke about herself, but it was clear to all that she revered her father, who had been an early feminist and had risked his position as a respected school official in the deeply conservative Cottbus by openly supporting the international women's suffrage movement. The fact that Käte seldom mentioned her mother may have been a sign that there had been some conflict; in any case, Käte never talked about her childhood in Cottbus or her youth as one of the very few female students in an almost exclusively male academic environment. Some of her comments suggested that she had taken great satisfaction in being an outstanding student and that she had probably worked twice as hard as her male classmates to prove her competence in the face of the almost certain daily disparagement in the classroom and later in the university lecture halls. It is likely that Käte's straight posture and regal bearing, with her hallmark stony expression on her face when she was annoyed, and her legendary ability to shut down offensive speech with an icy comment stemmed from early experiences in a hostile environment.

When I met Käte after her return to her old apartment in the Römerstadt, she must have been in her late sixties. Vera declared that Käte was unchanged since her Wiesbaden days, and indeed, with her broad shoulders and stout body, always dressed in long dark-hued gowns, and the slight limp in her deliberate gait, she cut a striking figure. With her strong, chiseled face, skin stretched taut across her temples and upper jaw, her prominent aquiline nose, high forehead and clear, probing eyes, she seemed ageless and removed from the tyranny of daily necessities. When she spoke about things with special intensity, which she often did, her vigorous white hair, always cut at chin length, would levitate with agitation as it framed her sculpted face and lent her an aura of compelling moral authority.

Vera completed her piano studies in Wiesbaden and continued on to Berlin, where she experienced great musical fulfillment in her studies with Arthur Schnabel but also lived through the agony of watching her mother fall helplessly into depression and succeed—on her third try—to end her life. Käte had observed Vera's extremely close emotional bond with her mother and had, in fact, come to know Else Schaefer quite well over the years in which Else had visited Vera often in Wiesbaden. Käte undoubtedly recognized in Else a woman of her own generation who was living the kind of life that Käte had managed to escape with the steady encouragement and support of her liberal father. Käte also must have recognized signs of Else's chronic and deepening depression, and this may have let her fear for her young and vulnerable student and motivated her to take a special interest in Vera's life after her graduation from the Pensionat Bernhard. It is also possible that Else, feeling her depression tighten its grip, feared that she would leave Vera orphaned someday and asked Käte to step in for her should she not live long. In any case, Vera and Käte stayed in close contact through the ordeal of Else's death, and it seems that Käte's strong emotional support during this traumatic time created a personal bond between the teacher and her former student that lasted until Käte's death many years later.

Through their continuing correspondence, Vera knew that Käte observed the growing threat of the Nazi movement with deep suspicion and growing fear, long before anyone else among Vera's family members and friends took note of the gathering disaster. When Hitler seized power after being named chancellor by President Paul von Hindenburg on January 30, 1933, Käte closed her institute because she knew that in the socially prominent position which she held in Wiesbaden, she would have to join the Nazi Party and demonstrate her loyalty to the regime or face certain political persecution. It must have been with aching sadness, controlled rage, and choking grief that she closed the school she had founded and led for twelve years. She sold the building, said goodbye to her staff, and moved to Frankfurt, where she had accepted the position of a fourth-grade teacher at the Römerstadt Elementary School. Here, in the anonymity of a public school for working-class children, she taught ten-year-olds to think for themselves and ask questions before accepting that everything they were told was always true.

Vera visited Käte in her new environment in Frankfurt and was horrified by the contrast between life in elegant Wiesbaden and the "socialist" housing settlement of the Römerstadt. When she expressed her sympathy about how Käte was forced to live now, she got to know a side in her former teacher's character that she had not seen before, although she could have hardly been surprised. Käte explained in a calm but firm voice that the new teaching assignment which she had chosen for herself was her effort to resist the Nazi regime. She added that she had thought very carefully about testing her courage to openly resist and had concluded that she had the strength to face death but not the torture to which opponents of the regime were routinely subjected. As Vera began to understand the true nature of Käte's plan to survive the Hitler years, Käte described to Vera how she had prepared for the predictable negative attention that she would receive from suspicious school officials and students' parents.

Käte had started a collection of Hitler propaganda photos and statuettes that were distributed widely and intended to satisfy the hunger of the *Führer's* millions of fans for memorabilia of their great leader. There was Hitler riding a magnificent white stallion, Hitler on his alpine mountain top terrace surveying his empire—alone, or with his deferential adjutants, Hitler striding through a meadow with his faithful German shepherd at his side, and Hitler reviewing his troops in the pose of a mythical Germanic hero. Käte also owned a large framed *Fuehrer* portrait, which was ready at all times to be hung at a moment's notice from a nail in a prominent place near the front door of her apartment. By the time of Vera's first visit to Käte's apartment, there had already been occasions to make good use of Käte's "survival equipment," once, when the local Nazi neighborhood watchman paid her an unannounced visit and retreated quickly when he saw the portrait, and another time, when a student's mother rang her doorbell to complain that her son was coming home with ideas that he could have only heard in school. Vera loved the idea of Käte's collection and quoted Käte's dry comment that if she and the collection survived the coming catastrophe, it would be worth a lot of money because all the real Nazis would have burned their own collections before the arrival of the Allies, and hers—the only one left intact—would become a museum piece, a testament to the Hitler cult and the banality of its paraphernalia.

Käte had also started to put together a large folder of posters, flyers, printed public announcements, notifications, proclamations, signs, and newspaper clippings that documented Germany's growing anti-Semitic harassment and vilification campaign as it rapidly transitioned from the rule of law to a totalitarian state. After Hitler had seized power on January 30, 1933, his first targets were the communists and socialists, whose ranks included many Jews. They were rounded up and detained in concentration camps for a brutal one-year "reeducation" course. By April 1, posters and flyers announced the countrywide *Judenboykott* against stores, attorneys' offices, and medical practices, beginning a relentless campaign to make life for Jews so difficult that they would voluntarily leave the country. On April 7, the government passed a law for the "restoration of the professional civil service," which forced the firing of tens of thousands of Jewish professionals. Membership in professional organizations like medical boards and the bar association, as well as access to universities and technical colleges, was blocked, and many organizations and clubs notified their Jewish members of their exclusion on the grounds that they were non-Aryan. Placards from 1934 to 1935 document how the lives of Jews were further restricted by laws forbidding access to movie theaters, concert halls, libraries, public swimming pools, and parks. Restaurants and cafés had signs in their windows barring Jews, and public announcements on bulletin boards urged citizens to report anyone who was seen frequenting a Jewish business.

Vera had very little contact with Käte after she moved to Paris with Harry. After their reunion in the Römerstadt in 1949, Käte unpacked her trove of historical documentation, which traced the systematic tightening of the anti-Semitic restrictions. Newspaper clippings from 1938 announce the levying of new, specifically anti-Semitic taxes; exorbitant punitive "exit taxes" are imposed on emigrating Jews, and the sale of properties formerly owned by Jews is listed in long, small-print newspaper columns. Measures intended to humiliate Jews included the announcement of restricted hours during which Jews could do their shopping as well as the decree which banned them from using public transportation. Beginning on January 1, 1939, Jewish men were required to add *Israel* to their name, while Jewish women were to adopt the name *Sara*. In 1941, the year in which I came into this world, Jews had to wear a yellow Star of David in public, and they received notices that their jewelry, family silver, art, and other valuable objects would be confiscated, followed by demands for their cars, bicycles, radios, typewriters, fur coats, and cameras. In the end, they had to give up their books and hand over their pets. When they had nothing left, they were evicted from their homes and assigned to *Judenhäuser*, where they waited in anguish for their deportations to the concentration camps.

Käte did survive the war, but I never got to see her "Hitler cult" collection. Maybe it was lost during Käte's several moves after her eviction by the American military, or she couldn't stand to look at it once she did not need it anymore and threw it away. What I did see soon after Käte was allowed to move back into her apartment was that she had boxes and boxes of books, which remained unopened for the time being because she had no bookshelves; I was also intrigued that she kept a tall stack of books on a nightstand next to her bed. I was probably ten years old by then, and I asked her why she had all these books next to her bed, when she could really be reading only one at a time. I was astounded when she explained that she was reading different books at different times and for different reasons and that she never got confused about what she had read in each book. I was obviously a very earnest and methodical young reader, starting one story at a time and following it right up to its end before starting the next one, believing that a book was like a plate of food that you finish because that is what you do with food.

Adding to my sense of wonder about Käte's ideas, I saw that one of the books in her stack had the title *Die Söhne Gottes* ("The Sons of God"). I remember my consternation at this title. There was no room in my head for accommodating such an idea since up to that moment, I had lived with the firm belief, based on everything I had heard so far, that God had only one son, and that was Jesus. I wondered who the other sons could possibly be, thinking that maybe Mary had given birth to more children. I did find out some time later, when Käte let me borrow the book, that the other sons were Mohamed, Lao Tse, the Buddha, and many other prophets, which I thought was a truly novel and daring idea. With my haphazard exposure to the standard teachings of Christianity, mostly through reading an occasional Bible story and attending a church service on Easter Sunday or Christmas as my only source of religious education thus far, I found the perspective taken by the author of Käte's book shocking in its implications. I began to understand dimly for the first time that much of what is commonly accepted as fact or truth might just be the result of seeing things in a certain way, and if we looked at things in another way, we might have to change our opinion on things. For quite a long time after this, I found the thought exciting that I had some secret, and mildly scandalous, ideas which would surely appall devout Christians, and I relished the thought that I was in possession of subversive information. Käte probably recognized that this book was a turning point in my cognitive development, and she gave it to me nine years later to take with me to America. The book has traveled in my steamer trunk across the Atlantic Ocean and—in several stages—across the American continent and has come to rest on a bookshelf in my home in California where I see it every day if I look in the right direction.

17

The Trial

Vera left the elegant but sedate Wiesbaden, famous for its healing waters and the luxurious respite that it offered to aristocrats and wealthy industrialists from all over Europe, and landed in the raucous Berlin of the mid-1930s, when the city was still clinging to its notoriety as the capital of perversion and decadence but was daily sinking deeper into the maw of the Nazi machine. Vera would not have described her arrival in Berlin in such Delphic terms. What she encountered was a vast sprawling city consisting of many individual townships, some of great wealth and others racked by grinding poverty, with dense traffic, and the kind of cultural diversity that she had only seen in passing on her brief student visits to Paris and London.

Vera found a studio apartment just large enough for the Steinway and set up her first improvised household, only to discover what it meant to be as unprepared for living on her own as she was. She didn't know how to tell when water boils, and years later, she regaled us with stories of burnt eggs, salty soups, and mushy vegetables, cooked after consulting with unintelligible recipes. She had no idea how to remove a stain from a blouse and once burned the shape of her iron onto the front of an evening gown that she was ironing for her appearance at a recital one hour later. Vera must have figured out how to survive such crises because she stayed on in Berlin with its dizzying nightly choices of concerts, solo recitals, operas, and theater performances; in spite of so many distractions, she remained focused on her piano studies, until her mother made her first suicide attempt in 1937.

Vera returned to Mannheim to be with her mother. Else had tried to drown herself but had been observed by people who rescued her in time. Else was hospitalized for a time and then released to her husband, Karl, who barricaded his fear for his wife's life behind a front of grumbling disapproval of her action. Vera would never talk about the details of the months she spent in Mannheim between Else's first failure and her ultimate success at suicide. On the third try, Else had shot herself in the chest while lying in her bed, and Vera found her, pale and unresponsive; pulled back the covers, and saw a sea of blood. Else died some days later of an embolism in her lungs. She was fifty-seven years old.

The gaps in Vera's story after Else's death remained blank pages for the rest of Vera's life, and they mark the total devastation that this event brought to Vera and the family. Vera was now essentially orphaned since she had lost in her mother her primary attachment figure and protector against her father's chronic anger, hardheadedness, and uncompromising insistence on always being right. Vera stayed on in Mannheim for reasons which, considered separately, seem unconvincing but when added up made sense. There was Vera's discomfort, soon after Else's funeral, at observing how Ms. Lenkewitz proceeded, with Karl's tacit approval, to reorganize the household, change familiar routines, go through Else's cupboards and cabinets, and begin to discard some of Else's things. Vera was determined to protect her mother's legacy by remaining present in the home environment in which her mother had raised her. There may also have been financial pressures on Karl, who may have been unable or unwilling to continue paying for Vera's costly music education in Berlin. And there was the proximity to Frankfurt, which allowed for frequent visits to see Käte in her new life in the Römerstadt.

Although Vera, in her blinding grief, had convinced herself that her sister Ilse was not particularly affected by Else's death, the opposite seems to have been true. Ilse's oldest daughter, Rosemary, today in her nineties, still talks about her mother's lifelong guilt for not having done more to help her mother. Ilse was haunted for the rest of her life by her memory of her mother's last visit in Bernau where she wanted to spend time with her young grandchildren whom she adored. Ilse remembered how, instead of being cheered by the company of the young children, Else's depression deepened, and the children would at times find their grandmother crying silently. It was decided that it would be unhealthy for the children to be around a person suffering from depression, and Else was asked to leave. When Rosemary suffered a severe bout of depression herself many years later, Ilse, now old and frail, came to stay with Rosemary and care for her, and on that occasion, she spoke about her guilt and remorse at having turned her mother away so long ago when she was ill.

Karl reacted to his wife's suicide in his characteristically gruff manner, rejecting all emotional approaches from the people around him and withdrawing into himself. He did not allow himself to grieve openly, did not offer consolation to his daughters, remained distant, and focused on running his company. Else had always wanted him to retire early so that they could buy a villa on the romantic Neckar River in Heidelberg, a spot she had dreamed about for years, especially when early financial success made Karl's retirement at a relatively early age a realistic prospect.

The dream of a comfortable, serene life in the idyllic Neckar Valley was destroyed by a series of reverses which were referred to in the family as *Der Prozess* ("the trial"). It all started when Karl was approached by an old and trusted friend, who had invented a typewriter with innovative features that would enhance the productivity of the typist. The inventor, who was well respected in the typewriter industry, wanted to manufacture this typewriter and submitted a well-thought-through business plan for this new venture. Karl agreed to cosign the loan papers and used certain high-value securities as collateral, with the stipulation to the bank that, should the venture fail, the bank must not sell these securities but instead accept other means by which Karl would make good on his guarantee of the loan. This was in 1926. As Else had secretly feared, the typewriter venture failed, and the inventor's company was unable to service its loans. By the time Karl was informed of this state of affairs, the bank had, contrary to the documented agreement, sold Karl's securities. Karl sued the bank and, after a year of litigating, won. The bank appealed the court's decision, and after another year of litigating and testimony by legal experts that the bank had acted in bad faith, the bank lost again. By this time, it was 1929, and the worldwide stock market crash had severely weakened the entire German financial system. When the bank lost for the third time in the highest appeals court, and Karl expected the vindication he had fought for so hard, he was informed that an emergency government mediation panel had been installed to settle this case. The panel found that the plaintiff, Karl Schaefer, had indeed suffered a severe financial loss due to the improper practices of the bank. The panel also found that the bank was so weakened by the international financial crisis that it would be at risk of becoming insolvent if forced to pay the restitution and penalties imposed by the court. This decision was based on the argument that the bank's insolvency would cause all of its small-scale depositors—workers, widows, and pensioners—to lose their savings and that the government could not allow that to happen. Karl Schaefer received a paltry sum of money as a symbolic restitution, and the case was closed.

It is hard to say what role this drawn-out legal case played in Else's deteriorating emotional state, but no one in the family had any doubt that this wrenching protracted court battle left the family wounded in lasting ways. It was clear that no one in the family was psychologically prepared to come to terms with this injustice. Karl had spent the three years of litigation refusing to even consider that he might lose his case, while Else had lived through these years suffering relentless anxiety, alternately clinging to hope and sinking into despair fueled by the long-covered-up anger and frustration that had accumulated in the course of her marriage. The tension created by the uncertainty of the trial's outcome shredded the fragile fabric which had held Karl and Else together, and it tore open floodgates of pent-up bitterness, disappointment, and lost hope. When the verdict of the highest appeals court was announced, and the finality of the judgment had to be accepted, Karl retreated further into himself, where he was undoubtedly tormented by feelings of rage and failure. He countered Else's accusations of having sacrificed her dream of an idyllic retirement, and her reproaches that he should have listened to her from the start, by shutting her out even more than before, and it was clear that this couple would never be able to come together as partners to shoulder the weight of an injustice such as the one inflicted on them.

18

The Auctions

When Käte received her certifications as a former occupant of the Römerstadt and returned to her apartment at Im Burgfeld 143, adjacent to Im Burgfeld 145, where we were now living, she had not seen Vera in eight years and must have found her marked by the trauma of the refugee experiences and the famine of the postwar years. She was probably touched by the sight of Vera trying to fill the role of a mother of three children, two of them energetic little boys, eight and five years old, Stefan in the third grade and René still home all day, impatiently waiting to turn six so that he could go to the first grade at his brother's school, and me, at ten, serious, alert, task oriented, unplayful, awkward, but not afraid to voice my opinion on whatever I saw going on around me. Käte's thoughts must have gone back to the time before the war when Vera told her about how she had met Harry in Mannheim in a social club of self-styled "cosmopolitan" young men and women who wanted to stay fluent in their foreign languages by conversing with one another in French and English one evening a week. Vera had always said that when she met Harry, it was not love at first sight on her part but that it was their common musical interest that drew them together. Vera was mourning her mother and found consolation in the chamber music pieces for piano and violin which they performed together, first in rehearsal, and later before small audiences.

Vera had also told Käte that Harry had not pursued advanced music studies but had instead followed his father's advice to train as a banker in Berlin for a couple of years before joining his father's international newspaper distribution firm in Cologne. Vera acknowledged that Harry did not develop the level of technical skill which she had achieved through her years of intensive study, but she also knew that his brilliant musicality made him a charismatic performer and a sharp critical listener who discerned the finest nuances in her playing and guided her toward a more powerful expression of the feelings that she brought to the music.

During their reunion, it would not have escaped Käte's attention that Vera's appearance had a new, matronly quality, although in lighthearted moments, her old girlish spontaneity still showed up. Käte had last seen me as a toddler, and she was probably curious how the former two-year-old had evolved in the midst of so much chaos and upheaval. And now here was Vera's intact family, survivors all, including Antoinette, settling into a place that would be Vera's home for the rest of her life.

Käte always said that she was deeply moved to see the Steinway again, which had recently recovered its voice. Vera played for Käte, and surely the music transported both women back to the *Pensionat Bernhard* in Wiesbaden, where Käte had enjoyed rich years of professional fulfillment, and Vera had aspired to great accomplishment, while the Nazi virus incubated and was then suddenly everywhere, upending lives, causing people to suspect one another, turn on one another, and send many fleeing for their lives. Käte probably found a new maturity now in Vera's playing, despite the inevitable loss in her technical skill due to the many years during which practicing had been impossible. It is likely that there was in Vera's playing also a new depth carved out by a pervasive, vague, restless unhappiness.

My brothers and I obviously did not have Käte's nuanced perception of our mother. After the arrival of the Steinway, we had quickly gotten used to Vera's piano playing, much like a steady backdrop to our day, and we forgot that the Steinway had not always been with us and that Vera had once spent her entire day seeing to her household and standing in line at the grocery store and the butcher shop and the vegetable stand to buy whatever was available for the meals that she would cook that day.

Hearing the piano, we always knew where our mother was, while she did not always know where we were. I was actually not hard to find since I loved to read, and the best place for undisturbed reading was my bed, as long as the boys were not there. It was harder to find the boys, who could be playing soccer with their neighborhood friends on the bastion below; they could also be playing in the cardboard and plywood fort they had built in the basement storage space assigned to our apartment, or they could be out seeking adventures in the fields below the bastion, where a parcel of land had been set aside to be subdivided into individual garden plots leased to apartment dwellers who yearned for a place to grow their own flowers and vegetables.

I know for a fact that Käte was pleased to see me go to school every day and study in Frau Hamann's little classroom. I recognize myself in the young person who woke up every morning with a firm sense of purpose, got dressed, took her school bag with a midmorning snack in it because she didn't want to bother with breakfast, walked to the bus stop five minutes away on the Römerstadtstrasse, took the bus to the streetcar terminal in Heddernheim, rode the packed streetcar down the Eschersheimer Landstrasse to downtown Frankfurt, and transferred to another streetcar that would take her to Frau Hamann's street, all this through a city which was still in the early stages of reconstruction, with entire city blocks where the teetering façades of houses bombed and burned five years earlier were eroding and sometimes collapsed on their own. Such rubble fields alternated with large construction sites, where the postwar concrete slab buildings, now despised for their ugliness, were thrown up in a hurry to meet the needs of the emerging economic boom of the 1950s.

Like so many people who reflect on their lives and marvel at the evolution of their sense of self, I am astonished to look back at early scenes of my life and recognize myself—the person I am now—in that young child's body, which seems much too small to contain the massive swelling and receding tides of emotion which have filled my adult body, and do so still.

When the Americans first entered Frankfurt in May 1945 and stationed large contingents of their troops in the newly vacated Römerstadt, they quickly built additional structures on its northern periphery where the densely developed suburb abutted the surrounding farmland. The American military installed large vehicle parking and maintenance facilities for their trucks, tanks, and jeeps, and put up long rows of vast storage sheds, whose concealed contents were protected by menacing concertina wire fencing. Small guardhouses manned by armed soldiers around the clock heightened the sense that valuable materials were stored there. With the gradual departure of many of the American soldiers from the Römerstadt, beginning in 1949, the motor pool was dismantled and moved elsewhere, and the contents of the sheds were transferred presumably to more secure sites. Unnoticed by the German people who were repopulating the Römerstadt, the sheds were now used as storage for something different, which arrived over the course of weeks in long lines of camouflaged trucks entering the fenced-off compound and was unloaded out of sight of any casual pedestrian walking along the fence.

Sometime after we had settled into our apartment, and Antoinette had been allotted her own room in the apartment beneath ours, which meant that we had more room upstairs, Vera found out what was being stored in the sheds. It was furniture, acres of furniture, all of it marked on the back in blue-stenciled letters *U.S. Military Property*, which were familiar from our Heidelberg years, when our own sparse furniture was stenciled in the same letters and color as we were evicted.

Rumors circulated that auctions would be held in which this furniture, removed from requisitioned German homes throughout the Rhein-Main region at the end of the war, was to be sold back to the German population. There were anxious weeks or months in which Vera watched for announcements regarding these auctions, and she struck up conversations with the soldiers in the guardhouses to see if they knew anything about them. Finally came the day on which the public was allowed to enter the first shed for a preliminary viewing of its contents.

I remember the startling sight of a maze of narrow corridors between walls of antique wardrobes, Beaux-Arts armoires, sturdy pine sideboards, hardwood highboys with gracefully turned legs, baroque credenzas on bulbous feet, vitrines looking hollow and bereft without their displays of crystal and porcelain treasures, functional chests of drawers, unassuming bureaus, ceiling-high carved oak bookshelves originally at home in a judge's study, modest kitchen cabinets, massive hope chests, peasants' hutches, and elegant writing desks for ladies of the court.

Next came a huge assembly of dining tables of every size and shape, style, and description—some with intricate mechanisms for adding extra leaves—followed by a huge gathering of chairs, some matching, most of them not, but all with their best foot forward as though awaiting hundreds of imaginary guests. Then came the sofas, lounges, tufted chaise longues, bombastic curved love seats with winged backs, the humble couches, and daybeds, their upholstery in various stages of wear and tear, and these, in turn, led to the domain of the bedroom furniture, mostly individual pieces but also entire sets matching down to their nightstands, some fit for princes, others more suitable for the simpler tastes of hardworking citizens seeking their well-earned good night's sleep in flannel bedding.

The auctions, when they finally came to pass, were heart-stopping affairs for the serious buyers who put up bids in the hope that their chosen object of desire did not have other fervent admirers who would drive up the cost of their purchase with their persistent counterbids. Vera's budget was small, and she was not given to impulsive spending. She knew that the auctions would be taking place at regular intervals over several months, one giant shed at a time, and the second and third sheds could contain even finer pieces, so she took her time and seldom bid against a competitor.

The pieces for which she had offered the winning bid arrived at our apartment at such a slow accretion rate that no one noticed when the line between "fully furnished" and "crammed" had been crossed. To anyone who had studied the original vision of the Römerstadt designers, which was to banish the stifling clutter of earlier eras in favor of spare, functional pieces in austere spaces, it would have been clear that their mission had failed, at least in our apartment. Photographs of family scenes show a domestic environment of overstuffed chairs surrounding a round table covered with embroidered linen and set with silver serving pieces for afternoon tea. Wallpaper with designs of baroque medallions, landscape paintings from Karl

Schaefer's art collection formerly stored in the farmer's barn in Wahlen, or windows draped with heavy brocade curtains form the background in these photos. Not visible in the photos are the plain linoleum floors, covered with overlapping oriental rugs, fraying and curling at the edges, which lent the apartment, built for the modern age, an air of faded elegance hinting at lost splendors.

In frequenting the auctions, Vera may have simply felt driven by the necessity to build an organized household, in which clothes, bedding, and the endless number of little things needed by a family of five in their daily living had their place. She must have shuddered at the fresh memories of how she had improvised each day in the Heidelberg apartment, where the task of coming up with enough food had dominated the daily agenda and matters having to do with organized storage of household items seemed like frivolous pursuits from a bygone era. The almost mythical role, however, which the auctions came to play in our family history clearly point to a deeper motivation. Vera saw a chance here to replace her own treasures from her past, which had been lost in stages, beginning with the complete destruction of her father's house in Mannheim, the repository of the furnishings and accessories of her mother's world. Karl had bought this house after Else's death and had furnished it down to the smallest detail with the things that had surrounded her in their apartment in the Beethovenstrasse. Whatever small possessions Vera had been able to acquire in Berlin and in Marschwitz were lost during her refugee travels, and the requisitioning of the sparse furnishings gathered in the Wolfsbrunnenweg house meant that she and Harry would have to start from nothing once again.

Among the auction items that were delivered to our apartment were two pieces which stood out from the other assorted tables, chairs, bookcases, and cabinets that were beginning to fill our four rooms. One piece was a large, intricately carved sideboard, dark with age, its interior spaces fragrant like ancient churches, with two finely chiseled doors across the front and, above the doors, three shallow drawers, the right and left one wide, the middle one narrow. The patina across the top of the sideboard, on the doors, and on the front of the drawers was worn smooth as satin by the hands of many generations of families who had stored their drinking mugs, plates, bowls, and eating utensils in it and had placed serving dishes with steaming food on its hardworking surface to serve to the people gathered at the nearby table. It was the hinges and locks on the doors, however, that immediately signaled to an observant eye that this hardware had been fashioned in a metalworking process of several centuries ago, by the skilled hands of an ironsmith who had fabricated this hardware for this particular set of doors. The sideboard was examined years later by an antique furniture appraiser who estimated that it dated back to the Thirty Years War era (1618–1648) and had most likely been made in the French region of Lorraine.

The other piece that stood out from the rest was a writing desk of the type commonly referred to as a "secretaire." It spoke a different language and told stories from a different world, most likely France just before the revolution of 1789. It was used to being admired and took its beauty in stride, showing off its magnificent inlaid geometric patterns of exotic woods and tolerating the casual playfulness with which its reclining lid and its three drawers were often opened and closed just for the sake of feeling the quality of the workmanship which had gone into its creation. While the somber-hued sideboard from Lorraine, solid and unpretentious, quietly embodied the integrity of its work ethic, this royal showpiece demanded attention for its lacquered panels with sunbursts, stars, diamonds, and rosettes glowing in lustrous shades of amber, rose, taupe, ochre, and coal. The interior behind the reclining lid resembled a jewelry box, with its miniature velvet-lined drawers, carved alcoves, silver inkwell, and secret compartments accessible only to the initiated. It seemed unthinkable that the writer sitting at this desk would not be dressed in courtly attire and wearing a white powdered wig.

Although Harry did not go to the auctions, he must have been pleased with the results of Vera's project. Faded small photos show him in rare casual clothing, in what looks like a knit pullover, lounging in an overstuffed chair in the music room, one of his two young sons leaning into him and the other one climbing into the chair with him. I remember family scenes of similar domestic contentment in the dining room across the hall from the kitchen, as on Sundays, when we all sat in a cheerful mood on our mismatched chairs at the new oval dining table hard up against the Thirty Years' War sideboard, Harry seated at one end of the table and Vera at the other. We were now eating meals which combined meat, potatoes, or noodles with fresh seasonal vegetables, all of which had, by 1950, become available in modestly stocked grocery stores without ration cards and long lines and at affordable prices. Vera shortened her piano practice on Sundays and cooked fairly elaborate dinners, usually containing Harry's favorite dishes. Among them was boiled beef, which, by Harry's decree, had to be served with horseradish sauce. The sight of Harry's plate heaped with fatty meat slices smothered in the thick white horseradish sauce invariably led to lively speculation by Stefan and René whether the slippery gelatinous clumps of boiled fat surrounding the meat slices should be considered fit for human consumption or might indeed be life-threatening and should be illegal since their appearance alone could bring on choking and suffocation, leading to a terrible death. This discussion, accompanied by peals of uproarious laughter, was a testimonial to the fact that the years of famine were now over, and diners of all ages could afford to become discerning in their food preferences.

19

Wilhelm Furtwängler's Dilemma

Harry had changed jobs and was now working as a reporter for the *Overseas Weekly*, a newspaper that had just been started in Frankfurt in 1950 by an American civilian, Marion von Rospach, and three male colleagues, who were expecting to finish their military service in a matter of weeks. With the outbreak of the Korean War in the same year, the men were detained in the Army, and Marion ran the paper by herself, initially out of her home, with a starting capital of $3,000. The newspaper was meant to serve not only the hundreds of thousands of American military personnel and their families stationed in West Germany but also the growing number of American civilian expatriates who had chosen to remain in Europe after their military service was over or who had come to Europe after the war to participate in the reconstruction effort.

Harry had no formal training in journalism since the Nazi regime had robbed him of any chance to obtain a university education, but he was a talented writer, and he quickly adjusted to his new work environment, which required the flexibility to accept constantly shifting work schedules and take assignments on a moment's notice. As the son of Willy Saarbach, owner of a firm which distributed international newspapers throughout Germany, Harry was at home in the world of print media, professional writing, and foreign languages. Owing to his childhood in Antoinette's multilingual household in Mainz, he spoke German, English, and French with perfect fluency—German and French with the effortless flow of a native speaker and English with a British accent of uncertain origin, possibly self-taught and intended to make an impression. His musical training, interpreter's skill, and literary education qualified him for the assignment to the newspaper's culture desk, and in that capacity, he was alerted whenever prominent Jewish musicians and writers were returning to Germany from the various countries to which they had fled during the Hitler years.

Many of these returning émigrés consented to lengthy interviews with Harry and welcomed the opportunity to talk about their stated reasons for returning and their often conflicted reasons for making that decision. Some said that they were coming back to stay. Others, usually those who had fled early enough to have missed the Nazi horror with its systematic humiliations, assaults, degradations, and deportations to the death camps, came for a few days on their way to other European destinations, casting a quick glance at what had become of the Germany which, less than a decade earlier, had exulted in its vision of total dominance over Europe and the complete eradication of the Jews.

A small number of the returning concentration camp survivors who had, after their liberation, been able to emigrate to Israel, Canada, or the U.S. came to visit, driven by an impulse to test their emotional resilience as they stared down the ghosts of the past. At the same time that these émigrés were taking their first uneasy steps as visitors in their native land, another large group of survivors of the persecution, along with hundreds of thousands of displaced persons from Eastern Europe, was still waiting in sprawling and crowded refugee camps, like the famous Friedland Refugee Center near the city of Göttingen, for visas to emigrate to the U.S., Argentina, Brazil, Chile, Canada, Australia, or New Zealand.

Harry's favorite assignments were his interviews of musicians and orchestra conductors. In the summer of 1950, word came that the celebrated conductor of the New York Philharmonic, Bruno Walter, was on a tour of several European countries, would be passing through Frankfurt, and had agreed to an interview with the *Overseas Weekly*. Harry was ecstatic. Bruno Walter, a native of Berlin, had enjoyed an illustrious conducting career in Germany and throughout Europe before fleeing the Nazi regime in 1933. He was revered by orchestras and audiences for his style of conducting, which relied on his personal warmth, empathy, humility, and genuine respectfulness toward his fellow musicians to bring out in each player in the orchestra the best performance he or she had ever given.

It is not hard to imagine Harry's nervousness and excitement as he prepared for the day on which he would interview Bruno Walter. He would have been concerned with matters of his appearance, might have had one of his best shirts professionally laundered and ironed for this special occasion, and may have decided that the purchase of a new suit and tie was necessary since the site of the interview was the *Hotel Frankfurter Hof*, a coldly elegant, pretentious, and utterly soulless place, which evoked with its Greek columns, gray curved portico, and chandeliered ostentation the opulence of the nineteenth-century founders' generation. It was the one hotel in Frankfurt at the time that was suitable for accommodating dignitaries and celebrities like Bruno Walter.

Harry came home after the interview with a glowing report that Bruno Walter had allowed the interview to quickly evolve from its official format to a deeply engaging conversation between two musicians, and at the end of the formal interview, it seems that Bruno Walter was so taken by Harry's knowledge of the classical symphonic repertoire that he continued the conversation as though it was a reunion of two colleagues. One topic led to another as Harry recalled minute details from orchestra performances he had attended in prewar Berlin in which Bruno Walter had conducted Mozart and Mahler, and there seems to have been a meeting of such kindred spirits that Harry, sensing how uncomfortable a guest would feel in the impersonal *Frankfurter Hof*, set aside reality, invited Bruno Walter to dinner at our apartment, and Bruno Walter accepted.

Vera's consternation at hearing about this invitation paralyzed her at first, and she was terrified by the task ahead of her. Like Harry, she revered Bruno Walter and was mortified at the thought of receiving him in our small apartment, but she rose to the occasion. There wasn't much time available to prepare for the visit since the world-famous conductor was expected in the next city on his tour in three or four days. A massive house-cleaning operation was launched, with Harry at the helm and all hands on deck, which included Stefan and René, who were put in charge of picking up everything from the floor so that floors could be waxed and rugs thoroughly vacuumed. The curved band of twelve windows in the music room had to be washed because the honored guest would most likely arrive before dark and should be shown the picturesque view of the Nidda Valley in the golden late-afternoon light. My job was to dust all level surfaces and to polish the silver serving pieces. There were also a white linen tablecloth and matching napkins to iron for the round table in the music room where the dinner would be served.

The bathroom was a special challenge. It was the place where all of us hung our bulging bathrobes, laundry bags, towels, and washrags from every available hook and nail, where all surfaces were covered with the detritus of daily grooming and where all our unsightly but indispensable household appliances were stored. This busy hub of a family's intimate rituals of personal hygiene had to be transformed into a spotless, uncluttered space that would not offend a guest of high distinction, let alone world renown.

Vera must have been bone-tired by the time she started cooking the dinner on the appointed day, but the anxiety probably energized her enough to help her get through the evening. Antoinette came up from her room downstairs and took charge of the children, with instructions for me to put on my best dress and be ready when called into the music room to be introduced to Bruno Walter. Meanwhile, Vera, dressed up and excited to meet the living music legend, was cooking a chicken dish with a French name, but judging from the leftovers, it looked a lot like ordinary chicken stew. It wasn't as elegant as Harry would have liked, and he made some critical comments the next day about chicken bones in the casserole, which seemed to have embarrassed him, but what I saw when I was called into the music room was that my parents and one of the most famous conductors in the world were just finishing a pleasant dinner, drinking wine, and deeply engaged in conversation, which they briefly interrupted so that my proud father, Harry, could introduce his nine-year-old daughter to the honored visitor. I curtsied and smiled thinly and said nothing until asked a question, which was at that time standard behavior for well-brought-up young girls. Harry said something about my being only nine years old but already studying material from the eighth grade, and Bruno Walter, who must have had young children introduced to him hundreds of times, spoke to me in a completely natural tone as though he had a genuine interest in who I was and what I thought. He seemed to be perfectly comfortable in our music room, as though there was no place he would rather be at that moment. With curiosity in his eyes, and his warm, reassuring smile and gentle voice, he asked me with earnest interest questions about my daily life, which I enjoyed answering, and what ensued was, in terms of minutes going by, a very short conversation which, in spite of its brevity, has reverberated in me for a lifetime. It continues to resonate in me to this day whenever I hear Bruno Walter mentioned by announcers of classical music radio programs in hushed tones as a towering master from the past.

Vera's and Harry's relief after the successful dinner for Bruno Walter emboldened Harry to repeat this experience, and in the course of his tenure at the Cultural Affairs Desk of the *Overseas Weekly*, he interviewed many writers and musicians, each representing a variation of the great theme of the time, which was the question how and where they had survived the Nazi years and at what cost. If they had remained in Germany, could their basic attitude toward the dictatorship be characterized as resistance, accommodation, or compliance with the regime?

Another famous orchestra conductor who accepted Harry's dinner invitation after a formal interview for the newspaper was Karl Böhm, who had been banned from performing in German and Austrian cities for two years after the war because of accusations that he had been a Nazi sympathizer. A native of Austria, he was accused of having advanced his career in Vienna by taking advantage of the expulsion of Jewish colleagues and colleagues who had been persecuted on political grounds and branded as enemies of the regime. In 1948, Karl Böhm was considered rehabilitated and allowed to resume his career. He went on to become one of the most sought-after conductors of the postwar era, appearing in the leading European concert halls and opera houses, as well as at Lincoln Center and the Metropolitan Opera in New York.

Harry was fully aware of the controversy surrounding Karl Böhm's career. If he was put off by this, he did not show it. After dinner, he repeated his proud father act, introduced me to the famous dinner guest and his wife, and accepted their benevolent comments on the pleasures of having children. The Böhms had one son, Karlheinz Böhm, who was a drama student at the time and later became one of the best-known movie stars and heartthrobs in the West German film industry.

Wilhelm Furtwängler had a different place on the spectrum of political positions taken by the musicians and artists who stayed on under Hitler. Furtwängler, like Bruno Walter, was a native of Berlin and had been the conductor of the *Berliner Philharmoniker* since 1922. He had an international career and was a frequent guest conductor of—among many other orchestras—the New York Philharmonic, which meant that he could have turned his back on the Nazi regime and left Germany without fear of losing his career and livelihood. Instead, he stayed at his post at the *Berliner Philharmonie* and accepted the appointment early on, in 1933, as vice president of the *Reichsmusikkammer*, the umbrella organization of German professional musicians, which would soon expel its Jewish members.

Book chapters, articles, and even a play have been written about the problematic decision by Wilhelm Furtwängler to remain in Berlin and allow himself to be used as a pawn by the Nazi propaganda machine. His devoted followers, themselves trapped in an increasingly isolated Germany heading toward the catastrophe, were grateful to him that he did not abandon them but continued to keep open for them what they felt was their last remaining refuge where they could hear the music that was the last thing left to sustain them.

Furtwängler's audiences understood the power of the concert hall to harness the rush of the sound waves created by the interweaving of timpani, horns, winds, and strings as they build powerful sound structures whose vibrations travel through the floor and the walls of the hall and turn it into one gigantic musical instrument. The listeners are cradled in this acoustic process as it heightens and then transforms their emotions, awakening deep compassion and consolation, along with delight and joy.

As the Nazis' grip on the cultural institutions in Germany tightened, the *Berliner Philharmoniker*'s audiences noticed that more and more longtime orchestra members were now absent and quietly replaced by new players, and it became public knowledge that Furtwängler was using his international contacts to secure jobs abroad for the Jewish members of his orchestra. In the early Nazi years, official exit visas were still granted on the basis of foreign job offers, and the musicians could safely depart with their families and a portion of their property after paying heavy departure taxes. By the end of the 1930s, the policies of persecution had become deadly, but by that time, the Jewish musicians of the orchestra had reportedly been saved through Furtwängler's quiet efforts.

With the fall of Berlin in 1945, Furtwängler joined the masses of refugees fleeing before the Red Army and making their way to the West. In 1946, Harry and Vera spotted him, pale, tired, and gaunt, stooped under the weight of a large backpack, walking through the Heidelberg railroad station. In that same year, after a bitter controversy, Wilhelm Furtwängler was acquitted of the charge of having collaborated with the Nazi regime, and in June 1947, he was permitted to perform again for the first time since the end of the war. He was reinstated as the principal conductor of the *Berlin Philharmonic* in 1952, one year after he spent an evening in Vera's and Harry's music room, and allowed his excited hosts to introduce their by then ten-year-old daughter to him. I curtsied as usual, and he stretched out his hand to shake mine. I remember his narrow oval face, high forehead, and thin, short-cropped white hair, and the probing expression of his eyes. He seemed weary but very kind in a formal sort of way.

It is likely that the dinner conversation revolved around plans for the future, with the prospect of exoneration and reinstatement in Berlin, rather than the painful topic of the Nazi past. Vera and Harry understood perfectly that accepting a conducting post at an American orchestra and leaving Germany as a protest against the Hitler regime would have meant abandoning his despairing audiences, and they were grateful to Furtwängler that he had stayed with them. Wilhelm Furtwängler died two years later, in 1954.

20

The Postwar Washing Machine

Harry and Vera enjoyed social gatherings and liked to have their friends come for tea or for dinner. It was not part of the urban culture in Germany to just drop in on one's friends, and visits were always in response to specific invitations. Guests would arrive punctually at five o'clock in the afternoon for tea in the music room, and these visits could stretch into the evening, in which case a supper was improvised. There were also invitations specifically for dinner, with simple meals and several glasses of wine smoothing a path for lively conversation. My brothers and I pursued our various after-school activities in the crowded dining/family room, usually in the company of Antoinette, our "Omi," who would once again come upstairs from her room in the apartment below to see to things. Vera usually admonished her to speak only French with us, an instruction that we all conspired to ignore. Antoinette was terribly intimidated by Vera and feared her exasperated reproaches if Vera heard her speak German with us, so she silently busied herself with ironing a week's worth of Harry's dress shirts, listening to us saying things in German, reminding us in a whisper that we were supposed to be saying these things in French, which, as we reminded her, we didn't know how to do. We were growing up hearing French spoken at home, usually when things were being discussed which the children should not know about, such as financial worries. We did know a handful of idiomatic French phrases and the standard curse words, but as we pointed out to Vera, this was not enough for a "real life" conversation, an observation that Vera promptly turned into an accusation to the effect that this was Antoinette's fault because she should have taught us enough French to be able to have a "real life" conversation.

The tension created by this interminable controversy raised Antoinette's anxiety every time she came upstairs, and it made her forget where she had just put her beautiful amethyst ring, after she had taken it off before setting up the ironing board. Antoinette's anxiety was further increased by her dilemma of what to use as a stand for the hot iron when she needed to set it down for a moment while stretched out a new section of wrinkled shirt on the ironing board. More often than not, she picked another one of Vera's pewter plates from a display shelf as a stand for the iron, forgetting that the melting temperature of pewter lies below the temperature of a hot iron, and the plate would curl, bend, and buckle just as its companion pieces had done when they were pressed into service as stands for the hot iron. These evenings of stilted French phrases and melted pewter plates inevitably ended with Antoinette's anguished search for her ring, which often turned into an organized treasure hunt. Promising sites where the ring had turned up during previous searches were the third of six cup hooks below the wall-hung china cabinet in the kitchen, the back of a utensil drawer behind the seldom used silver mocha spoons in the dining room, a small key rack on the far side of a bookshelf in the hallway, and a solitary shot glass keeping company with an assortment of salt-and-pepper shakers on the kitchen windowsill.

That parents and children had separate interests and pursued different activities, even in crowded apartments like ours, was understood as a given and was reflected in the prevailing view of that era that parents engage in their adult conversations, and children, if present, were to be silent—"seen but not heard"—or be assigned to separate areas for eating and play, so as not to disturb the adults. The idea that children's interests dominate the dinner conversation, influence their parents' choice of recreational activities, or better yet, determine family travel destinations, would have been considered highly inappropriate, bordering on the exotic.

It was therefore not unusual for my brothers and me to have eaten our supper earlier in the evening and gone to bed hearing the voices of our parents and their friends as they were finishing their supper, lighting up American cigarettes and sampling the first wines produced by Frieda de Millas, Vera's friend from her Wiesbaden days, who had lost her husband in the final days of the war. Frieda was now working to rebuild the family vineyards in the Rhine Valley and making her first small deliveries in person. The friends in the music room would now be settling in for hours of lively talk, which usually revolved around war memories and postwar experiences, and the current struggles to build a new existence in the midst of so much devastation and feverish regrowth. Laughter could often be heard through the wall, which did not surprise us since Vera and Harry and many of their friends had adopted a gallows' humor perspective on postwar life in all its bizarreness and had chosen to see the funny side in circumstances which might have driven others to despair. They were joined in this by some of Harry's old friends from Mainz and by Vera's childhood friend Sigrid and her husband, Winfried, who had been a career Navy officer and captain of a destroyer when the war ended. He had spent two years in a denazification camp before being cleared of any wrongdoing and released. He accepted a job as an office assistant in the bookkeeping department of a small cement factory in Bavaria, a job which he performed with humility and quiet dignity for many years, until he received his official retirement and a captain's pension from the new German Navy. He was an unassuming, quiet man who loved his wife and never stopped to think that Sigrid might experience his exclusive focus on her as oppressive and controlling. Vera invoked Winfried as the ideal husband whenever she was frustrated with things that Harry had done or not done. In such situations, Vera would comment in a reproachful tone that "Winfried would have never done such a thing," and "Winfried would have quickly solved the problem," or "Winfried would have known better." Harry simply ignored these comments, and in time, they became family jokes.

There were also Gerhard Taschner, concertmaster of the *Berliner Philharmoniker, and his wife, Gerda*. Vera and Gerda probably would not have been friends if it hadn't been for the friendship between their husbands, but one thing that they had in common was their utter helplessness in the face of the practical demands of housekeeping. They were known to commiserate with each other over the endless cycle of removing dust and dirt one moment and seeing it return and build up a short time later so that the previous cleaning was once again in vain. One day, somebody overheard Gerda saying, "Vera, do you like dirt?" Vera's reply has not been recorded, but Gerda's fatuous question became an instant classic in our household.

And there was the Baron von Reitzenstein, who turned out not to be a baron at all, with his Brazilian wife, both supposedly stranded in Frankfurt while waiting for their visas and his immigration papers from Brazil. The documents never arrived, their story turned out to be a hoax, and the couple vanished and was never heard from again. Another friend who visited occasionally and always came alone was Dr. Mahlberg, a distinguished older gentleman, tall, gaunt, and mysterious, at least to me, with an aura of exceptional dignity and deep psychic pain. He had lost his wife during the war in one of the deadliest bombing attacks on the city of Hamburg and was now frantically searching for his daughter, a beautiful young woman with movie-star looks according to the photo of her which he showed to anyone who might have met her or seen her somewhere. He had information that hinted at a connection between her and an American colonel known to be close to the Allied intelligence community, and he feared that she had become involved in Cold War espionage activities for which Frankfurt was known to be a magnet. Harry, and Vera especially, were very much taken by Dr. Mahlberg's desperate search and always offered him a warm welcome and the comfort of true friendship. When they didn't hear from him anymore, they feared that he had taken his life, but this was never established, and his fate has remained a mystery.

One particular friend, Fredy Wilheim, had been, before the war, the publisher of the respected *Historische Zeitung* in Berlin, an educational publication in the format of a regular newspaper that was dedicated to bringing history to life by reporting great historical events as though they had been witnessed by the journalist writing the article. There were gripping accounts of mob scenes in the streets of Paris, which led to the French Revolution in 1789, triumphant processions through the city of Rome in the first century BC celebrating yet another conquest on the northern and eastern frontiers of the empire, or the heart-stopping tension of the moment on April 18, 1521, when Martin Luther stood up to the entire Imperial Assembly of the Holy Roman Empire of German Nations in Worms who were pressuring him to renounce his ninety-five theses: "Here I stand. I can do no other. God help me!"

Fredy's newspaper was bombed out in the final months of the war, and he fled Berlin and landed in Frankfurt, where he was currently supporting himself and his family by selling "outboard" washing machines, which were essentially powerful vibrators hung over the edge of nearly overflowing bathtubs, agitating the soapy water in which lethargic clouds of dirty laundry floated for unspecified periods of time, until they looked clean enough to hang up and dry. Fredy's droll delivery in his native Berlin accent and cadence could make a simple reading of a weather report a hysterically funny comedy routine. When Fredy described his new contraption, and all the things that could go wrong if instructions were not followed to the letter, the laughter from the music room would pulse through the whole apartment as it escalated to shrieks and convulsive sobs, which let us imagine that the people in the room were splitting their sides, slapping their thighs, gasping for air, and wiping cascading tears from their cheeks.

Common topics were also the politics of the day, the state of the new federal republic, the Americans, the Rosenbergs, the Russians, the federal chancellor Konrad Adenauer, and the reemergence of well-known Nazi officials—after their ideological rehabilitation, of course—in West Germany's public life. It was common knowledge that after the end of the war, the Allies had detained thousands of functionaries and businessmen in so-called denazification camps, where they were brought before a tribunal to determine how actively they had supported the Hitler regime. It was also commonly known, and gave rise to the wide spread bitterness and scorn, that many of those camp detainees recruited friends or family to lie on their behalf and falsely portray them as resistors and dissidents and that the Allies were gullible enough to believe those stories and release the scoundrels, who were promptly certified as eligible for employment by ministries and public institutions charged with building the foundations of the new West German republic.

In these conversations, which often included Käte, it seemed inevitable that at one point or another, someone would bring up the topic of emigration, either reporting that yet another friend had recently departed for America or Australia or musing about his or her own intentions, hopes, or fears.

Käte had recently been able to finally reclaim her two-room apartment for herself, after her last assigned tenant, a young electrician recently certified as a journeyman, had emigrated to Canada. Käte and Wolfgang Störzer had formed a close friendship during the two years in which they shared the small apartment, and he had come to see in her a grandmotherly mentor. Although Käte insisted that she was too old to consider emigrating herself, she had promised Wolfgang that she would visit him once he had settled somewhere in Canada. Several years later, she went on a six-month voyage to visit him in Vancouver, where he had found a well-paying job, bought a mobile home because his work was likely to involve periodic moves, and discovered the magnificent scenery of coastal British Columbia. After her return, Käte gave riveting descriptions of her ocean voyage to Quebec and her transcontinental train trip through the eastern Canadian landscapes, which reminded her of regions in northern Europe, the midcontinental states with their vast horizons, the Rocky Mountains, and finally the Canadian West Coast. Wolfgang met her at the train station in Vancouver and drove here to Nanaimo, where he now lived and where she spent several months as his houseguest between road trips during which Wolfgang showed her small towns that reminded her of English villages, as well as remote stretches of forest and coastline, which, in their wildness, could initially overwhelm a visitor from western Europe.

Käte probably shared with Vera some of the deeper, and possibly conflicted, feelings she had as the date of her return to Frankfurt approached, but she left those out of the educational presentations of her memorable trip as I remember them. I was particularly impressed by the mobile home concept and found the idea that people could just pick up their home and move it—complete with furnishings, household items, and pictures on the walls—absolutely brilliant and typical of the ingenuity of a restless and freedom-seeking country built by immigrants.

Not all the muffled sounds from the music room were hilarious. Late one night, I woke up to angry voices yelling and shouting in the music room. I got up and crossed the hall into the kitchen, from where I could hear the loud argument more clearly. It was Vera and her father, Karl, who had obviously come to visit at a late hour, after we children had already gone to sleep. I could hear Harry's voice interjecting soothing words, but his efforts at diplomacy accomplished nothing, and right after I recrossed the hall to go back to my bed, Karl came storming out of the music room, closely followed by Harry, who was unable to prevent Karl from rushing toward the front door, opening it, and heading down the stairs.

Neither Vera nor Harry ever mentioned this incident, and I thought it was best if I did not let on that I had heard the argument. I knew about the long-standing conflicts between Vera and her father, and I had overheard many conversations about Karl's misguided efforts to rebuild his shipping company on an outdated business model. He had lost most of his freight barges and tugboats in the wartime air raids, and as late as 1950, the few ships which had not been destroyed and sunk were still waiting in dry dock in various shipyards while Karl, from the isolation of his now permanent home in Wahlen, negotiated with various banks for the financing of the necessary repairs and upgrades.

The biggest obstacle to going forward with the rebuilding of his company, and the repair of the ships, was the fundamental change that was taking place in the river transport industry. The system of having one tugboat tow a string of four or five barges connected by long cables was rapidly being phased out and replaced by fleets of owner-operated motorized barges, which were more easily maneuverable through the increasing river traffic on the Rhine than the long barge trains and could be much more responsive to freight hauling demand between Switzerland and Holland. Banks knew about this transformation of the river barge industry and tried to reason with Karl that his resistance to the changes in his industry was pointless. Karl's most prominent characteristic being intransigence, he dug in his heels, pointed to his forty years of experience as a leader in the shipping industry, and quoted a letter from his captains and mates in which the aging men stated that they wanted to remain loyal to his business model, just as he had been loyal to them throughout the years, keeping the fleet fully staffed during the good and the bad times of fluctuating revenues, and especially during the time of the Great Depression in the early thirties, when the barges traveled up and down the Rhine half-empty or were idle as they waited for shipping contracts in economically depressed river ports for months at a time.

With his stubbornness and angry outbursts, Karl succeeded in alienating every one of the bank officials who had tried to protect him from the predictable failure he was bringing on himself. His raging against the new realities in his life was almost certainly fueled by other painful experiences, such as the suicide of his wife and the bitter injustice of the highest appeals court ruling against his rightful claim, and in favor of the bank that was too big to fail. Another disappointment for Karl was the indifference of Ilse's three grown sons, who showed absolutely no interest in their grandfather's business and found him an amusing relic of a distant past. Sixty years later, on the eightieth birthday of one of the three grandsons, this trio of now old men regaled the family gathering with tales of how, on their visits in Wahlen during summer vacations, they would watch Karl finish his nightly supper with a course of well-ripened cheese scooped up with the curly edges of dry old bread slices and wash the delicacies down with a favorite wine. Laughing so hard that they could hardly speak, the brothers described how Karl, extremely nearsighted by then, mistook maggots escaping from the cheese and crawling around on his plate for bread crumbs, moistened the tip of his index finger with his tongue, and swept up the unfortunate microfauna together with the bread and cheese crumbs into a neat little ball, which he ate with the satisfaction of having cleaned his plate and let no food go to waste.

Although there was very little contact between Vera and Ilse, Karl's angry letters from Wahlen to both of his daughters gave rise to occasional family visits between the sisters and their families, especially after Ilse's husband, Richard, had returned from Russian captivity as a prisoner of war. Richard had miraculously survived the shelling of his car in Berlin in the last days of the war, had been taken prisoner, and worked as a doctor in a prisoner-of-war camp in Russia for several years before being released in return for a delicate medical procedure which he had performed at the request of the camp commander. Vera and Ilse had never been interested in their father's business and couldn't remember a single instance when Karl might have sought the opinion of any family member on any issue, business related or not, but the banks had contacted them, as designated heirs, in an attempt to find a way to persuade Karl to listen to reason.

It is possible that Karl's late-night visit in our apartment was brought about by the growing urgency to resolve the financing of the ships' repairs and that the controversy spilled over into related issues and finally ignited the mix of pent-up hurt and resentment like a tinderbox. Memories of earlier family dynamics may have flared up, like the passionate confrontations about religion that had led to shouting matches between Karl and his sister-in-law Franziska, who—unlike her sister Else—fought Karl tooth and nail over every detail of their irreconcilable positions on the Catholic church and its dark history. Franziska, an unmarried woman in the era when unmarried women were dismissively called spinsters, was a petite, ever cheerful and fun-loving woman with girlish mannerisms and tight blond curls surrounding her pretty face, changeless and ageless into her late seventies. Franziska had been part of Vera's youth, having spent weeks and months visiting her sister Else in Mannheim, especially once her parents, Ludwig and Pauline Meincke, had passed away after Franziska had faithfully cared for them until their deaths.

The legendary shouting matches between Karl and Franziska usually started innocuously enough with cautious comments at dinner, where Else would steer the conversation away from known land mines. Once dinner was over, however, and the family adjourned to the sitting room, Else could not rein in her husband or her sister once they started to engage in one of their skirmishes. Else and Vera would find reasons to leave the room, and Franziska seized the opportunity to once again defend her faith against the great infidel, who, she would admit freely, had proven himself to be a loyal provider and generous son-in-law but had to be checked at every pass when he attacked her church. Karl never turned down an opportunity to declare his hatred of organized religion, reciting an ever-growing list of crimes perpetrated by all Christian denominations, sects, cults, and, foremost among them, the popes in Rome, such as the current one, Pope Pius XII, who had collaborated with Hitler and turned a blind eye on the Nazi atrocities in the hope that a Hitler victory would check the advance of godless communism out of Russia. Citing dates and invoking historical facts, Karl would walk over into his study to retrieve a book for checking a reference, and Franziska followed him, which meant that the duel was now being fought in the study, making it safe for Else and Vera to return to the sitting room, from where they could hear the combatants go on for a good while longer, with Karl raising his voice and his undaunted sister-in-law's soprano shouting above him that, no matter what he had to say, she would never let him rob her of her faith.

Else must have winced at what her sister had just said. Franziska knew that when Karl and Else started making plans for their wedding, Karl had refused to set foot in a Catholic church, and that Else had, at Karl's insistence, agreed to marry him in a civil ceremony and would therefore, in her mind, be living in sin. This thought caused Else mortal anguish as everyone in the family could see, and in the end, Karl offered a compromise: Else could join the minuscule *Altkatholische Kirche*, which had proclaimed itself the true, authentic Catholic church, with its rejection of the celibacy of priests and the doctrine of papal infallibility, as it had been decreed at the First Vatican Council in 1870. The stormy debates over the infallibility doctrine have, in the course of the past 150 years, given way to many other bitterly fought controversies testing the Catholic church, but at the time when Else agreed to marry Karl in 1902, the doctrine was still recent, and feelings were raw.

After Else's death, Franziska never set foot in Karl's home again. Since the passing of her parents, she had become accustomed to living on her own and was supporting herself with secretarial and book-keeping jobs. With her love of life, which natives of the Rhineland region, like herself, claim as a birthright, and with her disarming sense of humor, inquisitive blue eyes, and graceful, petite figure, she had no trouble attracting suitors, but none of them made the grade as they routinely violated basic norms of decency by attempting a kiss on the first date and touching her slender legs during a romantic moment on a park bench, among other unspeakable acts. Vera would eagerly question Franziska after each of her frequent dates about any new depraved behaviors, and Franziska would pour out her disappointment to her sympathetic young niece about the churlish men who initially seemed so pleasant but would, in the course of an evening, inevitably reveal their true nature as lustful beasts.

The disruptions and upheaval caused by the struggle to survive the war separated Vera from her delightful maiden aunt, but during our Heidelberg years, they were reunited. It turned out that Franziska had found a safe haven in the little town of Schwetzingen near Heidelberg, where she was renting a room in the home of a mailman's family who had embraced her as one of their own. We took the streetcar to visit Franziska, and she often took us on walks through the famous Schwetzingen Park, which surrounded a miniature Versailles palace with its own baroque theater, whose faux marble walls and columns turned out to be made of cleverly stained and painted wood.

Vera said that Franziska had not aged a day since she had last seen her almost fifteen years earlier, and it seemed that the two women simply picked up where they had left off so long ago, laughing, teasing, joking, and maybe sometimes crying when no one else was around. René, then three years old, fell in love with Franziska and announced that when he was grown up, he would marry her. Our fascination with Franziska had something to do with the way in which Vera was transformed whenever she was around Franziska. In front of our eyes, Vera became the lighthearted, cheerful prankster of her youth, the girl who always emerged in her tales of her childhood in Mannheim, playing tricks on teachers, flirting with half-grown boys, scheming with her best friend Sigrid on how to annoy Sigrid's mean stepmother, cuddling with her mother, making faces at her father behind his back, and quizzing her maiden aunt about her latest disasters with debauched men.

Once, when Franziska talked half in jest about feeling old age coming on, with a hint that Vera should not expect her to live forever, Vera laughed boisterously the way children laugh at a birthday party when the clown stumbles and falls into the pool. Mixed in with her laughter, Vera announced that she was making an official declaration: "Titi, wenn du stirbst, dann lache ich mich tot!" ("While this idiomatic expression is difficult to translate literally, the closest English version is probably something like: 'When you die, I'll split my sides laughing.'") Franziska understood how Vera had meant this seemingly heartless remark and joined in Vera's laughter, all the while insisting that she would indeed die someday. I don't remember who else besides myself was present at this little scene, but it has remained vivid for me as an example of a loving relationship so secure that two people can acknowledge the coming heartbreak in the language of jesters.

After we moved to Frankfurt, we did not see Franziska again, in spite of frequently stated intentions to visit her, and then we received a black-rimmed envelope in the mail with a letter from Franziska's adopted family notifying us that she had died in her sleep.

Vera accompanying Harry on his way to
deployment to the Eastern Front in 1941.

Vera posing for the official photo of the baptism of her children,
Heidi and Stefan, in Marschwitz in November 1944.

Vera and Harry in Heidelberg after the "Hunger Winter" of 1946.

Vera and Heidi in Heidelberg in 1947.

Vera and her three children, Heidi Stefan,
and René in Heidelberg in 1948.

Harry at the Leipzig Book Fair in East Germany in 1956.

Vera at her piano in Frankfurt in 1959.

21

The Roman Milkman

As much as Harry loved the excitement of his job at the *Overseas Weekly*, which put him in frequent contact with the international crowd in Frankfurt and provided frequent occasions for late evenings of smoking, drinking, bridge playing, and storytelling with colleagues, he could no longer ignore the reality that his salary of seventy dollars a week, even with the favorable exchange rate of four marks to the dollar, was simply not enough to support a family with three children. The chronic shortage of money, and Vera's silent anger about the late evenings, where Harry occasionally lost money at his bridge games, must have begun to outweigh the fun of it all, and when he received an offer from an Italian businessman to join a newly formed venture, he accepted.

This meant that we were now going to move to Rome, the hometown of many of the people who, almost two thousand years ago, had lived and worked in the city of Nida, now buried fourteen feet below us. No one in the family had time to give this much thought as each of us faced too many immediate tasks. Vera was cautious and insisted that we keep the apartment and sublet it to a suitable tenant, while we were to live in Rome on a trial basis. Vera, who had grown up without ever having to worry about money, where it came from, and how it should be spent so that it would go as far as possible, had by default become the family's chief operating officer, planner, and bookkeeper for accounts both payable and receivable. She had taken over these functions because someone had to, and Harry had already demonstrated that he had even less experience and talent for the job than she did.

It made sense that Harry would drive to Rome first, start work on his new job, and find a place for us to live, while Vera searched for a suitable tenant who would be agreeable to being introduced to the other families in the apartment building as our relative; this was necessary to get around the Römerstadt rule which prohibited the subletting of a whole apartment. René, in the first grade, and Stefan, in the fourth, were facing a major disruption of their elementary school education, and my time in Frau Hamann's school would have to come to an end. Disruptions were something that all of us were used to, and what I remember of this rather dramatic move to a new country with a different language and unfamiliar living habits is that we weathered it remarkably well. It occurred to me only much later in my life, when I worked in a residential institution sheltering severely traumatized children, that stoic behavior can mask a disturbed attachment style. The frequent moves and losses of our earliest childhood had probably left us, at an unconscious level, feeling anxious and insecure, and we may have learned to shut down those feelings to avoid the pain that came with them.

In any case, I said goodbye to Frau Hamann, the boys didn't seem to mind saying goodbye to their friends at school, and we followed Vera's orders about which of our things we could pack and which would have to stay behind. It was peacetime, trains ran on time, and railroad tickets came with assigned seats, which really existed at the end of a brief search for the correct railroad car and seat numbers. We found our seats on the direct train from Copenhagen to Rome; filled all the overhead luggage racks around us with our suitcases, bags, and boxes; and settled in for the long journey of a day, a night, and another day. We crossed the border with Switzerland at nightfall; laughed at the almost unintelligible German dialect spoken by the Swiss border patrol officers as they meticulously studied every passport; traveled through the Swiss alpine landscapes in the dark; reached the border between Switzerland and Italy at dawn; listened to more passport checking, this time in Italian; arrived in Milan in midmorning, thinking we were close to our destination, and then continued down the long, bootleg-shaped Italian peninsula until the train finally, in the early evening of the second day, pulled into the recently completed Stazione Termini, Rome's famous, at that time ultramodern, railroad station with its dramatically cresting and sweeping roofline.

Harry met us on the platform. He had the car with him, a large black Citroen sedan with its vintage look of large swooping front fenders flanking an elaborate silver front grille bearing the famous double chevron ornament, chrome headlights perched on top of the fenders. There were four doors, the front doors opening into the headwind. This distinguished conveyance had room for not only the whole family but all of the luggage we had brought along. We were too wound up to notice the late summer heat, chattering about the long train trip and wanting to know what kind of a place Harry had found for us to live in. He and Vera had been communicating by mail as telephones were, at that time, still not a common feature in most people's homes, and we didn't have one in Frankfurt either. Vera had a general idea that we would be living, at least for the time being, in a rented house south of the city, on the Via Appia, the road built by Roman soldiers three hundred years before the birth of Christ as a military highway for their rapid marches designed to surprise and conquer Rome's neighbors to the south. Among the inhabitants of Nida, there had probably been more than a few who had walked on the Via Appia at an earlier time in their lives.

For a world-famous road, the Via Appia looked from a car window like a fairly ordinary country road, smoothly paved, with occasional patches of exposed cobblestone, winding its way through an iconic, softly rolling Mediterranean landscape of small fields, orchards, vineyards, olive groves, and the famous pines of Rome sheltering modest tile-roofed stone houses. Occasional stately villas could be seen in the dusk, usually half hidden by foliage and protected by tall, vine-festooned fences and sturdy gates.

It was completely dark by the time Harry suddenly made a right turn into a short driveway, stopped in front of an iron gate, got out of the car, pushed the gate open as though he lived there, got back in the car, and drove up a short gravel road to a white, two-story stone house whose thick walls seemed to squeeze its few small windows. Harry said that this was the house of a *senatore*, who was never there because he owned an apartment in Rome where he preferred to live, especially now that he was getting too old to make the trip to his country house. A caretaker and his wife lived in a small building across an overgrown courtyard, and we would be occupying the fully furnished second floor above the vacant first floor, with use of the kitchen, which was located in the basement and could be reached through a narrow passage leading to a set of timeworn stone steps.

The first few days, or maybe even weeks, went by in a fog. Distinct memories of scenes of daily life in the *Senatore*'s house emerge as I think back and visualize the whitewashed, spacious kitchen with a large wood-burning stove; massive cabinets; and open shelves with ceramic pottery and stacks of plates on them; a heavy wooden table with sturdy, straight legs; and rustic chairs to go with it. The person I still see cooking in the kitchen is not Vera but the caretaker's wife, a stout, older woman with braided hair and a white apron over a long brown skirt, who would have probably been very friendly if we had understood Italian. The language barrier stood between us, and I don't remember having any interactions with her, or her husband, which might have given me the feeling that I was getting to know them. I don't think I ever knew her name. She cooked our meals for us, and we came downstairs to pick them up and take them up to the second floor where we ate in an improvised dining room in the sweltering heat, with the windows open in hopes of a cooling wind. Since we were responsible for cleaning the rooms we used, she never came upstairs, at least not while we were there.

Vera loved the Italian night sky with the Milky Way and the prominent constellations with their defining stars, which a person growing up in Germany's cloudy climate rarely sees. In Frankfurt, I had never paid any attention to the night sky because there wasn't much to see, in part because of the moisture and haze in the air and because of the urban light pollution. Now in this rural area, away from city lights, looking up at the starry sky was a completely new experience, and when Vera pointed out Orion with his belt and sword, and his loyal dog Sirius in tow, Orion became a familiar presence for me, standing high in the winter sky. We didn't have binoculars, so we couldn't really see the fuzzy light halfway down Orion's sword, and it was much later in my life when I finally got to see the wondrous Orion Nebula through a telescope and learned that it is a place where stars are born.

Vera also loved the large overgrown garden with the lavender plants and lemon trees and kept quoting from the famous Goethe poem "Mignon's Song": "Kennst du das Land, wo die Zitronen blühn?" ("Do you know the land where the lemon trees bloom?") In that poem, Goethe had given voice to the age-old fascination that Italy holds for Germans who have traveled to Venice, Siena, Padua, Florence, and Rome ever since the Renaissance and before, seeking inspiration, knowledge, and immortal love. Vera could have gone on and on about the art and architecture and music of Italy and how Italy was the source of creativity and innovation for northern artists and composers, but such thoughts went over our heads. We were more interested in a beautiful large white dog who patrolled the thin wire fence along the road but did take time out here and there to socialize with us. He stood as tall as a large Labrador retriever, with a thick coat, floppy ears, a round nose and soft muzzle, intelligent eyes, and a bushy wagging tail, but with the purpose-driven personality of a German shepherd. It was a pastor Abruzzese, a shepherd dog from the Abruzzi mountains of central Italy, and he was very aware of his responsibility for securing property lines and keeping intruders out. He seemed to belong to the caretaker, who would feed him and whistle for him to come inside at nightfall. The dog was never called by a name, and we never learned if he had a name at all. In any case, this dog was also a seasoned warrior as we once observed when we were returning from a walk along the Via Appia and, approaching our driveway and the gate, saw a man on a bicycle pedaling along the loose and sagging wire fence, which caused the dog to race up and down the fence line, barking furiously. To our horror, the man on the bicycle whipped out a knife and hurled it at the dog, who had obviously experienced earlier attacks like this, deftly dodged the deadly projectile and then continued with his mission until the bicycle rider had retrieved his knife and disappeared down the road.

It was becoming clear that we would never feel at home in the *Senatore*'s house. Harry was in business meetings in the city all day and most evenings and therefore absent much of the time, which left us feeling isolated in the countryside without access to stores and other amenities, and there was no suitable school in the area for my brothers and me. We knew nobody, and it didn't seem likely that we would meet any of the families living nearby, given the language barrier and the significant distances between farmhouses in the area. We were probably no more than fifteen miles south of Rome's city limit, but when we heard Harry driving off in the morning on the crunching gravel driveway for yet another long day of business in Rome, we felt anxious and abandoned in a region that we experienced as remote and wild. We would see an occasional bus on the road, with passengers inside, but we felt so distant from the locals and so ignorant of their customs that getting on their bus seemed like too intrusive an act.

Vera and Harry must have talked about the emerging difficulties in our idyllic life in the country because there were several weekend trips to the city, with inspections of vacant apartments for rent in various neighborhoods. The hottest summer months, when people flee the stifling temperatures in the paved-over city for the beaches or the hilly countryside, were over, and besides, Vera had expected us to live in the city when she agreed to the move to Rome. Finding a suitable and affordable apartment was going to be a long, drawn-out process, but then an unsettling experience back at the *Senatore*'s house accelerated the search. It was late at night, after a powerful thunderstorm had broken the late summer heat, and we had opened all the windows on the second floor to let the cool breezes in. I don't know if it was Harry or Vera who thought to shine a flashlight into the dark garden with its dancing shadows of windblown shrubs, tree branches, and tall grasses, but what we all saw was eerie and chilling. As the beam of the flashlight wandered across the ground cover and overgrown paths, pairs of glowing red eyes stared up at us, first one pair here, then another pair there, and over to the right yet another. None of us admitted that we were scared, but we closed the windows and pulled the curtains. In the morning, Harry asked the caretaker in his steadily improving Italian what those animals were that we had seen from the window the night before and was told that these were the wolves. We immediately understood why the caretaker whistled his dog inside every evening.

After this experience, the search for an apartment in the city became a priority, and a suitable place was quickly found Viale Libia No. 25, on the fourth floor. Coming from the fabled Roman Empire's distant Germanic border region, we had now finally arrived in the capital of the greatest superpower of the ancient world, which had ruled Europe and the Middle East from Persia to Spain and Lybia, Tunisia, and Morocco to northern England. Now we were here, a short distance from the seat of government, the Forum, where the orders had been issued which the army commanders protecting the empire's borders obeyed as they implemented Roman foreign policy. In the halls and chambers of the Forum, the consuls of the Roman republic, and—after the fall of the republic—the emperors dictated the expansionist policies of endless military conquest until the Emperor Hadrian, in AD 120, changed course, declared an end to the politics of expansion, and followed his vision of consolidation, with secured borders, peace, and political stability.

The necessities of daily life quickly overtook these high-minded reflections, and the conversations that I now overheard were more about Vera's efforts to find schools for us and Harry's preoccupation with his business partners. Harry had made friends with several people since his earlier arrival in Rome, and based on their recommendations and helpful tips, markets and grocery stores, laundries and dry-cleaning shops, a hair salon and a post office where located, and in the end an international school for children aged six to twelve years old was also found. Stefan and René started school, but once again, my private school history made it difficult to determine which grade I should attend, and I agreed enthusiastically with the idea that I should take a year off altogether, study on my own the books that Vera would select for me, and help Vera with the household. The idea was that living in Rome was an intensive educational experience in its own right and that Frau Hamann had prepared me to work at a grade level for which I was too young anyway.

The prediction that experiencing ordinary daily life in Rome would be a rich educational experience proved to be accurate. I cannot remember doing any systematic homework there, but I observed and imitated the way of life of the locals, navigated the immediate neighborhood with its bakery and open market, then ventured a little farther, turning into an unfamiliar street and following it, until it intersected with a street I already knew, and where I recognized the names on signs and the words on advertisements. I wasn't particularly daring and branched out only slowly, but gradually I found other bakeries, so I could compare their breads and their prices, and I never got lost. The Italian liras were becoming as familiar to me as the German marks, and after a couple of months of exploring and rehearsing, I began to run the same local errands for Vera that I was used to doing back in the Römerstadt. I thought nothing of walking into the neighborhood grocery store on the Piazza Emerenziana with my little shopping list and a bundle of liras and felt comfortably accomplished when I climbed back up the four flights of stairs to our apartment with my purchases and some new words I had picked up on the street.

What made the shopping easy was that it worked in the same way that I was used to in Germany. The customer enters a store and walks up to the counter that separates the merchandize and the sales clerk from the shoppers. The sales clerk asks the customer what she wants and retrieves the wanted item, such as a can of peas, from a shelf behind her. If the customer needs three pounds of flour, the clerk opens the flour bin, dips a trowel into the bin, and fills a paper sack with the estimated quantity of flour, places the sack on a scale, adding or removing a few ounces until the desired weight is just right. This process is repeated with each new desired item, and a small pile of wrapped goods is accumulating on the counter until the shopping list has been completed. Then the clerk writes the cost of each purchased item on a small order form, performs a quick paper-and-pencil addition in her head, and announces the sum owed. The clerk and the customer chat for a moment, while the customer produces the money owed from her purse, and then the clerk turns to the next customer. After three or four visits by the same customer, the clerk remembers and greets the person with a few personal words, which in Rome tended to be much warmer and much more welcoming than what I was accustomed to at our *Latscha* grocery store in the Römerstadt.

Milk was delivered daily to almost all parties in the apartment house by Emiglio, a sturdy, rustic-looking man with dark tanned forearms, neck, and face, and an enthusiastic smile that was even more winning with its gaps, which added a hint of mischief to his grin. Emilio came every morning and placed a bottle of milk for each subscribing family on the lobby floor in front of the row of residents' mailboxes, collected the empty glass bottles placed there by the customers the night before, and rang every customer's downstairs doorbell to announce the delivery. I would go downstairs to pick up the milk, and one day, for whatever reason, I dropped the milk bottle, and of course, it broke on the tiled stairs. Emiglio was still in the building, saw my accident, laughed away the seriousness of the calamity, and handed me a fresh bottle. His words "Latte kaputt… va bene…va bene!" echo in my ear to this day. Vera was so impressed by this generosity that on the next day, she came downstairs with me to thank Emiglio, and they struck up a conversation in the course of which—enhanced by much lively gesturing—Emiglio expressed his abiding admiration and love for the Germans and their leader, on whose side he had fought during the war. As he shared his happy war memories, it clearly never occurred to him that Vera might not find herself on the side of his war comrades.

Emiglio has remained a vivid character in my childhood memories because he was the first non-German Nazi sympathizer I met. I had formed the idea as a child that only Germans could be Nazis, and if I left Germany, I would leave the Nazi curse behind me once and for all. Emiglio also became a living example for me of the paradox in human nature which makes it possible that a person can be decent and generous in one set of circumstances and in a different context relish the fight to advance ideologies that promote shocking cruelty to others. The discovery that the Nazi disease of nationalism, white supremacy, hatred, contempt, and violence toward marginalized groups had infected people in other European countries as well left me with a sense of disorientation and confirmed me in my plan to live someday in America, which was too far away from Europe to have Nazis. After all, the Americans had come across the Atlantic to fight and defeat the Nazis in Germany and were surely never going to tolerate Nazis, dictators and concentration camps in their country. Learning about Hitler's friend, Benito Mussolini, and the Italian fascists, also helped me understand why the Americans didn't land only in Normandy but also in Sicily, from where they had to fight their way up the Italian peninsula to defeat Mussolini's regime before joining the fight against Hitler's last remaining forces on German territory. I was intrigued to find that the word *fascist* is derived from the Latin word *fasces*, referring to bundles of twigs such as those carried by the dictator's special guard; this is an example of the countless ways in which ancient Rome is still alive in the way we live and speak two thousand years later.

While Stefan and René went off to school every morning, I stayed home with Vera and became more practiced in living like an ordinary inhabitant of the city, going to the post office, to the local park, and to the movies, where one of my favorites was *Il Ladro de Venezia* ("The Thief of Venice") because the language was straightforward, the action was obvious, and the lead actor was gorgeous. The movie theater around the corner was cheap, and once you had bought your ticket, they let you stay in the theater to watch the newsreel and the movie as often as you wanted; this was an excellent method (before television) for hearing the spoken language repeated until you had finally understood the gist of the dialogue.

My only friend during my year in Rome was Sofia, who came to our apartment with her grandmother once or twice a week. Her grandmother was Ricchetta, the sister of the *senatore*'s caretaker, whom Vera had hired to help her with the cleaning of our apartment. Ricchetta had agreed to come but was fearful of traveling by herself on the bus to Rome, where she had never been in her entire life. She was illiterate and needed help in deciphering the names of the streets leading to our building. For this reason, she had Sofia accompany her, which meant that Sofia was missing school on the days when her grandmother went to Rome to clean our apartment. Vera understood this and arranged activities for Sofia and me which had educational value for both of us. If there had been a piano in our furnished apartment, I am sure Vera would have given her piano lessons, but since that was not possible, she found books for us on Italian paintings, sculptures, churches with domes and elaborate bronze doors, Tuscan city halls, and Venetian palaces with their facades reflected in the Grand Canal. Works by Michelangelo, Leonardo da Vinci, Donatello, or Brunelleschi were just as unfamiliar to Sofia as they were to me, although we both recognized the Mona Lisa in a lineup of famous faces, and wondered why she was in Paris and not in Italy. Neither Vera nor I had come very far in our attempts at Italian fluency, and Sofia learned new German words at about the same rate as we learned new Italian words from her. Ricchetta seemed to approve of Sofia doing what looked like schoolwork, but she never joined our conversation to see what we were talking about or working on, and there was a hint in her glances that sitting at a table and looking at pictures in the middle of the day meant that you were wasting an opportunity to be outdoors doing necessary work that had to be finished before the sun went down.

It seems that our plan to lead an ordinary life in Rome succeeded. Unlike tourists, we never bothered to stand in line waiting to get a glimpse of famous sites. If there was a line, we changed plans because we could always come back at a better time when there would be no line. Bus rides to the dentist's office passed by the Colosseum and the Forum, Sunday afternoon walks in the cooler autumn temperatures led to the Spanish Steps or the Pantheon, and casual strolls across Saint Peter's Square with a folded newspaper just purchased at a newsstand in the shadow of the colonnade signaled one's status as a local resident.

Our ordinary living also included occasional visits to friends' houses. There was Abbas the Iranian, who once had us all come over to his one-room apartment in an old stone house that could only be reached by a precarious bridge across somebody else's courtyard. He had made some delicious Iranian pastry that was very sweet and sticky with honey-glazed nuts. Abbas worked for the Italian businessman who had offered Harry the opportunity to join his company. This Italian was a somewhat elusive figure, often out of town and out of reach, and to the extent that children sense their parents' unspoken anxieties and tension, I had begun to pick up an occasional hint that Harry was no longer entirely convinced that this Roman venture would lead to something substantial. There were other times, however, when our future in Rome seemed assured, as on the occasion of an invitation from the entrepreneur to join him and his wife for dinner at their home.

The entrepreneur and his wife made their home on the top floor of an eight-story residential building on the fashionable Monte Parioli. Crossing a beige marble lobby under the stern gaze of the concierge, we found the mirrored elevator and arrived moments later on the eighth floor directly in front of the apartment door, just as it was opened from inside by a young woman in a maid's uniform holding up a tray with a variety of drinks for arriving guests. What I remember most about the apartment's interior is that everything was white: white carpets on white marble floors, white leather sofas and chic chairs and tables, white walls and ceilings, white curtains, and a white poodle in the arms of the hostess, whose silver-white hair completed the composition of the scene. I had never seen anything like this apartment before and found it cold and pretentious, and somehow unsettling, without knowing why. Maybe I had already absorbed enough of the socialist Frankfurt spirit to feel an instant aversion to the conspicuous display of wealth, especially since I had noticed that there were many people living in poverty in other districts of the *Eternal City*. Fortunately, there were a lot of other guests deeply engrossed in their conversations, and nobody paid any attention to the three German children, who were quickly offered some food and games in a separate room, where we stayed until it was time to go home. When I saw the film *La Dolce Vita* years later, many of the movie sets reminded me of that preposterous Monte Parioli apartment, a stage for self-absorbed people seducing one another into believing that they were happy.

Casual strolls across Saint Peter's Square would occasionally lead to equally nonchalant visits inside Saint Peter's Basilica. Here is where Vera's belief was put to the test that by living in Rome, I would be getting an excellent education even if I wasn't going to school. She selected reading materials for me that discussed the history of the city, the history of how Rome became an empire, the history of the papacy, and the history of how Saint Peter's was built on top of a previous structure, which was thought to have been erected on top of the site where Saint Peter was executed. Lectures followed in which Vera explained how stonemasons used as their building materials recycled stones harvested from dilapidated temples and walls built during Imperial Roman times, how marble for the vast floors of the church had to be brought in on sleds pulled by teams of oxen or horses, how enormous bronze doors were cast and installed, how sculptures and ornaments had been pilfered from other antique public buildings and repurposed to adorn the enormous edifice, and how all this was paid for by a wicked scheme of selling certificates of forgiveness in heaven for sins committed on earth by the easily duped faithful. As I learned next, the German monk Martin Luther was so appalled by this fundraising practice that he spoke out against it with thunderous rage and caused the furor, which resulted in the Protestant Reformation. Paid with the enormous sums of money pouring in from well-to-do, mostly German sinners, Michelangelo had designed the dome and painted the *Last Supper* on the ceiling of the Sistine Chapel by the time the Reformation movement was underway.

In this intensive homeschooling, criticism was obviously encouraged, or at least tolerated. I remember how Vera spoke in an admiring tone about Bernini's grotesquely ornate *baldacchino* above the basilica's main altar, held up by four massive spiral-shaped columns. I was twelve years old and didn't know how to articulate my thoughts on esthetics, so I carried on about how awful I thought this *baldacchino* looked and how I didn't like it. Today I still don't like the look of the *baldacchino*, and the best reason I can give is that it makes me think of an Ottoman potentate's scandalously voluptuous four-poster bed.

The crypt below Saint Peter's was a place where a lot of European history could be learned. The remains of almost a hundred popes share the crypt with the thousand-year-old corpse of the German Emperor Otto II, with members of the Catholic Royal Stuart family of Scotland, with the composer Palestrina, and with the enigmatic Queen Christina of Sweden, who had given up her throne to travel in Europe, settled in Rome, and scandalized her Protestant countrymen by converting to Catholicism at a time when Catholics and Protestants had just fought a war for thirty years, finally ending in 1648, and leaving German lands in a state of such devastation that they would not recover for fifty years.

One of the popes in the crypt, Pius X, was laid out in a glass coffin for all to see that the previous thirty years since his death had caused no deterioration in the condition of his body, a sure sign that this pope enjoyed a special status in the world of spiritual perfection. A small plaque next to the glass coffin stated that a thin layer of silver was covering the pope's face to protect it from decay.

There were many things in Rome that could be regarded with a critical eye. The best example of how a hideous site could become a popular destination and object of admiration of tourists from around the world is the Colosseum. I found it inexplicable how awestruck tourists marveled at the fact that this giant arena still stands, listened to the guides who explained architectural complexities, and completely overlooked the signs and exhibits describing the events of systematic unimaginable cruelty which took place there. I want to believe to this day that there were in ancient Rome groups of abolitionists who resisted, denounced, and possibly tried to sabotage the spectacles of wholesale slaughter of prisoners and slaves as crowds roared their approval.

My favorite building in Rome was Hadrian's tomb, also called the Castel Sant'Angelo. The massive cylindrical fortress across the Tiber from Saint Peter's was built by the charismatic emperor Hadrian, whose political judgment led him to recognize that there had to be a limit to Rome's expansionism, lest the empire become ungovernable. Hadrian had established the first permanent borders for the empire and, in AD 120, had visited Nida—my hometown, so to speak—to inspect his troops as they were building the border fortifications that are meticulously maintained to this day as a field trip destination for Frankfurt's schoolchildren and their teachers. Hadrian was married for many years to his Empress Sabina, with whom he had adopted two sons. In midlife, he fell in love with Antinous, the most beautiful young man on earth; never got over his adored young lover's suicide;

and several years later died a slow death that was so painful that he begged a faithful servant—in vain—to end his misery by killing him. I was fascinated by this story in the way that young people today might be fascinated by the life and death of an aging rock star, and in my eyes, Hadrian's massive mausoleum perfectly expressed the power and appeal of this glamorous emperor.

There were limits to our casual access to Saint Peter's. Harry had the idea that we should go to church on Christmas Eve "like all good Christians" and that our local church would be Saint Peter's, and celebrating the mass would be our local pastor, the pope. When we got to Saint Peter's shortly before midnight, the vast piazza was unexpectedly quiet, as though we had come on the wrong day, and when Harry went ahead to ask about midnight mass, he was told that His Holiness Pope Pius XII was celebrating mass in the Sistine Chapel for the Diplomatic Corps only. I think we did some grumbling about the unfairness of it all but got over it fairly quickly. We walked home in the late night and probably commented more on the famous Roman cats owning the city after sundown than on the missed event.

The following week brought another unexpected experience. It was not surprising that, as midnight approached on New Year's Eve, the streets would be full of revelers, and the apartment doors in our building stayed open as people were coming and going, greeting one another with shouts, song, chanting, and laughing. What we were not prepared for was that at midnight, our neighbors began to hurl cups and saucers and plates, glasses, and bowls out of their windows and off their balconies, with no apparent concern for the safety of the pedestrians below. We need not have worried because this was obviously a well-established practice, and the people on the street below knew what was coming and how to avoid the hazards of the new year's first fifteen minutes. We found out from a neighbor who was amused by our consternation that Romans traditionally save up all the dishes broken in the course of the year and throw them down on the street to greet the new year with the thrill of the explosive impact.

On a sunny day in March, Harry and I were once again walking across Saint Peter's Square on our way to run an errand, when he overheard people around us saying that Stalin had just died. Harry was electrified by the news and hurried to a newsstand to see if there were some news bulletins available. The journalist in him was ready to jump on the story, but since he was no longer part of a news organization, I became the beneficiary of his impulse to report this momentous story, beginning with a dramatic account of the failed Russian Revolution in 1905, when the Tzar's soldiers opened fire on the crowd of demonstrators in front of the Hermitage Palace in Saint Petersburg, going on to describe Lenin's arrival at the Finnish Railway Station in Saint Petersburg after the Germans had helped him get there by transporting him and his band of fellow emigrés in a sealed train from his exile in Switzerland to the Baltic Sea, how this maneuver had its desired effect of taking the Russians out of World War I, how Josef Stalin came to power, how millions of Russians died due to Stalin's policies, how Hitler first signed a friendship pact with Stalin and then invaded Russia one month before I was born, and how more millions of Russian and German soldiers died in the ensuing Second World War in murderous battles too terrible to describe.

Since that memorable introduction to modern Russian history, I have read many accounts and seen many documentaries of the epic events in twentieth-century Russia, but Harry's gripping tale of human suffering, political intrigue, cruelty, and the insanity of war remains indelible and unique. It lives in my memory as a testament to his passion for the idea that a just and fair society depends on its newspapers to provide the people with true information about what is happening in their communities and in their government. Without newspapers and objective reporters, a community does not know itself, and its voters have no basis on which to make prudent decisions. Harry had seen firsthand as a young man what happens when the government spreads lies and people have no access to the true facts: large numbers of disappointed and resentful people swallow the propaganda that they want to believe, and they enthusiastically follow the leader who dazzles them with visions of restored greatness, while other groups lose interest in their government altogether and distract themselves in the hope that if they don't pay attention, the evil will pass with no harm done.

22

The True Believers

By the middle of June, with the summer heat reaching temperature measurements which seemed improbable and fantastical to people from northern climates, Harry and Vera decided that our future was not in Italy. There were probably a number of reasons for this decision, having to do with growing doubts about Harry's association with the Italian businessman, and Vera's unhappiness without her Steinway. One day, on relatively short notice, Harry's vintage Citroen was methodically loaded up with boxes and suitcases, leaving three small niches in the back seat for René, Stefan, and myself to nest in during the two-day return journey to Frankfurt. The three of us took the change, of course, in stride, and it seems that we were more drawn to resuming our life in Frankfurt than invested in our Italian experience. I initially missed the daily routine of wandering through our neighborhood open-air market and looking for novelty pasta shapes in the vendors' huge glass jars, walking to our bakery down the street, chatting with Emiglio, helping Ricchetta with the cleaning and watching Vera try out new Italian recipes while Sofia would talk about what was going on in her school. What has remained in my memory of our year in Rome is not a list of world-famous artworks, churches, and monuments but the general sense of having lived an ordinary life there, having blended in with the people around us, participating in quotidian routines among the descendants of the ancient Romans for whom, two thousand years ago, the word *quotidian* was a part of their everyday vocabulary and which, in fact, literally meant "every day." These ancestors had thought, spoken, argued, whispered, dreamed, shouted, sung, and cursed in Latin just as their compatriots did on the frontier in Nida, to which we were now returning.

The tenants of our apartment in Frankfurt still had a month to go on their lease when we returned from Rome, which meant that we dispersed to various temporary living quarters for a month. I went to live with a foster family in a village outside of Frankfurt and experienced a culture shock when I discovered that no matter how hard I tried to blend in with their routines and customs, I would never fit in. They were extremely religious, frequently referred to Bible stories and quoted scripture when discussing news stories and current events, and invoked the Word of God at every turn. They were naturally very interested to hear what I had seen in Rome, and on the second or third day, at the dinner table, when I got to the story of the pope in his glass coffin with his face covered by a layer of silver, they marveled at my good fortune to have been able to see this miracle. I assured them that the pope's silver face was not brought on by a miracle but by the hands of a human silversmith, a fact which I had learned from the small wall-mounted plaque near the glass coffin. As I said this, I immediately felt an uneasy silence in the room, followed by a cold wave of rejection as the family closed ranks and consigned me to a place outside their community, where they would view me as "the other," no longer meriting their compassion, and I suddenly understood how, in closed societies ruled by authoritarian leaders and dogmatic beliefs—secular or theocratic, the believers unite in upholding their articles of faith, strip the nonbelievers of their right to inclusion, and leave them to their fate, even if that fate means being dismissed, expelled, disowned, imprisoned, herded into gas chambers, or burned at the stake. There was no physical aggression toward me in that family, and they fulfilled their contract to provide me with room and board for the agreed-upon four weeks, but I never felt safe there, and I counted the days until I could leave that house.

It was this early, disturbing experience of living in a family setting that on the surface looked normal enough but masked the fact that I was a foreign body among them, an unsuccessful graft, that I often recalled in my work, decades later, with children living in foster and adoptive homes. The children couldn't say in words but drew in harrowing pictures how they felt like strangers in the families which their social worker had chosen for them. In my memory, the faces of my short-term foster parents are blurred, like faces of actors in an inconsequential, almost forgotten movie, but I can still feel the icy silence through which they banished me from their community of believers.

23

The Economic Miracle

Eventually, we were all reunited in our Römerstadt apartment, where the Steinway had remained silent for a year, and we found that nothing had changed in the building during our absence. The two first-floor apartments were still occupied by Herr und Frau Hartmann on the left, and Herr und Frau Fuchs across the landing on the right. Herr Hartmann was close to retiring from his lifelong job with the railroad, but Herr Fuchs had already retired from his municipal job as a security guard and could now devote his days to ensuring the security of the little park surrounding our building. Herr Fuchs considered the use of the park benches as goalposts for the neighborhood boys' soccer games a safety hazard; found the accompanying noise from the shouts, whistles, and cheers unacceptable; and dedicated his retirement to the prevention of soccer playing anywhere within his sight or earshot.

Upstairs, across the landing from our apartment, the Langes still lived behind their seldom opened front door and continued snubbing us as they had done since the day in 1949 when we first moved in, and they realized that they would now have to endure the disruption and the dirt caused by a family with three young children, two of them loud boys who leaped down the stairs four steps at a time. The rift between us and the elderly couple happened almost immediately, when Frau Lange demanded that Vera agree to a cleaning schedule for the shared wooden stairs between the second and third floor, which would state in writing that we sweep, wax, and polish the stairs twice as often as Frau Lange because we were clearly tracking in much more dirt and mud than she and her husband, who seldom went out. Vera refused to be ensnared in yet another house rule, of which there already were several, and insisted that we would adhere to the standard fifty-fifty schedule as set forth in the official rental agreement. When Frau Lange filed a formal complaint, an official opinion from the management confirmed Vera's position. From that day on and for the next thirty years, not another word was exchanged between the Langes and us, until Frau Lange died, and Herr Lange moved into a nursing home.

On the second floor, the apartment on the left was inhabited by a couple who were almost never home. It was assumed that they actually lived somewhere else, and there was some speculation about how they had to know someone high up in the ranks of the housing authority to be able to keep an unused apartment at a time of extreme housing shortages. In later years, they must have wanted to live in Frankfurt again because they were now observed coming and going regularly, and they seemed like a nice couple after all, greeting neighbors with a friendly smile and holding the heavy entry door to the building open if they saw someone behind them loaded down with heavy shopping bags.

In the other apartment on the second floor lived Antoinette, who was still renting the room that the apartment's principal tenant, Walter Bragge, had offered her five years earlier, when he needed to prove to the housing authority that his apartment was fully occupied and could not accommodate any more assigned tenants. Bragge was a tall man in his thirties, dark blond with a fatty, pockmarked complexion, and an odd gait, in which strutting morphed into slinking and created an eerie mix of menace and seduction. Bragge never held a regular job, disappeared and returned at odd hours, never talked about what he did for a living, adroitly redirected any questions about his personal life, and liked to hold forth on current events and political issues of the day. He spoke basic English and seemed to have regular contact with Americans, and it was suspected that he had in earlier years been a successful operator on the black market, with easy profits through the exchange of American cigarettes for expensive consumer goods, which he in turn sold to a variety of obscure customers. He had a wife when he first moved into his apartment, and then one day, she wasn't there anymore, and rumors flew that Bragge had sold his wife to an American for the price of a big shiny Studebaker, which he parked in full view of all the neighbors, taking up parking space which could have accommodated at least two Volkswagen beetles.

As the black market lost steam in West Germany's growing economy, Bragge was not able to make the leap into legitimacy, and he remained a petty huckster, trying his skills on one questionable scheme after another, and ruling his little kingdom, in which Antoinette held a stable, if somewhat exotic position, even after he brought home a new wife. He treated Antoinette with clumsy respect, tried to create the impression that he always spoke French with her, and used her delicate aura to decorate his life and lend it an international flair.

It was time for my brothers and me to go back to school. Stefan and René rejoined their old friends in the neighborhood public elementary school, and my unconventional educational path seemed to be continuing with my enrollment in the recently opened Waldorf School in downtown Frankfurt. The Waldorf School movement was created by Rudolf Steiner, the Austrian educator, scientist, and philosopher who envisioned a learning environment in which children could use their intellectual, artistic, and practical skills in an integrated and holistic manner, with imagination and creativity as the central focus. This development was to be facilitated through free play and mutual engagement, which, in turn, was to generate empathy and stimulate inquisitive thinking. It is easy to imagine that Vera, the primary decision-maker when it came to my education, would have found these ideas very compatible with her own thinking, overruling any concerns about the continuing cost of my private schooling. Vera, who, for reasons which she refused to discuss, had managed to circumvent the mandatory smallpox vaccination of her children, probably would have sympathized with the anti-vaccination views held today, in the year 2019, by many American Waldorf parents. While the Waldorf School has refused to take an official position on the measles vaccine controversy, parents have sued to overturn measures that bar unvaccinated children from schools. A

Waldorf parent was quoted in the June 15, 2019, issue of the *New York Times*: "We're taught to live in the present, and right now my children are healthy."

I didn't like the Waldorf* school from the minute I set foot in it. The ideas which Vera had found so appealing meant nothing to me. I wanted to be with other students in the type of conventional classroom that I would recognize from descriptions in books and magazines I had read and from the tales that my brothers would tell of their school days. I wanted the teacher in front of the blackboard to tell us what we were supposed to learn and ask us direct questions to see if we had understood the lesson. I wanted straightforward grades, a 1 meaning excellent and a 5 being a failing grade. I wanted to know exactly what I was supposed to study, and I wanted to know where I stood with my grade. I didn't know what to make of class periods where I wasn't sure what we were studying and what the teacher was talking about and where all the students' replies and comments were applauded as equally excellent. And I most certainly did not want to change into an odd outfit and dance shoes for the daily eurythmy class and wave a copper wand in the air while listening to ethereal flute music.

Looking back, my individual instruction by Fräulein von Pittoni, and Frau Hamann's teaching method, which amounted to independent studies in a common work setting, had taught me to approach learning tasks in a methodical, systematic way, one step at a time, with a quantitative assessment of each completed assignment. This style does not win over learners who thrive with a more playful, intuitive approach to new material, but it has served me well in a lifetime of study, especially in times when challenges were daunting and the obstacles on the path toward success seemed overwhelming. Fräulein von Pittoni and especially Frau Hamann were encouraging and supportive but could also be taskmasters who did not accept facile answers and careless work and let me know in kind but firm

---

* Rudolf Steiner's schools came to be known as Waldorf schools after one of his strongest supporters, the owner of the Waldorf-Astoria cigarette company in Stuttgart, opened a Steiner-designed school in 1919 for the children of the company's employees.

ways when I had not done my best. They had not been trained in a teaching method which tied a student's performance to the child's developmental readiness for the task. When they saw mistakes in their students' work, they circled them in red and expected the students to take an interest in the correction and learn from it.

At the Waldorf school, it didn't seem to matter if the students made an effort or not, and the students acted as though they knew that. The general feeling in the classrooms was, as far as I could sense, that the school needed the students more than the students needed the school.

Another reason why I felt out of place at the Waldorf school was that most of the students there seemed to come from a way of life unknown to me. What they had in common was that their families were part of the newly emerging affluent and privileged class in postwar Germany. Their clothes came from stores I had never heard of. Instead of small change, they carried wallets with bank notes, sometimes in a foreign currency left over from their most recent vacation trips. It was obvious from the way they talked about their routines at home that their families lived differently from mine. Their fathers were bankers and insurance executives, and their well-dressed mothers looked fit and played tennis while their housekeepers greeted them when they got home after school and supervised their after-school activities. I knew that I would feel insecure in any large and noisy communal learning environment since I had led a rather solitary student existence so far, but the degree to which I felt out of place among the Waldorf students left no doubt that my adjustment to the social demands of classroom life was in peril. I didn't have the vocabulary to articulate my sense of awkwardness in the midst of a bustling classroom full of banter and chatter, so I resorted to easy grievances and went home and complained that the kids were dumb or arrogant, that the teachers were weird, and that going to that school was a waste of time and money. My complaining was apparently effective because after a few months, Vera let me quit the Waldorf school. She must have noticed that my eyes no longer crossed, just as my eye doctor had predicted years earlier, which meant that there was no longer any reason why I should not attend public school.

The lengthy exit essay from my Waldorf teacher, with a discussion of my strengths and weaknesses, which included faint praise for my efforts and pale prospects for my potential success in life, contained no quantitative grades in specific subjects, something that I found extremely upsetting since I was certain that any public school I would transfer to would surely require them.

My experience with the affluence on display at the Waldorf school contributed to my general sense that Frankfurt had changed during our year away in Rome. There was now more new construction everywhere, and the shrinking islands of stark rubble heaps became mute war memorials among the noisy building sites, where roaring bulldozers, scraping backhoes, and churning cement trucks created an expanding landscape of renewal. There were more cars on the streets and more stores in the city center where the shoppers, now definitely better dressed, could marvel at the new designs in housewares, furniture, lamps, plumbing fixtures, or wallpaper. When Vera once embarked on a project of sewing curtains and needed the hardware to install the curtain rod, she was able to find a store specializing in a wide variety of drapery fabrics and hardware but had to wait a long time before a sales clerk had time for her because a customer, with her interior designer in tow, was demanding the full attention of the entire sales staff for her deliberations about the color scheme and decor of the nanny's room and how those colors and that decor could be integrated into the overall design of her brand-new bungalow-style house, creating a unifying feel while subtly announcing that this room was inhabited not by a family member but by a household employee.

Had I looked out on the street through the store's display windows instead of staring at the preposterously self-important customer, I would have seen a steady stream of pedestrians rushing past, men in suits with their fedoras, and women in dresses and coats with a variety of stylish hats, most adults at least twenty-five pounds heavier than they had been during the famine and the years of hardship after the end of the war. There would have been working-class people and groups of students or young mothers with baby carriages and elderly couples walking more deliberately, perhaps with a dachshund on a leash and looking for a place to sit down in the outdoor café next door. And there were the men who had survived the war, had returned from prisoner-of-war camps maybe only recently and were still adjusting to the new Germany, some blind, their armbands with the three dots signaling their disabled status, and the amputees who had learned, with the help of crutches, to walk on wooden pegs while they were waiting for the better prostheses of the future.

It is possible, of course, that what had changed in a year was not the city of Frankfurt but my ability to notice these things; it is a historical fact, however, that the West German economy had only recently begun to show the intended effects of the Marshall Plan, which had been anchored in an event which in 1953 already lay five years in the past and had worked its magic as predicted: the fabled Currency Reform (Die Währungsreform). Germans in 1953 may not have agreed on the exact day when the Second World War ended, but they knew the date of the currency reform, June 20, 1948, a Sunday, when the old German reichsmark was replaced by the newly minted Deutsche Mark. On that Sunday, all the local distribution stations where the populations had become accustomed to picking up their monthly food rationing cards were open for the unique business of handing out forty D-Marks to every person who could produce an official identification document, the *Kennkarte*. The old currency became extinct in West Germany on that Sunday, concluding an operation that had been meticulously planned by the U.S. government since 1946 for the purpose of restructuring the financial system underlying the anticipated eventual rebirth of the West German economy. By October 1947, the new money was ready to be printed in the United States, and in subsequent weeks, twenty-three thousand wooden crates containing the new West German currency were shipped on freighters across the Atlantic and by train from the port of Bremerhaven to Frankfurt, where it was stored, all five hundred tons of it, amounting to 5.7 billion D-Marks, in the basement of the old Reichsbank and then moved by heavily guarded trucks to the central banks of each of the West German states. From there, on June 20, the new money was distributed to a skeptical population, which promptly baptized it "Mickey Mouse dollars" and jokingly groaned that this had to be one more of the dubious schemes imposed by the military government. What even the most cynical doubters of the new money could not deny was that on the very next day, Monday, June 21, 1948, the previously empty shelves of desolate stores had overnight been filled with the merchandise previously withheld by the store owners out of distrust of the value of the old Reichsmark currency.

What historians of the postwar era point out, and what most Germans have forgotten or have never realized, is that the Soviets had been firmly opposed to the formation of a West German state and had suspected that this currency reform driven by the Americans was a precursor to the establishment of the Federal Republic of West Germany, which promptly occurred one year later. Therefore, on June 23, 1948, three days after the debut of the Deutsche Mark, the Russians retaliated by shutting down the power lines to the three western sectors of Berlin, and a day later, the entire rail and road system into and out of Berlin was closed. The head of the Soviet military government in the East German sector let it be known that these disruptions would remain in place until the West had agreed to cancel its plans for a West German state. The population of the western sectors of Berlin were trapped like islanders in a storm-tossed sea, and the Airlift began its legendary ten-month rescue mission. West Berliners did, in fact, jokingly refer to themselves as *Insulaner* ("islanders") for many years.

By 1953, any lingering doubts as to the need for the currency reform had long been dispelled, and its status as the foundation for the legendary revival of the German economy in the early fifties—often called the *Wirtschaftswunder* ("economic miracle")—was acknowledged by all. It was also clear that since that memorable third Sunday in June 1948, when the economic playing field was as level as it would ever be, because every person in West Germany owned the same paltry amount of 40 D-Marks, people with imagination, initiative, and an instinct for turning a profit seized the opportunities to propel themselves forward, while others clearly missed the boat, maybe because they were temperamentally unsuited for the relentless drive to compete and found risk-taking and deal-making repugnant. In any case, the egalitarian distribution of assets, repeated two weeks later with a handout of another 20 D-Marks, very quickly gave way to a much more uneven distribution in the population, and by 1953, modest-wage earners living in cramped apartments and taking their sack lunches to work every weekday on the streetcar could admire ostentatious wealth on display in jewelry stores, showrooms of Mercedes-Benz dealerships, and luxury restaurants, and read in the newspapers the latest gossip about the customers of these establishments, who were forming a rising moneyed class.

As the entitled behaviors of domineering customers in West German stores and other public venues showed, the deprivations of the immediate postwar era had, by 1953, become a distant memory. What dominated the conversation and energized people now was a race for financial success, visible in the forest of cranes marking construction sites throughout the cities and seen in the statistics published by the economics ministry, which tracked the steady increases in industrial productivity from the investments by the Marshall Plan. In a bitterly ironic twist, the factories of Nazi Germany, which had been destroyed by the Allied air raids during the war, were replaced by modern, state-of-the-art facilities which were able to function much more efficiently and therefore competitively, making them the envy of the French and British manufacturing companies who still operated with outdated prewar machinery.

If a survey had asked West Germans in 1953 what words they would use to describe the public mood, they probably would have mentioned a rush to produce, a need to hustle, to outdo one another, get ahead, stay busy, focus on the future, and avoid thoughts of the lost war.

There were two other words that also belonged into the vocabulary of daily conversation in German households like ours in the early fifties: *Wiedergutmachung* and *Lastenausgleich*. These words, classic examples of how the German language stretches to create new concepts with a chain of homely components, literally mean "making good again" and "fair distribution of burdens."

What was to be made good, or whole, again by the West German government's *Wiedergutmachungsprogramm* were the material losses of personal property and business assets suffered by civilians as a consequence of the war. In the case of my grandfather, Karl Schaefer, this meant his fleet of cargo barges and tugboats, his town house, and his company's offices in Mannheim, all of which had been destroyed in bombing raids. Karl's many contentious confrontations with the agency's administrators were often applauded by the family like scenes in a satire, especially when one of his adult grandsons had been present at a hearing and could give a first-hand report on how Karl tried with increasing frustration and rising agitation to explain to a dense and clueless case worker at the *Wiedergutmachungsamt* that he could not provide documentation of his ruined business assets because the business office, with all its documents, had been incinerated in the firestorms unleashed by the notorious incendiary bombs.

The Lastenausgleich had been instituted for the purpose of achieving a more even distribution of income in a postwar population in which the people with a special gift for sensing profit potential were accumulating extraordinary wealth in a relatively short time span, while other groups in the population remained cut off from the opportunities that would lead to financial success. The merits and pitfalls of these government programs, including the massive bureaucracy that administered restitution payments to Holocaust survivors living in Israel or in the many other countries to which they had fled, were freely discussed in newspaper editorials, radio commentaries, and in the general public. There seemed to be a tacit understanding that the best way to go forward as a post-Nazi society was to support the restitution policies of the young federal republic of West Germany. Cash payments to survivors were viewed as a necessary step toward reconciliation by a society which was still years away from being able to process in words the vast and unimaginable pain that the Nazi regime had inflicted on its victims. Financial restitution was paid to as many survivors as could be found scattered all over the world, but there was little verbal acknowledgment of the crimes that had not yet been named genocide and the Holocaust. Not until the student movement of 1968 publicly challenged holders of high offices in government, in the church, in industry and banking, in the universities, and in the judicial system, to disclose how they had spent the Nazi years, were former Nazi functionaries identified and called to account for their actions.

24

Real School

It was in this uneasy atmosphere of surface noise blanketing a deep, knowing silence in the population that I finally entered public school. The school system that I came to know in 1954 was a relic of the educational institutions of the nineteenth century, built on a strictly authoritarian social order in which the teacher ruled in the classroom like a dictator, and admission to the school was determined by a deeply entrenched class system. In this system, all children started their school career at the age of six in the so-called *Volksschule*. Toward the end of the fourth grade, those students whose parents saw their children as future adults with university degrees were made to take an exam to qualify for admission to the academically oriented *Gymnasium*. Parents who did not have academic aspirations for their children looked to the *Volksschule* as the stable path toward a solid future, providing instruction in basic math, social studies, writing skills, and of course, English. This prepared students for the four-year apprenticeship in a trade union-approved shop. The newly minted fourteen-year-old apprentices, proud of their status as job-holders with real paychecks, were required to attend the *Berufsschule* ("vocational school") for two afternoons a week to study the theoretical aspects of their chosen trades.

This system of rigorous training of a skilled, well-paid, and highly respected workforce had its roots in the late nineteenth century, after the industrial revolution had created a strong demand for workers with diverse technical competence. The emergence of a new generation of well-qualified young workers in the 1950s made the economic resurgence of West Germany possible; in fact, it led to such levels of success that there were not enough workers in Germany for all the jobs which had been created, and a guest worker program was instituted that drew tens of thousands of job seekers primarily from Turkey and Italy to work in German factories and shops.

While this tradition-bound educational system clearly had merit, it also perpetuated a rigid class system by dividing ten-year-olds into two groups and placing them on separate academic tracks. The future tradesmen and professionals parted ways as children to settle into separate social and cultural environments, without an opportunity for crossing class boundaries until many years later, when the American model of a much more accessible college education, with its option of "going back to school" after years of working in lower-level jobs, took hold in Germany.

The school in which I was enrolled was the municipal *Gymnasium* in the little town of Oberursel, on the northern outskirts of Frankfurt in the direction of our old Roman Limes. My educational history had been carefully reviewed by the Gymnasium's principal, and it was decided that I would likely benefit from being in a class with students of my age, which meant that I would attend the seventh grade, called the *Quarta*, in the ancient tradition of the Latin schools that educated the privileged boys in Western European countries since the Renaissance. Indeed, the school experience of students in the 1950s more closely resembled that of students from a century ago than what a student would encounter a mere decade later. We stood up when the teacher entered the classroom and remained standing until we were given permission to sit down. We stood up when called on to ask or answer a question, and we stood up again when the teacher left the classroom at the end of the period. We lined up for everything, raised our hands to ask permission to speak or go to the bathroom, followed directions as a matter of course, and feared the teacher's disapproval, especially when the disapproval was officially documented in the class record in the form of a dreaded written reprimand. Physical punishment had been banned after the war, but the need for authoritarian rule remained unquestioned.

The war had ended less than ten years earlier, and each of our teachers had his or her own personal history of how they had accommodated themselves to the Nazi regime. Just exactly how, parents like Vera and Harry wondered out loud, had these teachers survived the regime? They knew Käte's one-woman strategic resistance movement in our local elementary school but doubted that there had been many other teachers of her caliber and fortitude of spirit. Most teachers forty years or older must have started their careers during the Nazi era, which meant that they had to have been members of the Nazi Party to keep their jobs. If they had been drafted into the military early in the war, they had most likely seen rapid conquest of foreign territory at first, followed by a halt in the forward momentum, and eventual retreat on the eastern or the western fronts, participating in actions of which they could not have been proud. How each man squared his wartime behavior with his conscience must have affected his beliefs about the war. However, such questions were never raised, and it would be another fourteen years before university students, during the 1968 student riots, openly challenged their professors by disrupting their lectures and shouting, "Where were you during the Third Reich?"

Our history classes, more than other subjects, reflected these difficulties. Methodically, and with the intention of giving us a comprehensive understanding of how European culture and civilization had evolved, our version of Western history started with Mesopotamia and Egypt, and then lovingly studied the Greeks, their literature, the wisdom of Solon, the genius of democracy, Socrates's puckish philosophizing, Plato's elegant thought, and Aristotle's knowledge of everything. The second part of the school year dealt with the Romans, that belligerent upstart tribe halfway down the boot of Italy, who went from being a single village on the Tiber River to conquering all their rivals, even the mighty Carthaginians in North Africa. Of particular interest to the history teachers was the Roman version of democracy and how the Roman republic crumbled under the force of a breathtaking power grab. The republic's sad decline into a garish imperial dictatorship, and its inevitable ruin under the pressure of mass migrations from the north and the east, would carry the class right up to the summer vacation and the end of the school year.

The next school year's history class would skip about three hundred years of "dark ages in which nothing much happened" and pick up the story at the beginning of the Middle Ages, with explanations of how Charlemagne and his successors came to be heirs of the Roman emperors, and what led to the Protestant Reformation, a story which I had already heard in Rome from Vera in her inimitable way of bringing history to life. We learned to identify the main artworks and architectural wonders of Renaissance Italy, recite the horrendous statistics of Germany's Thirty Years War between the Protestants and the Catholics, make sense of the *Enlightenment*, trace the growth of the British Empire in which the sun never set, and write essays on the American Revolution, the French Revolution, and the Industrial Revolution. Just before the Russian Revolution in 1917, history ended with the arrival once again of summer vacation and the successful completion of the school year.

After this two-year sequence, we found ourselves, at the start of the next school year, back in Antiquity, and since we were now two years older and capable of a more nuanced perspective, we revisited the topics we had studied before, tried to visualize what the decline of empires actually looked like, studied the various forms of government which different nations had endured, and spent the subsequent two school years at the same pace, landing again conveniently in the neighborhood near the dawning of the twentieth century, which was, from the German perspective, the era of Emperor Wilhelm II, the one who brought us the First World War.

I never did learn how to recognize when an empire is dying, but I wonder if undreamed-of assaults on the United States Constitution and endless Brexit turmoil, in which the Queen herself is pandering to the grotesque buffoon in hopes of a trade deal, do not qualify as symptoms of a great decline.

Our teachers staggered under the weight of their mission to make three thousand years of history relevant to the life that their students now saw all around them, including the aftermath of Hitler's murderous regime, and they were clearly not prepared for the task. The enormity of the historical events of the first half of the twentieth century was overwhelming, and another fifty to seventy years needed to pass before a new generation of historians had enough distance to the events they were studying to allow them to breathe while they were doing their work.

Our own history teachers were paralyzed and blinded by what they had witnessed and survived, and they couldn't encourage discussion and independent thinking in their students because they had not experienced these freedoms themselves. Instead of drawing lessons from history and tracing the developments that led to the recent catastrophe—whose consequences were in full view every day—they hid behind the assignment of rote memorization of dates, place-names and conquerors' pedigrees, and labored over issues like the administrative accomplishments of the English King Henry VII and the piety of King Louis of France and without fail ran out of time every school year as we crossed into the twentieth century. Summer break and the end of the school year rescued these poor men and women who were charged with explaining something to us, which they were incapable of understanding themselves.

Our student teachers did not labor under such burdens. They were recent university graduates who had spent their childhoods in the Hitler era but came of age in the postwar years. They were the first generation to be free to experiment with open criticism and dissent, albeit with some caution. Furthermore, since they had still been children when the war ended, they could not be accused of being complicit in the crimes of the regime. They entered their chosen profession knowing that they were pioneering new teaching methods, and they brought with them the idealism of novices who were still nervous and excited to face their students every morning.

One of our student teachers has lived in my memory for all these decades, although I have forgotten his name. He was the student teacher in our American history class. He looked like an athlete and paced back and forth in front of the blackboard and up and down the aisle separating the left side of the classroom from the right side by the windows, asked questions so quickly that we didn't have time to stand up to deliver the answer, told us that he didn't care if we stood as long as we were thinking about his questions, and infected us all with his nervous energy. This teacher believed that the

American constitution was a work of genius, greater than the dome of Saint Peter's in Rome or the pyramids in Egypt, something that the world had never seen before, and he explained why he thought that. He said that in America, there is not just one power ruling the country, but there are three, and he named the president, who oversees the execution of the laws; the congress, which makes the laws; and the supreme court, which determines if the laws are applied in accordance with the Constitution. Pacing through the classroom with occasional bursts of enthusiasm, he explained that this system of three institutions checking and balancing one another was a guarantee against dictatorship, and he predicted that if this system were adopted by all countries, that would be the end of dictatorships everywhere.

I'm wondering if this young teacher remained in his chosen profession and if he is still alive. As the very old man that he would be by now, he would be witnessing the unthinkable: that there is a president now in America who proclaims that he can do anything he wants and, more unimaginable still, that about half of the people in America don't mind.

My favorite classes were always the English classes, no matter who taught them. To me, the English teachers didn't have to be interesting; they just needed to teach me how to speak grammatically correct English. I knew that the English I wanted to become fluent in was not the British-accented language that our teachers had learned during their studies in England before the war but the idiomatic American English I heard daily on the AFN radio station in Frankfurt, which broadcast a diverse program of news, sports, popular music, interviews with visiting American dignitaries and movie stars, educational programs, and a daily two-hour concert of classical music. The signature opening of that program was the great chorale at the beginning of the fourth movement of Johannes Brahms's First Symphony, which would fade away as a young private first class began announcing the pieces that he had selected for that afternoon's concert.

Frau Hamann had prepared me well for the *Gymnasium* curriculum. I had forgotten some things during my year in Rome, especially Latin grammar and verb forms, but living in the capital of the former Latin-speaking world and seeing the two-thousand-year-old "logo" of the Roman republic, the letters SPQR (short for *Senatus Populusque Romanus*) still used by the public works department of the city, had given me a sense of being on a familiar footing with Latin as a real language, in spite of the fact that there is no consensus on how it was pronounced. The only certainty I felt was that the Latin language could not possibly have sounded the way our German-accented teachers pronounced it.

Finding myself in a classroom with twenty or twenty-five other students proved to be a manageable challenge. A class photo shows a cluster of twelve—and thirteen-year-olds enduring the usual call to smile for the photographer and responding with various versions of contrived facial expressions. My face is unsmiling, as usual, but I am not the only student looking awkward and uncomfortable in that photo. What I remember about being in that class is that my entry into public school was uneventful, that I liked most of the other students, and that I took the whole experience in stride. I struggled with math, as I had always done, but we helped one another, and I made friends with students who appreciated my helping them with their English homework in return for their help with math.

Oberursel had not yet become a place where newly affluent businessmen from Frankfurt were building their first postwar villas and condos. It was still a small provincial town with a way of life that had not changed much in a hundred years, having been spared the Allied bombing raids and ground battles which had destroyed much of Frankfurt and caused so much upheaval in the population. The Gymnasium was housed in an unlovely nineteenth-century three-story brick structure and drew students from families of local municipal employees, professionals, merchants, and tradesmen who wanted their children to be educated for a solid, successful life but not necessarily for the life of luxury and excess that seemed to foment in the fevered growth of the resurgent large cities like Frankfurt.

Some of my friends were Frank Reichard, who could find Albania on the map and knew that its capital was named Tirana, and Inge Brasch, whose parents were a lot like my parents, although

I wouldn't have been able to say in what way and who later married an Englishman and moved to the remote Hebrides Islands in the North Atlantic, and Christiane Thamm, whose father was a butcher and owned his own shop, inherited from his father. Christiane was a large, strong girl with an open, friendly face, long curly dark-blond hair in loose pigtails, and a natural, unforced, matter-of-fact friendliness that melted whatever defenses and resistance my insecurity may have put up to this new friendship. Our contact consisted of daily chats during recess and mutual help with the homework in the classes we attended together. Most families, including mine, did not yet have telephones, so during the weekends and vacations we did not have any communication. One summer, I wrote her a letter and invited her to visit me, an invitation that was meant more as a flourish at the end of a chatty letter than a serious plan, and I didn't expect her to accept it, but on the day suggested in my invitation, here she was. She had taken the streetcar and the bus, and found me washing dishes in the kitchen and hiding my surprise. She either pretended not to notice how flustered I was, or she really did not notice my embarrassment; in any case, she picked up a towel in the most natural gesture, dried the dishes as I finished rinsing them, wiped down our tiny counter and the stove, and then asked where we kept the mop since she assumed that I would finish the job by mopping the kitchen floor. I hadn't planned to do the floor that day, especially with her being there, but she assured me in her matter-of-fact sort of way that the kitchen wasn't finished until the floor was mopped and that this is what she is used to doing at her home. She reached for the mop I was holding, dipped it into the bucket of water as though we were a seasoned team, and she was taking over from me and proceeded to mop the kitchen floor so expertly that I was in awe—of her skill and of her natural grace with which she had shown me how to do it better without making me feel less competent.

During the rest of the afternoon, Christiane effortlessly fit herself into our household, overlooked the clutter in the family room, tolerated my brothers' attention-seeking interruptions with good humor, commented on the sounds of Vera playing the piano behind the lace-curtained glass door, and radiated a warm sense of interest and friendship, making it clear that she had not expected to be entertained in any way but had come to spend an ordinary day with me in my home. The memory of Christiane's visit has remained vivid for all these many decades, and to this day, I mop my kitchen floor and think of her and wonder how her life turned out.

I never went to Christiane's house, but I always imagined that her homelife was unproblematic and orderly, with a father who worked regular hours in his shop and came home at the same time every evening and a mother who ran a well-organized household where everything was in its place, and things happened on time and predictably. I burnished this image of normal family living as my worries about our own family's circumstances grew.

25

The Telephone

Harry had taken a job as a sales representative of an international publisher of scientific journals and textbooks, which required him to travel a great deal. It didn't occur to me that there might be a connection between his prolonged absences and Vera's gradually deteriorating health. What I noticed was that occasionally, and then more and more frequently, she was still in bed when I came home from school at about two or three in the afternoon. Stefan and René had already been home from school, had made themselves sandwiches, and were off playing soccer with their friends in the neighborhood. Vera explained that she felt too weak to get up, but she responded well to verbal encouragement and offers to make tea and buttered toast with jam. After she had eaten something, she seemed to feel better and was even able to play the piano for a while before going to the kitchen and cooking something for dinner, which had by now become our main meal of the day, just as I had seen in the American families beneath our windows before they all moved away. After dinner, she said she was exhausted and went to bed before we did. Sometimes, her symptoms included severe stomach cramps, which usually came on during the night. A doctor had recommended hot compresses to ease the cramping, and I quickly learned that when I heard Vera start to moan in her bed, I needed to get a bowl of hot water, dip a towel into the hot water, wring it out, and place it on Vera's stomach while it is still steaming, cover it with a sheet of rubberized material, pile blankets on top of her and wait for her to relax with the soothing heat, at which point I returned to my bed and immediately went back to sleep.

Attending to Vera's fluctuating health needs became an unquestioned part of my life during much of my teenage years. Her physical symptoms, which ranged from hardly noticeable and easily dismissible to moderate and even severe impairment, clearly lowered her self-confidence, and it shaped my sense of myself as a person who had to be capable of carrying on and maintaining control when things were threatening to fall apart.

Several doctors were consulted over time, and at first, the diagnosis was a "nervous disorder," but then came an opinion that there was an "adrenal insufficiency," which in turn was replaced by suspicions of an underperforming thyroid. A new doctor who was known for his success in treating gastrointestinal disorders was consulted, and he cited the effectiveness of the hot compresses on Vera's stomach as evidence that he was on the right track. Harry would accompany Vera on a few of her doctor's appointments, but he had not been home often enough to observe some of her most severe symptoms, and he said that his presence at these consultations accomplished nothing. We knew that Harry was generally ill at ease in matters related to medical problems, those of others as well as his own.

One dramatic deviation from the familiar range of Vera's symptoms occurred when Stefan and René and I came home from school one day and found an ambulance parked in front of our building and a medical team in our apartment just as they were carrying Vera on a stretcher out of her bedroom, blood dripping from the stretcher, her face pale and waxy. She was unresponsive, and the straining medics ignored us and focused on getting her down the stairs and into the ambulance as quickly as possible. They succeeded in their lifesaving mission, and several days later, Vera had recovered enough from the severe blood loss to be discharged from the hospital. She returned home, where life managed to return to normal, and this incident was added to the list of topics which no one in the family would talk about. To this day, I do not know who discovered Vera as she was bleeding out and called for help, and I don't remember if Harry was home during her recovery, but I do know from piecing things together which I heard over the years that Vera had an abortion, a procedure which was illegal at the time and had to be performed in secret back-alley locations by questionable practitioners.

Vera might not have survived the aftermath of the abortion if we had not had a telephone by that time. It was a heavy black Bakelite dial phone attached to the wall with a thick black spiral cord. It came with the assigned number 57 25 32, which Vera kept until the end of her life. It was delivered and installed one day during one of Harry's absences, and it sat fairly ignored on a designated side table, with one of us occasionally lifting up the bulky receiver from its cradle and listening to the dial tone and then hanging up the receiver again because we couldn't think of anyone to call. When Harry got home and saw that the telephone had been installed, he was ecstatic and called everyone whose phone number he knew, which amounted to about six people. I knew nobody's phone number, and neither did Stefan and René. Vera must have found the phone practical, but she made very little use of it until the day when the phone made it possible for someone to call for critically needed medical help.

Vera finally found a doctor whose treatment was slowly but noticeably having an effect. It was a neurologist, which was the term then in use in Germany to refer to psychiatrists. Frau Doktor Nehle was a medical doctor who specialized in mental disorders and their effects on physical functioning. Vera went three times a week on the bus and the streetcar to see Dr. Nehle in her busy practice near downtown Frankfurt. From my own life's work in later years, I know that the treatment which Dr. Nehle provided was what we call today psychotherapy, and I wouldn't need to see her clinical notes to imagine how Dr. Nehle proceeded in treating Vera's symptoms. She surely diagnosed major depression as the overriding presenting problem and probably worked in a style pioneered by Sigmund Freud, listening to Vera talk about her current suffering and its origins in her childhood, her deeply conflicted relationship with her father, her mother's suicide, and her husband's infidelity. Vera formed a strong bond with Dr. Nehle and credited her with saving her life by making her feel heard in her despair.

Dr. Nehle did not rule out the possibility that Vera's symptoms could be due to a medical disorder, but she concentrated on treating

Vera for depression, and the positive results of this approach were clearly visible. After several months of consistently attending therapy sessions, Vera's aches and pains went away, her mood lightened, she took an interest in what we were doing, cooked more elaborate meals, and returned to her regular daily piano practice. Since Dr. Nehle's treatment was not covered by our health insurance, Vera paid for the treatment out of the household budget, which she always managed as frugally as possible but couldn't prevent from being insufficient to cover all expenses. It is likely that Vera, once she was feeling better, ended the therapy to avoid further expense, with the predictable result that her depression symptoms returned, and our household deteriorated again. Not until several years later did I recognize the pattern that Vera had far fewer health issues when she was seeing Dr. Nehle regularly and became bedridden again when she stopped therapy to save money. Renewed therapy would again bring relief, raising Vera's hopes that this time, she really could manage on her own and safely terminate therapy, only to find a repeat of the cycle.

Whether Harry participated in the decisions to end or resume Vera's therapy is uncertain, as is so much else about his comings and goings and his extensive travel schedule during those years. I distinctly remember the days when he was home, usually during the last week of each month, when lengthy, detailed reports of his travels and meetings with bookstore owners and university libraries were due at the Manhattan offices of the American publishing house, Harry's employer. Harry would take over the family room and especially the big dining table, which he covered with the unpacked contents of several heavy briefcases. There were notebooks, brochures, letters, envelopes, pages torn out of telephone directories, maps, receipts from hotels, gas stations, and restaurants, almost illegible handwritten addresses and directions how to get there, and lists of names of people he had spoken with or would try to contact in the future. Everything in this chaotic assemblage made sense to him, and out of it he created well-formulated end-of-month reports, which he hammered out at an impressive rate with his two index fingers on a portable Remington typewriter, cigarette hanging from his lips and a cup of bitter black coffee within reach.

It was hard to know if Harry hated this task or if it reminded him enough of his days as a journalist to give him a trace of satisfaction as the stack of bulging envelopes stuffed with his reports grew in front of him. With the end of the chore finally in sight, there would only be three more, and then only two more, and finally just one more report to do, and he would be done until the end of the next month. I recall every detail of this ritual because I had a role to play in the process. It was my job to punch three holes into the margins of the fragile onion skin carbon copies of Harry's reports and to file them in the appropriate three-ring binders. I took pride in the growing library of Harry's business correspondence, which, when filed correctly and in chronological order, could be read like a novel, or at least like an engaging travel log.

Living now in a hyperconnected world in which everyone can reach everyone else by voice or text with their cell phones, it seems hard to believe that our homely black telephone apparatus was not put to use for keeping our family connected while Harry was traveling, but the fact is that I have no memory of Harry calling from out of town to speak with Vera, the boys, or myself. I found out that he was home when I got up in the morning and saw his travel bags in the hallway, and a few days later, I figured he had left again when I came home from school and his car was gone, and Vera was playing the piano past the time when she would usually stop to cook something for dinner. What I do remember is that I once sent him a chatty letter in which I mentioned in passing that I, or Stefan, or maybe René, had spilled some liquid in a hard-to-reach spot, maybe behind a radiator, and in an awkward attempt at humor, I reassured him not to worry because it would have dried by the time he came home. I remember this so clearly because he wrote me back in a gruff tone that this was an unacceptable attitude and that he expected more maturity from me. This may explain why I don't remember writing him any more letters during those years.

In another memory from that time, I come home from school, stop on the second floor to spend a little time with Antoinette, which I often do, and find her wringing her hands and dissolved in tears. She doesn't want to tell me what has happened but eventually lets on that Vera is furious and that she only meant well and had not wanted to offend anyone. I cannot get her to say anything more, and I feel terribly sorry for her. When I go upstairs, Vera's face is hard like a stone, and she refuses to answer any questions.

In time, it dawns on me what has happened. One of the two women with whom Harry had shared his initial two-room apartment in the Römerstadt back in 1948, the same apartment in which Käte had lived until the Americans came, had written Antoinette a letter introducing herself as the mother of Harry's five-year-old daughter. The woman, Rosemarie Saupe, wanted to know if Antoinette would like to meet this little granddaughter, and Antoinette had written back and said yes. Antoinette must have thought that the chances of Vera finding out about these visitors were slim, and she dearly wanted to meet her unknown grandchild. As bad luck would have it, Vera ran into the visitors as they said goodbye to Antoinette at her front door, and a scene followed which must have been awful.

Months later, as I did my daily chore of going downstairs to get the mail, I saw among bills and other correspondence a handwritten envelope addressed to Vera, with a return address and the name Saupe. I feared another scene and decided to prevent it by tearing the letter down the middle but then, thinking better of it, hid the torn halves in the bottom of my underwear drawer. A year or more later, Vera received a phone call from an elderly couple who asked her if she received their letter with their deepest regret and apologies for their daughter Rosemarie's inexcusable behavior. Vera told me about the phone call, and I confessed that I had hidden the letter because I thought that it came from the woman whom Vera detested so much. It turned out that the letter I had smuggled out of sight was from the woman's parents, who begged Vera to forgive them and assured her that they had been so appalled by their daughter's shameful behavior that they had disowned her and her child.

Vera never said anything about the feelings with which she read that letter, but she told me that it was a good thing that I had kept it. It may have given her some satisfaction that the woman who had been a party to Harry's infidelity was harshly punished. As a daughter of the bourgeois patriarchy, Vera had absorbed many of the norms, standards, and prejudices of her social class, which included protecting the status of the legitimate wife and her offspring and condemning "the other woman" for her perfidious designs on the "helpless" husband. The idea that marital infidelity could be symptomatic of problems in the spousal relationship and should therefore be openly addressed by the couple was anathema for a number of reasons: "Adultery is a sin, period! The adulterer is guilty, and the cheated-on party is innocent. No amount of talking is going to change that!" Or "What will people think if we admit that we have problems?" Or "We know we need help. But there is no one to turn to." Or "Even if there is someone to talk to, I don't even know how to describe what I am feeling, or why I do certain things."

At the time when Vera and Harry were suffering the emotional pain of growing alienation between them, the psychological study of family and spousal functioning was not even in its infancy; in fact, it had barely been conceived. Similarly, the clinical understanding of post-traumatic stress disorder, from which a large part of the postwar population, including Vera and Harry, were suffering, was at a very early stage. Psychoanalytic treatment for neuroses, as pioneered by Freud and Jung and their students, was known to exist in America but was reserved for people who could afford the extravagant cost, and it was not seen as an option for large segments of the general population. Depression, anxiety, and many other disorders were endured in private, often medicated with alcohol and held in check by the fear that if the hidden problems were to come to light, they would cause loss of social standing and stain one's reputation.

26

The Prophet's Curse

My brothers and I lived in different worlds even as we fitted ourselves into the cramped spaces in that airy top-floor apartment designed for the modern life of clear lines, fluid movement, and minimized effort. A handyman had been hired to build a wall dividing our previously shared room into two small chambers, which reduced the chronic teasing and bickering but also accentuated the differences in the roles we had learned to play in the family configuration.

Stefan and René had always been lumped together as "the boys" (*die Jungens*), and their alliance was cemented by their devotion to soccer, as celebrated weekly in the games played by the Frankfurt soccer club *Eintracht* against the top teams from other West German clubs. Stefan's and René's enthusiasm for playing soccer absorbed all their time and attention, and they feverishly awaited the sports segment of the Sunday evening radio news to hear the summary of the weekend's soccer results from all the First League's games. Results would be received either with abject groans or full-throated jubilation. Stefan and René played soccer with neighborhood friends every afternoon, and all day on weekends, unless they took the streetcar or rode their bikes for considerable distances to watch other youth teams play. Local matches with four or five players took place in the forbidden little park downstairs. Their adversarial relationship with the "soccer cops Hartmann and Fuchs" had hardened into a relentless feud with a lengthy history of either Herr Hartmann or Herr Fuchs stomping onto the playing field and confiscating the ball.

When a number of balls had been taken out of commission in this way, Herr Fuchs would take them to the local police station as evidence of the malefactors' persistent wrongdoing and lodge a formal complaint. Vera and Harry promptly received a notification from the precinct station to present themselves and their sons for a lecture on respecting the peace and quiet to which their neighbors were entitled. In return for apologies and promises to play their sport from now on only on official soccer fields and swallowing their objections that the nearest soccer field was one hour's bike ride away, the boys and their friends, who had come along for moral support, were handed a sack with all of their playing balls, which ranged from expensive soccer balls—favorite gifts from Christmases past—to beat-up and lifelessly thudding rubber globes. Predictably, within a few days, the promises were forgotten, the whole theater repeated itself, and in time, Stefan and René accumulated a weighty record as scofflaws, which made them candidates for the status of juvenile delinquents and forced Vera to have to appear with her sons in juvenile court several times over the years.

Stefan and René paid their tormentors back with periodic pranks. One of their more ingenuous pranks became an instant legend, dividing neighbors into two camps. In one camp were gathered all those neighbors who seethed in their outrage over the insolence of today's youth, while in the opposing camp people chuckled and secretly admired the cleverness of the deed and furtively enjoyed seeing the petty authoritarians on the first floor of the building Im Burgfeld 145 reduced to panic and hysteria.

What Stefan and René had done was actually quite elegant in its simplicity of design and dramatic effect. One evening, after dark, they strung a cable across the first-floor landing, tying the knobs of the two opposite front doors to the Hartmann and Fuchs apartments together so that neither the Fuchs nor the Hartmann family members could open their front doors from the inside. The boys then reached into the fuse boxes mounted near the two front doors and switched off the fuses to the power supply in the apartments. The idea was to have the apartments go dark, which would induce the inhabitants to want to step outside their apartment doors to access their power panels and reset the fuses. When the hapless apartment dwellers found that their doors would not open and they were trapped in their pitch-black rooms and then heard hollering and door banging coming from their neighbors across the landing, they had an experience which they would not soon forget.

I don't remember Harry being home that evening. What I do remember is police sirens coming closer and then wailing on the street in front of our building. Vera and I ran to the kitchen window to look down and saw a police car with its lights flashing in the dark and two police officers running into our building. Moments later, one of the police officers returned to the patrol car and turned off the siren and lights, and after what seemed like a long time, the second officer came out of our building, and the officers drove off. Stefan and René had joined us and looked out the window as well; they never let on with even a glance that they knew exactly what was causing the commotion downstairs.

What really embedded itself in my memory about this incident is the eerie tone in Mr. Fuchs's rageful voice as it echoed within the concrete walls of the staircase all the way up to the third floor:

"Frau Saarbach, Ihre Söhne sind Verbrecher!"

The three rasping and gurgling *r*'s in the word *Verbrecher*, and the operatic high note of the 'ö' sound in *Söhne*—like a bassoon gone mad—rose up as if from a deep well, frightening like the curse of a prophet especially when compared to the softly rounded English syllables of *your sons are criminals*.

27

Clara Wieck

Käte was well aware of Vera's precarious health, Harry's long absences, and the different ways in which the strain within the family was affecting my brothers and me. If she had asked me, I would have denied that I was feeling any strain at all because my life seemed so normal to me. I never gave any thought to the possibility that there was something odd about my iron resolve to learn to speak English like an American and move to America. Käte may have wondered how serious I was about this. She would invite me to come over and see her, and I spent afternoons with her, telling her about the books I had recently read and movies I had seen, and we made plans to see a new exhibit at some museum, reminiscing about the time in 1950 when she had taken me to see the famous Nofretete bust on its tour through German cities for the purpose of kick-starting postwar German cultural life. At the time, the three-thousand-five-hundred-year-old Egyptian queen had meant little to me, until Käte explained why she thought I would be interested in Nofretete's story: "This woman was married to the Pharaoh Echnaton, who was so powerful that he was even able to abolish Egypt's old gods and replace them with his single sun god, yet here she is, on her own, more famous than he is, the most famous woman in history. Wherever she shows up, people want to see her, like a movie star." What I had been able to see for myself was that her traveling exhibit created great excitement comparable to the enthusiasm which the King Tut exhibit generated years later; King Tut, incidentally, was Nofretete's stepson.

Käte also took me to visit the rebuilt house in the bombed-out part of Frankfurt's historic district, where Johann Wolfgang von

Goethe was born and had lived until he went off to the university and never came back except for brief visits to appease his mother. After the material, spiritual, and intellectual devastation brought on by two world wars, Goethe still rules in the realm of German letters, although his function as the patron saint of so many German cultural institutions is becoming somewhat perfunctory and abstract.

As a passionate teacher, Käte had always taken an interest in my education, and one summer she assembled a reading list for me of the core works of nineteenth-century German literature, so that she could help me understand the key concepts of literary Romanticism. Sadly, she had overestimated my fourteen-year-old intellect. I can still see myself, struggling to get through the early pages of the first selection on the list as my eyes glazed over, and I could not remember what I had just read, no matter how many times I read it. Käte was more confused than disappointed by my failure, asking herself—as she told Vera—if she had maybe chosen the wrong books for me to read, much like a scientist questions her methodology and not the subject if an experiment fails.

I caused Vera a similar disappointment with my resistance to her plan to teach me how to play the piano. After her Steinway had arrived in 1949, Vera envisioned giving me piano lessons, and for about a year, there was an hour per week set aside for my introduction to reading music, proper relaxation of my tense arms and hands before being allowed to even touch the keys, and eventual permission to play the simplest pieces by Diabelli. Vera insisted on correct posture, deeply relaxed breathing, and fluid wrist and finger movements as the foundation of a worthy performance, and she did not compromise on her principles. So every time I put my hands on the keys to play some notes, she would lift up my right wrist and hold it suspended above the keys, softly telling me to let my hand and my fingers become heavier and heavier and giving the weight of my entire arm over to her. Then just as she was about to place my relaxed fingers on the keyboard so she could coax them into the intimate moment of connecting with the keys, I would tense up with impatience and play a quick tune, only to have her lift up my wrist again and repeat the whole procedure. This began to look to me as though

I would be forever stuck in the same finger exercises and the same Diabelli tunes, and my interest turned to other activities.

Later, Vera periodically asked me if I wanted to try piano lessons again, and I believe she offered the same to Stefan and René, but we did not take her up on her invitations. She wisely refrained from exerting pressure on us since that would almost certainly have led to power struggles. Looking back, I should of course have taken the piano lessons she had offered me, and I have regretted my resistance all my life, but I also understood that I needed my resistance as a shield to protect myself from becoming trapped in conflicted emotional dependencies. If anyone had asked me why I was refusing to study the piano, and had promised never to tell anyone what I said, I think I would have explained that I didn't want to have a life like Vera's. So instead of learning to play the piano, I learned to listen to it, primarily from the kitchen, where I spent a substantial amount of my time over the years of my adolescence.

Working in the kitchen was not an assigned chore as it is in well-organized households where responsibilities are distributed among family members according to their age, skills, and maturity. Vera and Harry were never organized enough to come up with such a plan. I found myself cleaning up the kitchen simply because it desperately needed to be done, and no one else was doing it. It was similar to the many times when Vera was ill, and no one else was around to provide the care she needed, so I volunteered because I knew what to do. I didn't enjoy it, but I didn't question it either; it was simply the way things presented themselves. An advantage to never having been assigned the cleaning or nursing tasks was that they did not trigger my oppositional impulse, which is always quick to spring to life when authority figures start issuing orders.

As a small child, I had never had a dollhouse, so initially, I practiced the typical kitchen tasks—washing dishes, drying glasses to prevent water stains, polishing utensils, stacking saucers and plates, hanging the eight cups on their eight hooks, wiping surfaces, and scrubbing the sink with the same loving attention to detail that I observed fifty years later in my little granddaughter, Julia, when she played with her toy kitchen. It did not take long, however, before frustration set in over the inevitable disorder which would soon spread again over every surface as Vera cooked dinner, and Harry—if he was home—and the boys came in for snacks and left their debris lying around. Since there was only room for eight dinner plates, eight salad plates, and eight bowls in the carefully calibrated wall-hung cabinet, by the end of each day, the cabinet was empty, and its contents, smeared with food remnants, piled up in the sink and on every last inch of counter space, waiting for the elves to come and clean up the mess. The elves never arrived, and for a while, I took pride in the speed with which I was able to turn chaos into order. Predictably, my sense of accomplishment dulled over time, but the skills I learned from routinely restoring organization to a system in disarray have served me well in a variety of situations throughout my life, including the various kitchens in which I have cooked dinner over the years.

Julia's toy kitchen came with miniature furniture pieces that could be positioned in many different ways, allowing for imaginative reconfigurations of her little kingdom. The Frankfurt Kitchen, by contrast, was fixed in the rigid installation of its prefab components. Instead of having a liberating effect on the use of the kitchen by offering opportunities for inventing new uses of existing space and creating whimsical touches that expressed individual preferences, the Frankfurt Kitchen condemned the operator of the "kitchen machine" to the monotony of mindless repetition of the same steps—the only steps possible within the tyranny of the calculated design.

What saved me from sinking into self-pity and chronic resentment of the never-ending kitchen chore was that the numbing routine of it all freed up my mind for thinking about other things and for listening to the music being played on the Steinway in the adjoining music room. Unaware that what I was hearing was part of the standard repertoire of a piano recitalist, I followed the pieces as they were played through for the first time, accompanied by humming, singing, and various exclamations by the completely absorbed musician. Next came the second playing of the piece, from the beginning, now with frequent interruptions and pauses to read notations on the score or jot down new ones, and then numerous repetitions of particularly difficult passages. With continuing exposure to the arduous work of an exacting musician, I learned to listen closely, and was able to detect the changes which a musical piece underwent as Vera explored it, dissected it, put it back together, and experimented with it in other ways, all of which revealed the astonishing complexity of a composition. I noticed the tension between the musician's impulse to express her own emotions and the imperative to respect the composer's intentions. In some pieces, like Beethoven's short and impetuous *Rage over the Lost Penny*, the composer's intention is made perfectly clear, and is even pointed out in the title of the piece. In longer and weightier works, such as Beethoven's Waldstein Sonata, dramatic runs, wild eruptions, and quickly surging and then subsiding energy waves leave a lot of room for personal interpretation. Great pianists, like Arthur Schnabel and others after him, have said that throughout their careers, they return time and again to the study of Beethoven's thirty-two piano sonatas, and the consensus among musicians and audiences is that these pieces cover the range of human experience throughout a lifetime. Pianists who describe their experience playing these sonatas seem to be in agreement that over the decades of studying this music, their understanding of Beethoven's works has undergone changes as their own emotional development grew.

Playing house in my grown-up kitchen and fantasizing about the whimsical, zany, unique kitchens which I would have in my future life, I listened to Vera exploring and revisiting much of the piano literature of the so-called classical period, essentially from Johann Sebastian Bach to Johannes Brahms. Vera was very much drawn to the music of Robert Schumann and talked about his life and early death while hospitalized for severe depression as though she had known him personally. She spoke with admiration and warm familiarity about Schumann's wife, the famous pianist Clara Wieck, daughter of the great piano teacher Friedrich Wieck, and his prize student. Clara had married Robert, the love of her life, against her father's strong objections and in spite of his dire warnings about the young composer's emotional instability. When Robert died after having been sequestered in an isolated mental hospital for more than two years, he left Clara a widowed mother of eight children. Clara's income from her concert tours had been the primary financial support for the growing family even when Robert was still working at home, and now she became the sole support of her large household by going on lengthy tours playing Robert's music, and especially the famous piano concerto with its passionate opening statement from the soloist.

Maybe what Vera admired in Clara Schumann was the same initiative and resolve that she had observed in her friend Anneliese Reiche, who had given birth to her little American son in Heidelberg in 1946, in the same maternity ward and on the same day on which Vera delivered René. The American baby boy had arrived at a desperate moment in his mother's life, and Vera always remembered how Anneliese had rejected all self-pity, taken action, made some hard decisions, enrolled in a teacher training program, and became a highly respected educator, as did Clara, who pursued her exhausting concert career, including a tour of the United States in 1874, until she was offered a teaching position at the prestigious *Hoch Music Conservatory* in Frankfurt, where she worked with her students until her death from a stroke in 1896. Whenever Anneliese Reiche or Clara Schumann came up in Vera's conversations, she freely commented that she would have never been able to accomplish what these independent women did.

The story of Clara Schumann's life held a fascination for Vera which suggested that she strongly identified with Clara and was conflicted about the actions of Clara's father, who had seen early symptoms of mental illness in his student Robert Schumann and had forbidden any further contact between Robert and his daughter. Vera was clearly torn between admiring Clara for her determination in pursuing what she wanted and understanding Wieck's intransigent opposition to his daughter's choice of a husband, threatening to disown her if she married Schumann. Vera almost certainly also knew about Marie, the Schumanns' oldest child, who dedicated her life to helping her mother raise the younger children, and running her mother's household during Clara's many long absences. This piece of biographical information about the Schumann family, fraught with implications for her own household, must have promptly slipped into Vera's subconscious along with so many of her yearnings, fears, and projections, and she never mentioned Marie, neither as a role model for me nor as a cautionary tale.

In any case, Vera clearly felt a strong affinity for the Schumanns, in spite of the significant differences that existed between Clara's life and her own. She threw herself into performing Robert's music, obsessively practicing his compositions for solo piano, and especially the Carnaval Suite with its melodious, idle meandering along whimsical paths at times so obscure that it was easy to vacillate, become distracted by competing impulses, and get lost in a world of subjective experiences. Vera immersed herself in the musical expression of Robert's emotional life as she took on Clara's role as interpreter of the adored Robert's music, and it must have been jolting for Vera to step out of that intense musical immersion every evening and attend to her own household with her unsteadfast husband and three growing children.

When, in 1955, a marketing genius at a classical music label introduced the concept of recording piano concertos minus the soloist's part, allowing aspiring concert pianists to practice their solo parts alone in their rehearsal rooms with recorded orchestral accompaniment, Vera was able to play Robert's piano concerto with the full effect of an orchestral performance; its thunderous passages reverberated through our apartment building and streamed out through the open windows to the little park below, where at times a small gathering of classical music lovers sat on the benches, listening with knowing smiles and applauding at the conclusion of the concerto. Whenever that happened, Stefan and René and their friends went off to play soccer elsewhere.

There were also Franz Schubert's finely chiseled and probing piano pieces and Felix Mendelsohn's amiable *Seventeen Variations*, endlessly inventive Mozart sonatas, good-natured Haydn pieces, stately Händel compositions, the bold, unadorned sound of Johannes Brahms, and the inventions, preludes and fugues, partitas, suites, and variations by Johann Sebastian Bach. Whenever Vera played a Bach piece, my freely roaming thoughts gathered themselves into a sharp beam and focused on every note. I found Bach's music absolutely compelling, without having any idea what it was that caused me to resonate with it so strongly. What I heard in this music awakened in me thoughts that I could not articulate, and feelings that I could not name, but which gave me the assurance that for me, too, there would be a path to follow through life. Not for decades did I have the time to actually study Bach's music, to try to understand its structural elements and the many ways in which his orchestral and choral voices are interwoven, and to find that his compositions for solo instruments were made of that same texture. I celebrated Bach's birthday every March 21 and for years pondered the intricacies of obtaining a visa for traveling to East Germany, so that I could visit some of the towns where Bach had lived and worked. Then in 1989, the Berlin Wall fell, the East German government collapsed along with the Soviet Union, and I could freely travel to the city of Eisenach to visit the house where Bach lived as a child; and then on to Arnstadt, where he got his first job at seventeen as the church organist; and to Leipzig, where he ruled over the musical life of the city as the Thomaskantor and famously quarreled with the city council. However, it was in the Frankfurt Kitchen where I first heard the steady beating heart that pulses through Bach's music, affirming, sustaining, reassuring, and consoling me.

Vera played Bach as though we were still living in the nineteenth century, with lilting melodies, pleasing phrases, and ingratiating modulations. The effect of this interpretive style, quite common at the time, was that Bach's music sounded romantic, with an occasional lapse into turgid intonation. I knew nothing about music history and had only a vague idea of Bach's personality and life story, mostly inferred from the well-known portrait of a stern older man in a powdered wig that appears on countless album covers and dust jackets of Bach biographies, but everything inside me resisted this sentimental style of playing Bach's music. Vera didn't pay much attention to what I had to say about the music I was hearing, and I eventually learned to keep my strong opinions on this matter to myself, until a young Canadian pianist named Glenn Gould burst on the music scene in 1955 and swept the keyboard clean. Vera detested Gould's architectural approach to playing Bach and compared it to the mechanical clatter of a sewing machine, a scathing criticism that was the majority opinion among musicians at that time. Harry shared that opinion as well, but since he never expressed much interest in Bach, let alone the world of baroque music into which Bach had been born, his attitude toward this controversy was mostly dismissive and indifferent. Vera didn't understand what I meant by Gould's insistence on emotional honesty, and she couldn't appreciate his clearheaded and unrelenting search for precision and transparency. I instantly joined the growing number of Gould's European fans and found myself arguing with Vera without having the musical vocabulary to make myself understood, with the frustrating result that she remained completely unimpressed by my sweeping and uncompromising declaration that Gould's way was the only way to play Bach.

To this day, music has remained an essential part of my daily life, and I experience music in a deeply personal way, as a much more effective pathway for communicating complex emotions than discursive language. I have always loved hearing music in the process of being rehearsed, where I can hear critical passages played, halted, repeated, fine-tuned, started again, until another interruption is necessary for studying a different phrase or for discussing a slight alteration in a tempo.

During the 1950s, the recording company *Columbia Records* discovered that there was a significant interest in concert rehearsals of classical music, and a number of prominent conductors, including Bruno Walter, allowed their rehearsals with famous orchestras and soloists to be recorded and published. These recordings can today be found in thrift stores and estate sales as an older generation of music lovers passes away and their households are dissolved.

28

Anne Frank

Anne Frank was born in Frankfurt. She was four years old in 1933, when her father, Otto Frank, moved his family from Frankfurt to Amsterdam to escape the rapidly escalating harassment and persecution by the Nazis. Although the family continued to speak German at home, Anne and her older sister, Margot, quickly learned Dutch in their new schools in Amsterdam, and Dutch became their primary language in which they made new friends at school and in their neighborhood and enjoyed normal childhood experiences until May 1940, when Hitler's military invaded the Netherlands. Otto and Edith Frank tried to protect their girls from the reality of the Nazi threat, but their reassurances could not prevent Anne and Margot from noticing that Jews were singled out by having to wear the Star of David on their coats, which banned them by Nazi decree from movie theaters, parks, swimming pools, libraries, museums, restaurants, and stores.

When the deportations of Jews from Holland to Nazi concentration camps in Germany and Poland began, the Franks realized they were trapped, and by 1942, when I was one year old, their only recourse for escaping deportation was to go into hiding. A secret place was found in the building where Otto Frank had worked, with cramped quarters behind a swinging bookcase. The Franks would share this space with another Jewish family for two years and one month, from July 5, 1942, to August 4, 1944, when they were betrayed by a Dutch informer and arrested by the Gestapo, Hitler's secret police. The Franks were put on the last train to leave the Netherlands for Auschwitz. Anne and Margot were separated from their parents and sent to the North German concentration camp Bergen-Belsen, where they died of typhus in February or early March 1945, a few weeks before they would have been liberated by British troops.

Anne had been given a diary as a birthday present when she turned thirteen on June 12, 1942. She loved this present and immediately began making entries during her last month of freedom, before the family went into hiding in July, and then chronicled her life in her hiding place until the day the family was arrested. She wrote the diary in Dutch. One of the women who had provided the hiding place for the family, Otto Frank's secretary Miep Gies, found the diary and kept it safe until she could give it to Otto Frank, the only surviving family member, in 1947. Otto Frank decided to publish his daughter's diary in 1948, and by 1952, the diary had been translated into dozens of languages, including English and German, and was widely available. It was read, silently, by many people in West Germany who had barely begun to grasp the enormity of the Nazi atrocities and horrors perpetrated in their name.

I remember people talking about Anne Frank's diary and acknowledging that they had read it. Saying that they had read it did not lead to the customary discussions among readers about the merits of a current popular book or even a summary of the story. There was nothing to say that could have possibly been appropriate to describe one's feelings about the desperate plight of a young girl who had for twenty-five months tried to live her life despite unrelenting panic at being discovered in her cramped hiding place. The reader, who knows that Anne will not survive, gets to share her life as she tiptoes softly across the floor, careful not to have her footsteps heard below; as she forms a friendship with the son of the other Jewish family in the secret rooms behind the bookcase; and as she argues with her mother and has long talks with her father. If the reader is German, Anne's diary becomes an excruciatingly painful accusatory document, stirring guilt and raising questions which seventy years of soul-searching and remorse have still not laid to rest.

At the time when I read the diary, I had already figured out that the Saarbachs were Jews. Sometime earlier, I had overheard a conversation between Vera and a visiting friend in which the friend made some comments about how Harry had survived the Nazi years, and there was in her tone the same sense of wonder that I had heard elsewhere when people talked about how some Jews had managed to live through what would later be called the Holocaust. When Harry came home that night, I was still doing some homework for my English class, and I seized the occasion to ask him the harmless vocabulary question: "The word *Jewish* means *jüdisch* in German, doesn't it?" He looked at me, puzzled at first, then with a flicker of simultaneous resignation and relief across his face, said, "Yes, that's right." After that brief moment of truth, many fragments of family stories began to fit together like pieces of a broken plate, and I felt a powerful jolt as if rocked by a tectonic shift. The way in which I had up to that point tried to make sense of myself no longer seemed to fit, and a new understanding of myself dawned in me and promised to lead me in a darker, more authentic direction. I remember that after that odd exchange between Harry and me, the topic of our family's Jewish roots came up more often in conversations, and it had lost its mystique of unspeakability.

All this meant that I was reading Anne Frank's diary with the knowledge that her life could have been mine. At fourteen, more or less at the same age as Anne when she was recording her daily life, I could relate to her frustrations over the trivia which I recognized from my own life, but more importantly, I was horrified by the thought that Anne was forced to live in a hidden space that could be discovered at any moment as a result of the slightest mistake or the evil intent of someone who hated her and her family and wanted them dead. I immersed myself in her life, and my mind wandered from my kitchen in Frankfurt, Anne's hometown, to her prison behind the wall of books in Amsterdam, and there were many times when in my imagination I was in Amsterdam, experiencing the ever-present fear, inevitable anger, excruciating boredom, insane longing to be outdoors, the rage at the injustice of it all, and the emotional exhaustion brought on by this never-ending torture.

I never mentioned to anyone how strongly I identified with Anne, and I saw no point in talking about my horror at what happened to her. I locked these feelings away in the deepest recesses of my consciousness, where they played havoc with healthy boundaries in my emerging adolescent identity. Looking back, I find that the way I let my identity drift toward merging with the identity of the imprisoned girl in Amsterdam made me vulnerable to Anne's trauma and left me with symptoms commonly associated with post-traumatic stress, such as chronic anxiety, flashbacks—of imagined events in my case—and avoidance. I never opened the pages of Anne's diary again, and every January 27, when television news and documentary makers accompany the aging Holocaust survivors as they travel to Auschwitz to observe yet another anniversary of its liberation, I feel the same anxiety-driven resistance to making this pilgrimage myself.

Compounding this emotional vulnerability was an additional layer of feelings for which the term *survivor guilt* has been coined. Unlike Anne, I was spared the cruel confinement to which she had been subjected, and while reading her diary with her innocently hopeful expectations for a better future, I was leading a life in which I was free to come and go without fear, knowing all along how her life would end. Like a despicable voyeur, I had access to her most private thoughts and feelings and knew that everything she dreaded would come to pass. With the perspective of an observer who is witnessing a victim's desperate fight for survival, I knew what the end would look like. In solidarity with her suffering, I imagined myself in her place, hiding, being discovered and arrested, crammed into a freight train packed beyond capacity with other terrified human beings transported to their deaths, and I felt disoriented and detached from my safe life in school or in the kitchen or in my bed at night, no longer hearing the piano music coming from the next room and frozen in the void beyond the imaginable, which reverberated with the shattering question why Anne Frank died and I didn't.

My intense reaction to Anne Frank's diary was probably shared by many people in West Germany as they absorbed the steady stream of photos of Nazi atrocities published in newspapers and magazines since the early months after the end of the war, and continuing for decades with reports of freshly uncovered sites of war crimes appearing in documentaries to this day. The term *survivor guilt* came into use to refer to an obsessive preoccupation with unanswerable questions, usually beginning with "Why?" as in "Why did some people die while others lived?" or "Why was I spared?" More recently, a syndrome has been identified that has come to be thought of as *generational trauma*, in which a person exhibits the symptoms of post-traumatic stress without having been directly exposed to actual trauma. It has been proposed that exposure to the victims and survivors of prolonged trauma can trigger hyperarousal of empathy and a blurring of identity boundaries. In an informal discussion of a survey of politicians who admitted that they had guilt feelings after the failure of their policies, the international relations scholar Janne Nolan once commented that "your conscience is a living, breathing organism that you cannot mess with too many times before you become a broken person." Just like someone who is haunted by a guilty conscience, someone who is deeply immersed in an intensely empathic relationship with a victim and haunted by the imagery of the victim's suffering, may also experience disturbing psychological effects and "break" as a result of repeatedly overloading her "living and breathing empathy organism." What broke in me after reading Anne Frank's diary was my connection to Germany. I was overwhelmed by the scale of the mass murder that Germany's inhabitants had been groomed by their diabolical regime to accept. Like a visitor in a house of horrors, who stumbles through dark spaces and recoils from the ghastly images beckoning from every direction, I felt trapped in a nightmare scenario which I knew perfectly well was not a nightmare at all but real life, and I could not come to terms with it except to resolve to flee at the first opportunity.

I don't know if time heals, but it creates safer distances. In recent years, I have traveled in Europe in the company of family members, including my granddaughter, Julia, eleven years old on one of those trips, and once, to my momentary consternation, I found her reading Anne Frank's diary while sitting comfortably in a sleek, modern German train compartment. Julia was engrossed in the book, and she asked questions after she finished it, but her reading experience was a healthy combination of empathy and eagerness to learn about a terrible time in Germany, which she tried to fathom without becoming a part of it and losing herself in it.

29

Jeans and Cowboy Boots and Camel Cigarettes

While many West Germans in the 1950s were still mired in their self-pity as victims of their own war, and just beginning to grasp the enormity of the crimes committed in their name by the Hitler regime, the cultural environment around them was changing with astonishing speed. A new generation, born during the years before the war, had spent their adolescence in a destroyed country sharing starvation rations with the traumatized surviving remnants of their families. Ten years after the end of the war, these young people were now adults, and they were searching for new ideas and new role models for how to look and what to like. They rejected the moral standards and behavioral norms of their parents' and grandparents' generations, and found inspiration in the parallel culture that had settled in all around them: the Americans. Adopting the American culture meant wearing jeans and cowboy boots, eating canned foods, drinking Coca-Cola, listening to Bill Haley's "Rock Around the Clock" on their transistor radios and smoking Camel cigarettes whenever they could get them. Striking this pose became a vehicle for self-expression as well as rejection of traditional German culture, which was now thoroughly discredited and despised because of its earlier function as a sentimental backdrop to Nazi propaganda imagery.

The Americans, whose lifestyle seemed so compelling, were present in daily life for all of us to see. Their abundant Thanksgiving holiday reminded everyone that Germans had also once celebrated their gratitude for successful harvests in an *Erntedankfest*, whose observance ceased in the previous century with the migration of rural populations to the industrializing cities, where the notion of a harvest festival was seen as quaint and outdated. The red-robed fat old Santa Claus at the center of the American Christmas was initially difficult to absorb into the Christchild-centered fabric of the German Christmas magic, but the jolly old flying sleigh driver and his fabled reindeer could not be kept at bay for long.

Perhaps most visible was the way the Americans celebrated their Fourth of July holiday. We enjoyed their fireworks, heard their military bands play their national anthem on the AFN radio station, and saw American flags in all sizes waving from apartment windows, rooftops and balconies, and fluttering from cars in city traffic. For Germans, after the catastrophe of 1945, patriotism had died. It had become a word that made people cringe, and for which there was no longer any use. Parents didn't have to explain to their children what the word meant, because children didn't hear anyone using the word. The way the Americans expressed their unabashed pride in their country filled me with wonder, although I also felt a faint sense of unease which I would have been unable to put into words if someone had questioned me. However, it did occur to me even then that the United States was such a young country with a relatively short history, and that it simply had not existed long enough to experience the collective trauma that renders the idea of patriotism meaningless to a completely exhausted and hollowed-out population.

It was difficult to resist the attraction of the American way of life all around us, which brought refrigerators, washing machines and clothes dryers, radios and television sets, and a parade of kitchen and household appliances of beguiling design, reflecting the American business principle that "ugliness doesn't sell." American-designed cars and airplanes and IBM office machines dictated to the world how these things should look. American English became the language in which the world did business and conducted scientific research. The American art of advertising had developed the code for how goods were marketed, and the people who needed things, expressed tastes and preferences, or showed interest in new products were called consumers. These consumers were closely observed, their purchasing behavior analyzed by increasingly sophisticated statistical methods, and advertising campaigns were launched on the basis of such studies, with the inherent manipulation and deception cleverly disguised.

The German language became Americanized to the point that a sentence had to contain at least one or two English words to be judged worthy of attention. If the Germans' newly adopted Americanization could be ridiculed for its mindless imitation and forfeiture of authenticity, or criticized as a convenient distraction for a population that didn't want to think about its hideous past, it also brought a previous gift—the idea of a liberal democracy with its emphasis on human rights. In 1948, one year before my Jeep ride to Frankfurt, when the United States had just created the clandestine new currency *Deutsche Mark* for the soon-to-be-installed West German Federal Republic, which in turn had provoked the Soviet blockade of Berlin and the subsequent Berlin Airlift, the United Nations Commission on Human Rights had published its *Universal Declaration of Human Rights*. This document states that human rights are grounded in the dignity inherent in every human being and that these human rights include free speech, the right to assembly, free exercise of religion, and the right of recognition as a person before the law.

The person who headed the UN Commission on Human Rights was Eleanor Roosevelt, widow of the American President Franklin D. Roosevelt. Since her days as first lady, Eleanor Roosevelt had advocated for the rights of women and disenfranchised groups. She didn't hold an office, but she learned how to use the power of her position to advance progress in the great issues of her time, and she was well-known and admired by people who looked to America for leadership in making justice, emancipation, and equal rights a reality in the world. I heard people around me mentioning Eleanor Roosevelt as a person whom they revered, and even though I knew almost nothing about her life, I understood that she had enormous influence, which she used for supporting causes which I later recognized as part of the women's movement and the civil rights struggle.

The AFN radio station played an important role in the Americanization process since it was widely listened to by many of the young Germans who had learned English in school and were seeking an alternative to the insipid, Nazi-tainted popular entertainment offered up by German radio stations. Besides its obligatory news programs, the AFN played a wide variety of music to console homesick soldiers from all parts of the U.S. I wore out the pages of my stained, dog-eared English/German dictionary, looking up words that I could barely understand as they were sung, crooned, wailed, belted out, cried, shouted, hollered, and screamed to the accompaniment of country and western bands, early rock bands, rhythm and blues bands, jazz and swing bands, bluegrass bands, and at the Grand Ole Opry in Nashville, Tennessee. And then, of course, there were the recorded performances of the Seventh Army Symphony Orchestra and the classical music program every weekday evening. The AFN also broadcast favorite radio shows from back home, like the *Great Guildersleeve* and *The Lone Ranger*, interspersed with short educational presentations.

One of those educational programs was the *Primer on Communism*, a daily fifteen-minute piece that would be repeated in the afternoon and again in the evening. It dispensed cautionary tales of the pernicious effects of communist rule and contrasted it with descriptions of the American system of government that had so inspired one of our student teachers in Oberursel: the three branches of government—the executive, legislative, and judicial—each of which was there to check the other two, creating a balancing mechanism for preventing power grabs by any one branch of government. Brief examples were cited which illustrated how this balancing mechanism had worked in the past, and the genius of the creators of this political system never went unmentioned. The *Primer on Communism* always ended with a reminder that, in contrast to all other forms of government, and especially communism, America is governed by the rule of law, and no one is above the law.

These uplifting messages were read by an announcer with the voice of an eager, confident, upstanding, and trustworthy young heir to the great tradition of liberty and justice for all. Such lively little bits of information added some much appreciated color to the dusty lessons on the American revolution presented by our history teachers.

Those teachers would have categorically and unequivocally rejected out of hand the possibility that sixty-five years into the future, an American president would sit like a king in his oval throne room and declare that "I can do whatever I want. I have all the power," and hint at remaining in office indefinitely.

30

My Grandfather's Clock

My grandfather Karl Schaefer was not one to want to have anything to do with Americanization. He didn't have to look any further for reasons to reject the American influence than the rate at which packaging materials were wasted by this throwaway culture, which valued convenience more than conservation of natural resources. Karl was angry because he had been unable to bring his shipping business back to life, and his remaining outdated river barges, damaged during air raids in the war, had been sold for scrap after accruing astronomical fees while waiting in dry dock for repairs that no one was willing to finance. After his bankruptcy, Karl gave up on ever returning to Mannheim, and he remained in his house on the edge of the forest in Wahlen, where his personal isolation grew as the village of Wahlen became harder to reach after the closing down of the railroad line that had formerly provided a thin but consistent connection with the outside world.

Karl died in 1956, exhausted after a hard fight in which he ordered his heart to keep beating although it was too diseased to go any further. In line with his lifelong rejection of religion, he had left instructions in his will that there would be no church service of any kind, and so the funeral party of some sixty or more people stood on a cold winter day at the gate of the little country cemetery, waiting for the coffin to arrive so that the small planned ceremony could begin. Standing in the wind shadow of the cemetery wall, I recalled some of my visits to Wahlen after the end of the war, when there was so little food, and Vera brought us to her father's house hoping that the local farmers were supplying Herr Direktor Schaefer from

Mannheim with more food than his and his housekeeper's ration cards entitled them to, which was indeed the case.

One of my favorite moments on those visits was Karl's nightly ritual of winding up the enormous, dark wooden grandfather clock in the dining room. He would open the tall slender door, stop the ponderously swinging brass pendulum, and reach up into the dark cabinet to catch hold of a weight in the shape of a shining brass cylinder at the end of a brass chain. Pulling this weight down caused the other end of the chain, equally weighted by another cylinder, to come up from the base of the clock housing. The idea was to undo the work that the weighted chain segment on the left had done in the past twenty-four hours as it applied the force of gravity to slowly hoist the other weight upward, causing the chain to move the gears in the clock hidden behind the upper clock housing. Karl would then restart the pendulum with a hand movement of such gentleness that it seemed as though he was nudging a momentarily lifeless creature to breathe again. The pendulum started up again with its dark velvet metronome sound, moving the hands of the clock forward on their journey around the dial until they triggered a soft baritone gong at the top of the hour. I loved how the metronome sound of the pendulum spread reassurance through the house that the world would remain stable for another night and day.

In another memory associating clocks with this emotionally gnarled grandfather, I recall Vera telling me how Karl had been intrigued by my infant development from birth and how he measured my growth by my emerging interest in his gold pocket watch, which he dangled over my crib to see if I would respond to the shiny object. I did respond, and by age one, I reportedly sought him out, let him pick me up, and set me down on the massive oak desk in his study, next to his stacks of business papers, while he sat down and let me hold the gold watch and listen to its ticking. He occasionally opened first the front lid to let me watch the busy second hand run circles around the minute hand and the hour hand and then opened the back lid, which revealed the inner workings of the tiny gears. I can imagine how intrigued I must have been by this watch, and he seems to have approved of a toddler who showed an appreciation for the workings of a clock.

In the group of mourners waiting for the hearse with Karl in his simple pine coffin were several of his Dutch barge captains, long retired, in their seaman's dress uniforms. They carried the coffin up a short distance on a curving gravel driveway to the straight footpath leading to the freshly dug grave. There they placed the coffin on a bier and stepped back to allow a kind-looking older man in a dark suit and tie to conduct a brief generic funeral ceremony, after which they stepped up, one by one, to deliver eulogies to Karl, their employer for decades. They spoke of Director Schaefer as a man who had steered his company on a steadfast course through turbulent times, had kept them on the payroll during times when the barges were idle, and had been a fair and loyal boss, generous, responsible, and honest. I don't remember if the word *trust* appeared in any of the short eulogies, but what I heard in the words of these men was that they had trusted Karl and repaid him with their loyalty. One of the captains was the father of Fräulein Lenkewitz, who had, at her father's request, traveled from Rotterdam to Karl's home in Mannheim to assist Karl in the days immediately after Else's death and had remained as his housekeeper and caregiver for twenty years until the end of his life. I recall this memory of my grandfather's funeral at a time in history when modern business models all but prevent such loyal relationships between business owners and the people who work for them, generating a new model in which people are forced to be permanently alert to signs that they are about to be replaced.

I did not personally know any of the barge captains, although I had heard their names over the years, nor did I know the tiny, frail woman in her black overcoat and a wisp of a black veil covering her white hair, who leaned on the arm of a sturdy, compact man in a black suit as they walked through the cemetery gate and followed the other mourners to Karl's grave. It turned out that this was Karl's widowed sister, Johanna, with her son, Julius. I was surprised that Karl had a sister whom no one had ever mentioned, and I was even more amazed to find out that she lived in Frankfurt, about an hour away from us by streetcar, at the other end of town, in a run-down working-class neighborhood. I naturally suspected that a great scandal had caused a rift between the Schaefer siblings many decades ago, but Vera's minimal explanations alluded to a much quieter, though in its own way equally scandalous drifting apart. Karl had married into a family of significantly higher social standing, who, though financially unstable, had bestowed a higher social status on him, and he had made his acquired family the beneficiaries of his increasing wealth. Karl seems to have provided some financial assistance to his sister from time to time, but his wife and her family had received most of his attention, and no one thought to include the quiet, diminutive, working-class Johanna and her only child, Julius, in the family circle and its frequent genteel gatherings. Now Johanna, accompanied by Julius, had made her way from Frankfurt through a maze of train and bus connections to her brother's funeral in a remote rural cemetery, where she was acknowledged briefly by her nieces, Ilse and Vera, and then departed, leaning on Julius's arm, before anyone remembered to invite her to the small reception after the funeral.

I never saw Johanna again, but I did get to know Julius many years later. He and Vera had become friends after his retirement from his lifelong job as a machinist for one of the region's largest engine-building companies. As a confirmed bachelor, and especially after the death of his mother, Julius had made his work the center of his life, and after his obligatory retirement, he found himself adrift and lonely. I suspect that it was Julius who initiated the contact with Vera because it was not in Vera's character to reach out on her own. During one of my visits in Frankfurt, I noticed that Julius visited Vera faithfully every Thursday afternoon. Vera made the tea, Julius brought the pastries, and the two cousins, who had for decades lived in the same city but worlds apart, talked about their lives, their memories, their hopes and fears, and the practical challenges that come with aging and living alone. Vera and Julius were in their seventies by then, and when Vera had a stroke and afterward struggled with some language impairment, Julius came for tea twice and sometimes three times a week, smuggled speech therapy exercises into their conversation, and cheered her up with his dry humor. Vera and Julius included me in some of their afternoon teas, and I could see that they had formed a bond that expressed itself in an easy, trusting familiarity. At the end of one of those afternoons, I thanked Julius for his loyalty to my mother, but he waved me off and declared that he was visiting Vera to learn what it is like to have a stroke.

Several years later, after Vera had passed away, Julius suffered a stroke himself. I visited him in the hospital and found him paralyzed on one side, but in good spirits, at least on the surface. Unforgettably, one of the first things he said to me with a chuckle was that he had always been curious how it felt to have had a stroke, but not that curious.

At Karl Schaefer's funeral, it was hard to tell if Vera was affected by her father's death. Once Karl's coffin had been lowered into the ground, she and Harry took their place near the start of the line of mourners at the open grave, waiting to take their turn to sink a shovel into a mound of freshly dug moist earth and drop the rich black soil on the coffin. She looked composed and purposeful and seemed focused on bringing this ritual to a dignified conclusion. When it was my turn, I reached for the shovel and followed the example of those who had gone ahead of me. As I heard the clumps of earth land on the coffin below, I experienced an indescribable emotion that transported me back to medieval scenes of Death swinging his scythe, grinning in a terrifying grimace, and rattling his skeleton under his hooded black cape. As a participant in the ritual of "earth to earth and dust to dust," I felt a connection with the long line of ancestors before me who had taken part in this ancient death ceremony at the edge of an open grave. I understood in a new way how, since the earliest days, humans have tried to come to terms with the power of that moment when the heartbeat stops and gives way to a great release, after which there is suddenly nothing but the crushing absence of someone who will not return.

Before this funeral, by contrast, I had been exposed to death on an immense, impersonal scale: in a catalog of hellish statistics, hundreds of thousands of civilians had died in bombing raids from Dresden to Hiroshima, thousands more had gone down in torpedoed ships, millions of soldiers had died in epic battles on Russian and European soil, more millions of prisoners had been worked to death, starved and beaten to death, gassed to death, and murdered in other monstrous ways. This had been my abstract acquaintance with death until I attended my grandfather's funeral. There, a unique person was laid to rest, who had been known for his individual character traits (as a domineering patriarch, for example, and as a fair-minded entrepreneur, a generous employer, and a reliable, if often cantankerous, friend). His death was marked with a solemn ceremony, and his coffin was at the center of the proceedings. I had a personal connection to the old man whose body was lowered into the ground, and I experienced his passing as a natural completion of a long life, unlike the uncountable war dead, whose lives—abstract and anonymous in the vastness of their numbers—had been destroyed by weapons, starvation, persecution, and imprisonment.

31

The Sewing Basket

Back in Frankfurt, my life was busy. At fifteen, I had now been in public school for three years and learned important lessons about group dynamics and classroom politics. When I started public school in the seventh grade, I had the innocent expectations of a newcomer to a kindergarten class who is shocked to find that some of the kids are mean or set you up to get you in trouble with the teacher or make fun of you behind your back. I had seen some of that during my brief stay in the Waldorf school, but since I was sure that I would not be there for long, I ignored the cliques and the petty cabals. Now at the *Gymnasium* in Oberursel, it was different because I liked the school and wanted to be part of it. I liked many of the students in my classes and gradually learned to find a balance between being swayed by their opinions and standing up for my own ideas. I soon found out that I was not going to thrive in heated confrontations because I wasn't a quick thinker and that I did better when I let an opponent talk for a while and then suggested the possibility that another way of seeing the situation might also lead to a resolution.

I observed with detached interest how certain students gained status among their peers rather effortlessly, while others made clumsy attempts to attract attention and ended up looking pathetic. In my years of individualized instruction, I had never had the experience of getting teased by other children, with the exception of my brothers, of course, and I was at a complete loss of what to do when I found myself the target of jokes. In my confusion, I remained silent because I didn't know what to say, which may have given me the appearance of being unfazed because the teasing happened less often and even-

222

tually stopped. In time, I adopted the strategy of some of the other students who made fun of themselves first, which stole the momentum from their would-be tormentors.

What I did notice about my interactions with other students was that I lacked competitive drive. I became a liability for any team that wanted to win a board game or a card game, a spelling contest, or any kind of race, because I didn't care if I won or lost. I was more interested in observing my teammates and their opponents doing whatever the contest required than exerting myself to outdo them and win. On the rare occasions when I did win something, I didn't enjoy the attention, and when I lost, I didn't care. It is hard to know if my early individualized education has anything to do with my inability to take contests seriously, or if there is some genetic mutation at work, in which case I am destined to land on a very short and unsuccessful branch of the evolutionary tree. For whatever reason, the joy of following a competition of any kind has always eluded me, and my only ally in this lonely point of view is the legendary rabbi who, when invited to watch a soccer game to appreciate the beauty of the sport, replied, "I have the solution—give the other team a ball too."

A particularly interesting challenge was how to navigate among the friendships and cliques that had been formed before I joined the class. It was fascinating to watch what happened when two best friends turned on each other after one of them had struck up a friendship with a new student in class. I didn't know what to make of the merciless teasing and gossip whenever a boy and a girl were observed liking each other, and I was determined not to let myself ever get into that situation.

Some of my other lessons, usually learned by younger children on the battlegrounds of elementary school, had to do with when to speak up and when to stay quiet, how much attention to seek versus keeping one's own counsel, when to persist in an argument and when to let something go. After a few awkward attempts to experiment with overly forward and argumentative behaviors, I found it safer to seek a more muted observer role, in which I remained for the duration of my school years. In this role I felt most at home, and I slowly earned a reputation as a steady and responsible student.

After a year, I was offered the job of editor of the student news-paper *Der Stift*, which required that I solicit articles from other students, keep production and publication deadlines, seek ads from local merchants, and have the paper typed, mimeographed, stapled together, and distributed on time. At first, I embraced my role as manager, admonishing the paper's student writers to submit their articles on time as promised, pleading and begging for timely delivery of their journalistic endeavors, listening to their latest excuses, and extending the deadline one more time, until I discovered that it was much easier to just write the bulk of the paper's content myself, especially the editorials, travelogues, and reviews of recent books, movies, and concerts. When the retired old gentleman, who had been an office clerk and professional typist during his working life, fell ill and could not type the students' articles anymore, I also typed all twelve pages of the paper at home on Harry's typewriter. My quirky solution to the problem of the consistently tardy writers signaled very early that I would never be a successful manager of an organization, but thrived as an independent worker, and this has been true all my life.

As I gradually caught up with my classmates in what we call today *social competence*, I found myself more than once involved in a group dynamic that stirred impulses in me of which I was later ashamed. One classroom incident still has the power to make me cringe whenever I think about it. It involved a shy girl of slight build, unremarkable appearance, and quiet demeanor who had recently transferred into our class. I do not remember her name, but I have a clear memory that we gravitated toward one another like kindred spirits. She invited me to her home once, where I met an amiable elderly couple, the man tall and thin, with white hair and stooped shoulders, the woman much shorter, smiling kindly and offering me hot chocolate. My friend had introduced me to them and called them her mother and father, although it seemed to me that they were probably her grandparents. The family lived on the second or third floor of a half-timbered house on a cobblestone street in the old part of Oberursel, and in this apartment they had created what looked like a well-appointed nineteenth-century bourgeois interior, frozen in time, complete with a ticking grandfather clock. In this odd setting, the family looked and acted like the people portrayed by the painters of the Romantic school, the mother in a dark woolen frock with a white lace collar, the father in his sweater vest over a pleated shirt and old-fashioned tie, mild mannered, hospitable, and kind. I remember being shown an exquisite, intricately woven rectangular sewing basket, with its tufted lid and interior lined in sky-blue silk, holding little boxes of hemming pins with their colorful heads, and safety pins, thin sewing needles and thick embroidery needles, knitting needles and a crochet hook, a tape measure, thimbles, scissors, bobbins, a wooden darning egg, and a rainbow array of threads and yarns on a dozen spools. My friend had recently received this sewing basket as a birthday present from her parents, and I admired it with genuine appreciation because I knew from experience how frustrating it is to embark on a sewing project and be unable to find a needle, a thimble, or the scissors in a disorganized household.

To my surprise, I saw this wonderful sewing basket several days later on my friend's desk in our classroom. Maybe she had brought the basket to school for an elective arts and crafts class, perhaps to show it to the teacher of that class. She had obviously left the classroom for recess and had not yet returned by the time a group of students were wandering back into the room from recess and gathered around her basket. At first, their comments reflected their curiosity, but then they started to make fun of this old-fashioned object as a relic of the quaint domesticity of a bygone era. As more students returned from recess, the group surrounding the basket grew larger, the jokes became funnier but also more heartless, and the laughter began to feed on itself. There was something contagious in this escalating group dynamic, and I found myself joining in the laughter until I saw my friend coming through the door and looking at her classmates ridiculing her treasure. In her momentary eye contact with me, I could read her pain and her disappointment in me, and while my face was burning with shame, I immediately understood the hurt that my betrayal had caused her. I didn't know for days what to do, and by the time I figured out that at least I could try to apologize to her and tell her how sorry I was for having participated in that ugly scene, she had stopped coming to school.

This scene, with the moment when our eyes met, has accompanied me throughout my life and has filled me with deep suspicion of the dynamics which drive group behavior. Larger, more sinister versions of this process occur daily in ordinary life and give rise to justified fear of what heinous behaviors people are capable of, when their judgment and sense of decency are swept away in a surge of group energy. In my work, many years later, as a psychologist, I have studied the research, observed examples of group behavior in many different settings, and seen how people can act contrary to their own beliefs and betray their moral cores when the power of an agitated group snuffs out their conscience and sweeps them away like the debris riding the crest of a tidal wave.

32

Hermann and Thusnelda

In the decade since the end of the war, the German school system had been rebuilt enough to be able to expand the curriculum by adding field trips, and even an annual four-day class trip, to restore a sample of *normality* to the lives of postwar children, who had so far experienced schools as sites where scarcity of resources was the norm and lack of space forced teachers to improvise at every turn. The day trips usually took students to local museums, which had rushed to reopen as quickly as possible after the war to create a sense of cultural continuity for the population, even if the buildings' exteriors were still showing signs of war damage and the exhibits on the inside were put together in haste.

The seventh-grade classes always went to the Senckenberg Museum of Natural History in Frankfurt, a massive structure with an imposing portal leading into the museum's central building, which was flanked by wings housing more exhibits, research facilities, and labs. Today, this museum has regained its place among the premier natural history museums in the world, with an elegantly restored exterior and magnificent exhibition spaces, but in the 1950s, it was a distressed-looking building, colorless and uninviting, housing its treasured dinosaur collections as best it could and promising better days for its vast holdings that had miraculously survived air raids and streets battles.

I still see myself as one of about twenty-five thirteen-year-olds, led by two teachers, entering the Senckenberg on a gray, cold, rainy day and finding that the lights inside the drab exhibit halls were so dim and the huge rooms with their three-story high ceilings so drafty that I wanted to be back outside, where it would be positively warm and cheerful by comparison. I quickly lost interest in the gallery of dinosaur skeletons and wandered off through a narrow corridor into a much smaller room, where I found a small exhibit in a glass case with a drawing of a human embryo. Our biology books did not cover human reproduction, and pictures of embryos curled up in wombs were in the midfifties viewed by unprepared adolescents with the same tingling feeling of having stumbled on something forbidden and dirty that teenagers today might experience when they inadvertently open a pornography site on their smartphone. The exhibit traced the fetal development of the new human being in the womb from its conception to its exit through the birth canal, and I studied the sequence of panels with a mixture of disbelief, embarrassment, and fascination. I eventually rejoined my classmates, who were still milling among the different sauruses, and I alerted my friends to the exhibit I had discovered. We knew that we could not all disappear without this being noticed, so we asked the teachers for permission to take a short detour and include the human reproduction exhibit in the day's program. Permission was sternly denied by the mortified educators who had reason to fear that their curious students would ask all kinds of questions which they were—decades before sex education arrived in schools—completely unprepared to answer.

This little scene, hilarious in its awkwardness, serves as a marker for the level of avoidance with which the topic of sexuality was treated in the West German postwar society as a whole, and in my family in particular. Looking back, I marvel how easily I accepted my menstruation as a fact of life without making a connection to the mechanics of reproductive biology. I hadn't figured it out, and no one explained it to me. For me, menstruation had a practical advantage in that it served as a convenient excuse not to participate in physical education classes for one week every month, and I thought the discomfort was definitely worth it. As for the biology of reproduction, it seemed interesting but couldn't possibly apply to me.

In the eighth grade, the obligatory school field trip destination was the site of the nearby Taunus Mountains and the partially restored Roman border wall, military fortifications, and museum. Living in the Römerstadt on top of the buried ruins of Nida, and then having lived in Rome, I felt at home among the museum's displays of familiar objects of Roman design, such as weapons, tools, utensils, all standard equipment of the tens of thousands of legionaries who had over the years built and maintained this outpost on the northeastern border of the empire. A guide explained that the great Roman consul and general Gaius Marius had revolutionized the legionaries' operations as a fighting force by liberating them from their slow-moving supply trains. Marius ordered his legionaries to carry all their weapons and supplies on their backs, and he trained them to become an agile, rapidly moving force, able to march up to twenty-five miles a day, much faster than an enemy could put defensive fortifications in place against surprise attacks or a siege. I thought of my family's return from Rome, which had taken two whole days of driving on fast highways up the Italian peninsula, crossing the vast plain of the Po River, climbing the mountainous terrain of the Alps, following high-altitude passes across the Alps, descending on the other side, and continuing north through Switzerland into Bavaria, traveling a few hundred kilometers more up the Rhine Valley, and arriving in Frankfurt exhausted and glad to be finally able to get out of the car. I found it unimaginable that a hundred battalions of soldiers with heavy backpacks would leave Rome on foot to march to the northern border, ready to engage in battle or to work on wall construction and maintenance, but the historical evidence has shown that this is how the empire was defended and new territories were conquered.

In the museum's glass cases were also many objects that had clearly belonged to the women and children living in the family quarters outside the military garrison, proving that the legionaries were often deployed for lengthy tours of duty that could go on for many years, giving them time to form relationships with local women and raising their children as Roman citizens. Astonishing as this archaeological exhibit of Roman border installations is to this day, our class was visibly bored as we dutifully trudged along the recommended path from one site to the next, and everybody agreed afterward that the class trip to the nearby ski area, planned for the first snowfall of the upcoming winter semester, would be much more exciting.

God only knows where I got the skis and poles that I brought to the bus where the class gathered to embark on our ski day. They looked like the skis of the other students—long narrow wooden boards, bent upward in front, their hinged steel contraptions ready to capture my heavy leather boots. Attaching boots to skis by way of the contraptions rendered me essentially immobile. Eventually, I accepted the encouragement of some well-meaning onlookers to begin by sliding each foot forward by a few inches and to prevent the complete immobilization that would happen if I let the skis cross in front of me. With tiny sliding tiptoes, I gingerly made my way up a small rise, and when I reached the top, I again listened to someone cheering me on, and in a moment of false courage, I pushed myself off with the poles and experienced the giddy feeling of total sur-render to the force of gravity, felt the gentle slope gliding beneath my feet, conquered my fear of losing my balance, allowed myself a moment of incredulous euphoria, and then came to rest on level ground, overjoyed that I was still on my feet. I stood motionless, but before I could even wonder what I should do next, I heard the sound of cracking wood, looked down, and saw that I was straddling a small creek with a thin ice crust partially hidden under no more than an inch of snow. I watched in disbelief as the splintering and breaking ends of my skis—both front and back—bit into the soft banks of the creek and slowly sank under the burden of my weight, and I felt icy water pouring into my boots. It did occur to me that I needed to separate myself from the truncated skis, and I bent down to extricate my boots from the stranglehold of the steel traps, but my frozen hands wrestled with them in vain until I attracted the attention of a helpful soul who was able to loosen their death grip, and I could climb out of the icy slush. There was really nothing that the teachers could do about my predicament, so they advised me to spend the rest of the day walking around briskly to stoke the furnace of my youth-ful circulation, which would keep my feet warm and dry my socks and boots from the inside out. This method actually worked, and by the time our bus had transported us back to our school in the late afternoon, and I then made my way home on the familiar streetcar as usual, I felt tired but reasonably fit, the water in my boots was warm, and I was pleased with the way I had weathered this experience. It did turn out, however, to be the last time that I ever attached my feet to a pair of skis.

By the time I reached the ninth grade (the Obertertia, as it was still called), the Oberursel Gymnasium had joined many other schools in the Frankfurt region in reviving the tradition of the annual four-day river trip on the Rhine. If the teachers aimed to flood us with historical information and drill us so we would remember everything about this trip for the rest of our lives, they succeeded, at least in my case, because every time I take this popular river cruise with my American family, I have to fight the impulse to turn into a tour guide and deliver lectures on the geology of the Rhine River gorge and on the history of the Roman towns lining the river's left bank, which were founded when the river was the natural boundary of the Roman Empire. I could go on to talk about the architecture of the churches on the river, the castle ruins perched on rocky outcroppings above the river, and the many legends and fairy tales that have their origin on this river. A patient audience would then get to hear the story of the Germanic heroes and villains of the Nibelungenlied, and this could swerve into the saga of the Loreley sitting on her rock high above the site where the river gorge narrows and the water becomes treacherous, and where so many sailors wrecked their ships and lost their lives because they were distracted by the beautiful woman combing her long blond hair high above the churning waves. If the patient audience actually wanted to hear this crash course in German mythology and national ethos, I would eventually be interrupted by the warbling loudspeakers intoning the famous song of the Loreley just as the cruise ship rounds the curve at the foot of "Loreley's Rock":

> Ich weiss nicht was soll es bedeuten, daß ich so
> traurig bin,
> Ein Lied aus alten Zeiten, es geht mir nicht aus
> dem Sinn.
> ("I don't know why I am so sad,
> a song of old will not leave me in peace.")

Finally, the day of our class trip was here. Our heads filled with knowledge and our backpacks stuffed with the required travel items, our class met early one morning at the Frankfurt railroad station, and we took the train to nearby Wiesbaden, much as we would today. Wiesbaden, since Roman times famous for its mineral waters, had in recent centuries become a glamorous resort destination for international royalty and celebrities, especially after the city built a world-class gambling casino in the nineteenth century. After the war, the American military government chose Wiesbaden over Frankfurt as the new capital of the state of Hessen, leaving Frankfurt to redirect its ambitions and become a center of international trade and finance instead.

From Wiesbaden, we took the bus to the cruise line's dock in Biebrich on the Rhine and boarded the ship. It was this little river port of Biebrich where my grandfather Karl Schaefer had grown up, where as a fourteen-year-old he dropped out of school after his father had died so that he could support his mother and his younger siblings and where he worked long hours as an apprentice in a freight hauling company to learn the Rhine River shipping business, until he founded his own firm and built a fleet of barges and tugboats. The building where he worked as an apprentice from early Monday morning until late Saturday night still stands and today houses a fine restaurant where three-course lunches are served on white linen tablecloths matching intricately folded linen napkins tucked into crystal wineglasses.

Our class had dutifully studied the assignments on the geology and history of the Rhine Valley, but we balked at the sentimentality of the poetry and the legends, their message of patriotic pride, and the nationalism inherent in the reverence for "Vater Rhein." We thought that the idea of a river as a "father" was preposterous to begin with, and endowing a river with the magical power to whip up nationalist impulses was dangerous and needed to be opposed. We had grown into a generation of youthful doubters and questioners, and while we were too young to formulate deep insights on what had gone so horribly wrong in the country we had been born into, we intuitively knew that there was little to be proud of, and nothing to celebrate, in the hellish destruction and ruins that we had inherited. We could see all around us a country in the process of being rebuilt, but we also wondered how it was possible that so many high-level government positions were held by people who had formerly been prominent functionaries during the Nazi regime. We couldn't understand how the Catholic church in Germany, officially silent during the Hitler years because it considered communism a greater evil than fascism, now had a strong influence on the leading political party, the Christian Democratic Union, and its first federal chancellor, Konrad Adenauer. We knew about the controversies and the public debates whether the new federal republic should have a flag, a military, and a national anthem, and many of us wanted nothing to do with patriotic emblems, collective singing of hymns, and a rebirth of the German military apparatus. What we did appreciate were the sciences, and geology in particular, because we had a dynamic geology teacher who was enthusiastic about new methods for dating rock formations and estimating the age of the earth and the relative youth of the river's course. We sneered and groaned and rolled our eyes when the teaching materials extolled the glorious role of "Father Rhine" in the many wars between Germany and France over the centuries and how the river supposedly personified an essential aspect of the way Germans feel about themselves.

It took our cruise ship most of the day to reach our destination. The ship was spacious, with a large restaurant below deck for passengers who wanted to look at the landscape through picture windows, and a wide-open deck above with chairs, tables, and benches offering a wind-blown view of barge traffic, riverside towns, and robber baron castle ruins on nearly every crag and precipice. The river, after having lounged on the broad plain between Wiesbaden and Mainz, suddenly changed course and threw its weight against the tectonically uplifted plateau to the northwest, carving away at it until it had dug itself a broad winding path between steep escarpments. Digging its bed deeper and deeper, the river has left behind narrow shelves which are now, in the modern geologic era, covered by a string of historic towns and villages at the foot of steep vineyards, connected by busy highways and railroad tracks on both banks. This looks picturesque from the decks of tourist boats on a sunny afternoon, as toy trains dart into and out of tunnels blasted into the mountainside, and miniature cars and trucks buzz along at the river's edge, but when the cruise passengers disembark and want to take a walk through town, they quickly reach crosswalks where drivers are unwilling to stop for pedestrians who get disoriented in the steady drone of the highway traffic as they feel the ground vibrate under their feet when the long freight trains roar through the gorge.

Our ship finally passed below Loreley's steep rock, her song came on over the loudspeakers, and we promptly embarrassed our teachers and offended some of our fellow passengers with our mocking and disparaging comments and rude noises. We laughed too loud and did pantomimes of fair maidens combing their long golden hair, stoking the raucous adolescent humor that had us in its grip, but to the relief of tourists and crew, our stop came into view soon after we rounded Loreley's rock, and our teachers pointed out the castle perched above the small town of Saint Goarshausen, where we would be spending the next three nights in the castle's youth hostel.

This meant that the first real test of this class trip was about to begin. Dinner for a hungry crowd of fourteen-year-olds, who were still complaining about the hike up the steep trail to the castle, couldn't come fast enough, but once the large bowls and platters arrived on the rustic wooden tables at which we were seated, everything fell into place, plates heaped with warm food were passed from hand to hand until everyone was served, and a feeling of comfort settled in. I don't know what I had expected, but I remember feeling a sense of relief and a quick impulse of cautious optimism that this trip might turn out to be easier to tolerate than I had feared, given my social awkwardness and general inclination to withdraw to a place in the back row from which to observe group activities in which I did not want to participate.

Our teachers seemed to have anticipated potential turbulence, which is probably why they had put together a program for our two-day stay in such detail that there was no opportunity to stray. As a result, the days went by in a blur of hikes and castle tours complete with dungeons, torture chambers, war machinery, storerooms for provisions to outlast lengthy sieges, knights' quarters and stables for their horses, and the baron's Great Hall. Our meals were not hurried, but timed to keep us moving and out of trouble, so that the only activity not on the organizational chart were glances across the court-yard to the crumbling battlements where a group of young masons and stonecutters were working on masonry repairs. At the end of two days, the consensus among the girls was that the fellow with the mustache and a flirtatious grin was the cutest.

The after-dinner entertainment of the third evening did stand out. In a small open-air theater, a local actors' ensemble presented a dramatic telling of the story of Hermann, the valiant Germanic prince from the Cherusker tribe, who brought the most powerful man on earth, the Roman emperor Augustus, to his knees. The site where the story took place was the unstable northeast border region of the Roman Empire in the first century AD not very far from where we found ourselves at that very moment. According to the story, Hermann followed the example of many other young tribal leaders of the day and went to Rome to perfect his Latin and to enjoy the fashionable urban lifestyle in the empire's capital. Averse to the corrupt ways of the Roman elites, Hermann, now Arminius, joined the military and rose through the officers' ranks, until he led a legion in several cam-paigns with such bravery that he came to the attention of the Emperor Augustus himself, who made him an honorary Roman citizen in spite of the fact that his tribe lived outside the borders of the empire.

Hermann, however, had come to Rome with a plan. In his heart, he had remained a true Cherusker, and he did not like the changes which Roman rule had brought to the Germanic lands. Returning home, he burned with shame—as the narrator put it with theatrical fervor—when he saw that his countrymen were forced to pay taxes to their Imperial occupiers and serve in the Roman military in foreign wars half a world away.

What happened in Hermann's life next brought out such fervor in our actors that their delivery changed from a lively telling of a tale to a solemn declamation of a great national epic, an origin story in the language of myth: "It happened in the ninth year of our Lord, when Jesus was a nine-year-old lad, and had probably already started working in his father's carpentry shop, that Quintilius Varus became the Roman governor in the Rhine border region." The narrator described Varus as a harsh man, accomplished but arrogant and prideful, whose methods for pacifying the border included disowning the local people and robbing them of their customs, their laws, and even their language. This obviously brought on great hatred of the foreign regime, but no one dared to offer open resistance because the empire was too powerful.

In this desperate time, Hermann became the savior of German freedom. He had secretly gathered a council of the best men of the Germanic tribes, and all present agreed that the Roman occupiers were to be attacked and killed. An incident had to be staged that would motivate Varus to mobilize his legions and lead the twenty thousand men into a trap, where the combined forces of the tribes would ambush and annihilate them. To that end, Hermann used his stature as Arminius, the decorated veteran commander of Roman troops in earlier campaigns, to gain entry into Varus's camp and win Varus's trust with his manly bearing. The plan succeeded, and Varus came to rely on his adjutant Arminius's counsel more than that of his other advisers, in spite of their warnings.

The little theater company was so effective in presenting Hermann's story that our cynical attitude toward "Father Rhine" themes and the Germanic cultural legacy lost some of its hard edge. The audience of youthful hostelers eagerly followed the action, especially when a love interest complicated the plot. Hermann had fallen in love with Thusnelda, whose beauty and virtue were unmatched in the land. She was known to oppose the Roman occupation, but her father Segest worked for the Romans and hoped to rise to high political office under their rule. When Hermann asked Segest for Thusnelda's hand, Segest refused, and the couple eloped. Segest swore eternal vengeance, went to Varus, and warned him not to trust Arminius. But Varus despised Segest and ignored him.

A short time later, according to plan, several tribes living at some distance from the Rhine staged an uprising, and as Hermann had predicted, Varus immediately mobilized all three of his legions to put down the rebellion. Hermann accompanied Varus for a time and then requested leave to assemble additional soldiers as reinforcements. This was a ruse. Hermann met up with a large force of Germanic fighters who followed the Roman soldiers into the wildest part of the notorious Teutoburger Forest, where they ambushed the legionaries at the end of a long day of marching with their heavy loads of weapons and equipment. The narrator made much of the pouring rain and howling winds in which the Roman legionaries fought for their lives, but he raised his voice into fateful intonation as he pointed out that the Germans fought for the cause of their freedom and that the mission gave them the supernatural powers they needed to destroy Varus's huge army. Varus could not accept the reality of his defeat and threw himself on his sword to escape the humiliation, and in Rome, Augustus was heard to beat his forehead against the wall and plead, 'Varus, Varus, give me back my legions.'

The story ended badly for Hermann and Thusnelda. After a short period of peace, the Germanic tribes went back to fighting each other, which induced Augustus to send another army to the north to reestablish Roman rule. The evil Segest offered the Romans his undying loyalty and handed Thusnelda over to them, knowing that she would be taken to Rome and exhibited as a war trophy. Thusnelda endured the shame of being displayed among the spoils of war in a triumphant parade through the streets of Rome, and she died a short time later. Not long after that, Hermann was assassinated by one of his countrymen, who accused him of plotting a power grab.

After three days of incessant organized activity and very little sleep, we were tired. We had been away from home long enough, and we had seen more things than we could possibly be expected to discuss in the inevitable essays that we would be assigned once we were back in the classroom. Unschooled as we were in critical thinking, none of us asked the question how German history would have turned out differently, if the Roman legions had defeated Arminius, and had expanded the Empire deep into the Baltic region, or possibly into Scandinavia. How might German history have unfolded, if the technologically advanced urban culture of the Romans had advanced beyond the Rhineland, spread all over central Europe, and put an end to the tribal fiefdoms and their incessant conflicts between petty local warlords?

33

Capable

One of the constants in my years of growing up in Frankfurt was the uncertainty of never knowing what to expect when I got home. I must have learned to shut off any anxious thoughts of what might be happening at home while I wasn't there, and often enough, I came home to the familiar scenario of Vera practicing the piano as usual and my brothers playing soccer, or still at school, so that I could say to myself that there was really nothing to worry about. At other times, I would come home from school to find Vera and Harry still in pajamas and bathrobes, sitting in the music room, cups of coffee, cigarettes, and breakfast dishes on the table, listening to music on the radio or record player, debating the fine points of a performance and recalling earlier performances of the same piece. But then there were the days when I would come home to find Vera in bed, and no sign of Stefan and René, and I went into my automatic response mode, straightening up things, getting a sense from Vera about how she was feeling and what might help her get up and face the day. She had recurring bouts of a mystery illness, whose primary symptom was, as she put it, "indescribable weakness and tiredness."

Seeing Vera looking wan and helpless triggered a nameless, unbearable feeling in me from which I could only get relief by an all-out flight into action. Years later, I realized that the unbearable feeling I couldn't name was absolute terror that I could someday become incapacitated myself. I am convinced that this fear is the origin of my lifelong idea that if I wanted to be known for something, it didn't need to be honesty or loyalty or any of the other classic virtues, but it should be that I was capable. Being capable meant using good practical judgment in assessing a situation and knowing what needs to be done and what doesn't. It meant knowing how long to pursue a goal and when to stop. It meant self-reliance and asking for help only when absolutely necessary. To not be capable meant falling into despondency, condemned to being at the mercy of others, not being in charge of one's own life. Becoming incapable has remained my great existential dread throughout my life.

To give myself courage in the face of Vera's frightening immobile state, I would announce in a matter-of-fact tone that it was now time to get up and walk over to the music room, where we would be having some tea, and I would tell her about my day in school. Vera was suddenly able to focus what little strength she could muster to stand up, walk over to the music room, and sink into her well-worn upholstered wing chair. Inevitably, the tea, and the butter and jam on the toast that came with it, along with my practical, task-oriented conversation elevated her mood and her energy level sufficiently that the afternoon ended with piano music and led Vera to act on her often-stated resolution, directed at me, but probably also meant to steady herself through difficult times: "Whatever else happens, make sure there is dinner on the table for your family every day." Since Harry was so rarely home, especially at dinnertime, this left Stefan and René and myself to constitute the family she invoked. She would then step from the music room into the kitchen, ignore the chaos that had taken over once again, put a frying pan on the stove, and retrieve boiled potatoes, onions, eggs, cheese, and various other ingredients from the refrigerator for yet another variation of a dish that could best be described as a fried potato omelet, and which usually turned out to be very good.

When I came home in the late afternoon from the four-day Rhine River trip, I found Vera in a state which was more alarming than what I was used to. She was in her wing chair, her legs on a hassock, bundled up in a blanket, her head turned to one side, eyes closed, pale and seemingly lifeless. Leaning over her, beside herself with helpless agitation, was Antoinette, who told me that she had found Vera in this same condition in the morning, when she had come upstairs for some trivial errand and had tried without success to call Vera's doctor, and then another doctor, on the telephone. Antoinette did not have a telephone in her room downstairs and had never used ours, which meant that she had been left to frantically guess how to operate a device that was a mystery to her.

Help did arrive shortly after I got home, in the person of a doctor dispatched by a nearby hospital, who determined that Vera's blood pressure was very low, but heart function was within the normal range, and gave Vera an injection and wrote a prescription for medication. Within a short time, Vera started to show some signs of returning life, and by late evening, she was able to talk about her odd experience, of which she actually remembered very little, and which was on the following day diagnosed by her regular doctor as "probably a vascular disturbance."

Only several days later did Vera mention that while I was on the class trip, Harry had been home for a couple of days and that she had found him distracted and nervous. It took several more days before she told me that Harry, who was once again out of town, had been diagnosed with lung cancer and that a well-known surgeon, Professor Zenker from the University of Marburg Medical School, had agreed to accept Harry as his patient but that a date for the surgery had not yet been set. She was undecided about whether to tell Stefan and René about this, possibly because she didn't trust herself to find the right tone with them as she explained to them that their father had a very serious illness without frightening them too much.

The small, picturesque university town of Marburg is about two hours north of Frankfurt. Once a date for the surgery was set, Vera prepared to travel to Marburg with Harry and to remain in Marburg until Harry was well on his way to recovery from the surgery and the status of the cancer and Harry's prognosis had been determined.

During the time leading up to the surgery, the mood in the family was tense. Harry took me aside once for that melodramatic moment when the dying parent tells the firstborn to take care of the mother and younger siblings. What I remember about that moment was that I was suddenly burning with anger as he explained to me that I would now have to be mature and responsible and help Vera if he didn't survive the operation. I realized how inappropriate an angry outburst would be at this key moment in the melodrama, so I resorted to my familiar strategy of walling myself off behind my unsmiling face. I was decades older by the time I finally found the words to go with that unforgotten anger. They would have sounded, in English translation, something like: "What in the world do you think I have been doing all this time?"

Stefan and René came and went as they always did, with sporadic school attendance, playing soccer and reading their comic books, spending time with their friends who didn't do well in school either and whose families were held together by their widowed mothers. Some of the neighborhood boys had accepted that their fathers, whom they did not remember, died in the war, while others remained open to the possibility that their fathers, ten years after the end of the war, might still be detained in prisoner-of-war camps in Siberia. In any case, this platoon of friends grew up together on the same street and were at home on their improvised soccer fields and on Sunday afternoons headed out to the big stadium at the other end of the city, across the *Main River*, where the Frankfurt soccer club *Eintracht* competed with the other big West German teams for the leadership in their league.

There was an occasion, during the Soccer World Championship in 1954, when Stefan's and René's total absorption with soccer drew us all into their world as they alerted us every day to how the West German team was rising through all the qualifying games, all the way to the finals, where the Germans would face Hungary, a game which the Germans were expected to lose. This legendary game was broadcast from Bern, Switzerland, to the whole world through millions of radios and early television sets. We were all gathered around our big black-lacquered family radio in the music room, which normally spread the music of the Berlin Philharmonic, the Salzburg Summer Music Festival, or the annual Wagner extravaganza from Bayreuth through the apartment, but here we were, listening to the sports announcer whose descriptions were so vivid that we felt as though we were seeing the game with our own eyes. When in the final minute—in pouring rain—the goalie Tony Turek blocked a ball and kept the score at 3 to 2 for Germany, the stadium exploded in ecstasy, the announcer was overcome by emotion and sobbed into the microphone: "Tony, du bist ein Fussballgott," and tears of joy were wiped from flushed cheeks in countless homes, restaurants, beer halls, and village squares. This unlikely victory by the German soccer virtuosos came to be seen as the first occasion since the capitulation in 1945 in which the world community perceived Germany in a positive light instead of the land of "Death, a Master Craftsman from Germany," as the poet Paul Celan had written in his "Death Fugue." The grateful enthusiasm for the German national soccer team, its legendary captain Fritz Walter, its revered coach Sepp Herberger, and Tony the "Soccer God," touched something in Vera, Harry, and myself as we started to understand Stefan's and René's passion for their sport a little better. Käte, however, remained unmoved as she pointed out Sepp Herberger's Nazi past as head coach of the national soccer team during the Hitler years.

I don't remember when I first heard the name Paddy, but all of a sudden, this name was a living presence in our family, bringing on tension, triggering conflict, and conjuring the word *divorce* in desperate moments when Vera turned to me because she didn't have anyone else to talk to in her anxiety and agitation. Paddy's name had initially come up as one of Harry's colleagues in the textbook publishing business. As Harry's surgery date was set and drew closer, Harry and Vera quarreled repeatedly over issues that sounded like they were related to his postsurgery medical care but turned out to have to do with Paddy's wish to visit Harry at the hospital. Vera spent five days at Harry's bedside, then came home to relieve Antoinette from taking care of the household. She found out some time later that immediately after her departure, Paddy had arrived at Harry's bedside and had stayed with him for the remainder of his hospital stay, before he returned to Frankfurt to continue his recovery at home with us. He brought with him the good news that his surgery, which involved forcing open his rib cage to gain access to his lungs, and considered back then a high-wire act much like the early open-heart surgeries were in the 1970s, had succeeded in removing the entire tumor. He told us that his surgeon had given him a guardedly optimistic prognosis, but he didn't say a word about whether his health crisis was inspiring him to look at life in a new way; review some of his habits, like smoking two packs of cigarettes a day; and perhaps to make some changes in what we would today call his life-style. We were alarmed when we saw him smoke cigarettes again after his recovery from surgery, but a direct link between smoking and lung cancer had not yet been established by the health science of the 1950s, and with his assurances that there was nothing to worry about, the crisis slipped into the past.

34

The Höchst Palace

At the beginning of the tenth grade, a new student came into our class who had just returned from Detroit, Michigan, where she had spent a year in the foreign exchange student program of the American Field Service. Her name was Margret, and she created something of a sensation in the class since she was the first student we met who had been in America. I was intrigued from the moment I saw her and looked for signs that she was somehow different as a consequence of having lived in America. She looked and dressed like a regular German sixteen-year-old, came to school in a straight skirt, blouse and jacket, nylons and leather shoes with stacked heels, and no makeup. I don't remember if I was disappointed that Margret wasn't wearing socks and sneakers, Capri shorts or a pert shirtwaist dress, permed hair, and nail polish, but the English that came out of her mouth during our daily English class was everything I hoped for—authentic American English, totally fluent and effortless, spiked with little pieces of slang, delivered with such convincing ease that our English teacher's insistence on textbook grammar and proper pronunciation became irrelevant. She was the one who had actually lived in the land where American was spoken, and her prestige as an international traveler let her prevail unquestioned.

Even if Margret had not lived in America, she would have stood out among us because of her disarmingly natural and secure way of moving through the classroom and expressing her opinions freely to teachers and students alike. I wished that I had known her before she went on her student exchange year, so I could determine whether her extraordinarily secure sense of self and her cheerful optimism were natural gifts or learned in America, the land of equality where, as we had read, students have the right to speak up and where social rank and class distinctions don't exist.

Margret was not a standard beauty. She was chubby, with a soft round face, a small, pretty nose, inquisitive hazel eyes, and short, dark blond hair cut in no particular style. What made everyone around her notice and enjoy her presence was the expression on her face when she came into a room, when she walked up to someone and started a conversation, when she responded to someone who wanted her attention, when she greeted someone or said goodbye. This expression, a blend of curiosity, warmth, concern for others, and enjoyment of life, animated Margret's face during her waking hours and was present, if subdued, even at times when she was ill or in pain.

As we got to know each other, I learned that Margret's homelife wasn't easy either; she said that she was much closer to her kindly, soft-spoken father than to her mother, who frequently had affairs with other men and didn't care who knew it. We didn't talk much about our families because we were focused on our imagined future in America. Margret loved talking about her life with her Detroit family, and she happily described all the details of a day in an American high school that I wanted to know. She had lived in Detroit with a black family, who had made her feel as though she had finally come home. The American Field Service had originally placed her with a white family, but something had gone wrong with the paperwork, and when the AFS asked her if she would like to live with a Negro family (it *was 1956!*), she enthusiastically agreed. It seems that she instantly felt at home in the new family and called the parents Mom and Dad, as they had offered. She referred to the son and daughter in the family as her brother and sister and embraced the family's habits and routines so quickly that neighbors and friends talked about the family's "three kids." The "three kids" went to the same high school, leaving the house every morning shortly after the parents had left for their jobs in different car assembly plants, and on Sunday, the family went to church together and then met for a big dinner with relatives living not far away.

Margret managed to make all this sound like a fairy tale while at the same time giving unvarnished descriptions of the conditions which defined life for black Americans in the 1950s: segregated schools, segregated housing, segregated swimming pools and water fountains, segregated bathrooms, segregated lunch counters, restaurants, and hotels. The loving tone in which she spoke about her experiences in Black America disguised the pain and anger created by the daily injustices she saw and felt and heard about, such as the lynching and mutilation of Emmett Till just a year earlier, in 1955, just because he had whistled at a white woman, and it confused me as I struggled to acknowledge that such things existed in America right now, not a hundred years ago. I had read *Uncle Tom's Cabin* and *Gone with the Wind*, and stories of the Underground Railroad, as well as selected speeches by Frederick Douglass, and I thought that the North's victory in the Civil War had ended the misery of the enslaved people, especially after the legislation named *Reconstruction* was passed by Congress. The thought briefly crossed my mind that the Jeep driver who picked up Vera and myself during the downpour on the Autobahn on-ramp might not have stopped for us if we were Black. From across the Atlantic Ocean, it had been easy for me to come away with the impression that the horrors of slavery were long gone and that racism with its ideology of white supremacy and discrimination against anyone not white was largely a thing of the past. I don't remember at what point I realized that the Americans I had observed as they were living their attractive lives in front of us were all white, but I do recall the moment when I felt ashamed that I had not even noticed who was missing in this pretty portrait of America.

For Margret, the AFN radio station provided a connection to her adopted homeland, even as it continued to be my source of music, world news from the American perspective, and a broad range of half-hour comedy shows and melodramas. Understanding Jack Benny's and Bob Hope's jokes brought me a big step closer to mastering American English with its many ways in which one word can mean different things, and sentences seem to flow freely without obeying the rules I had studied in my grammar books. The dialogue in the melodramas seemed to me to resemble the sorts of things that people would actually say to one another in their daily American lives, and I filled many notebooks with sentences copied from those shows, looking forward to saying such things at appropriate moments myself once I would be living in America. In addition to the daily two-hour classical music concert, there were a lot of country music programs, including the Grand Ole Opry from the Reiman Auditorium in Nashville on Saturday evenings and a jazz hour on most nights. All these programs were hosted by disk jockeys who invited their listeners to send in requests for their favorite songs or instrumental pieces. Margret and I decided to test this invitation and submitted some requests, and within a week or so, we were stunned to hear our first names spoken on the air by handsome-sounding young men who were playing our songs just for us.

It was probably Margret who had the breathtaking idea to actu-ally visit the AFN studios and meet the people with the mesmerizing voices. The AFN studios were in Höchst, a small city some twelve miles downriver from Frankfurt, and once we started talking about actually doing this, we quickly came up with a plan. I was going to use my legitimate status as the editor of the student newspaper *Der Stift*, appoint Margret as my assistant, and write a letter to the station, legitimized by our school's letterhead, with a request for an interview. Again, we were amazed to receive in fairly short order an official reply granting our request and offering several time slots for possible interviews.

Our excitement was intense. The AFN studios were housed in the Höchst Palace, a compound of undistinguished buildings, some of which dated back to the seventeenth century. The palace, in the middle of town near the Main River, had at one time been the res-idence of a local aristocratic family, then a consolation prize for a deposed bishop, and in the early 1900s became the family home of a wealthy industrialist. After the war, it looked just as battle-scarred as the surrounding urban landscape, but the proximity to Frankfurt allowed Höchst to latch on to the 1950s building boom going on upriver in Frankfurt. It helped that the U.S. military had occupied the ungainly palace since the end of the war and was using it as head-quarters of the AFN, accommodating the technical requirements of a large radio station and housing the entire staff. As the site from which the American political and cultural presence was broadcast to a large part of Western Europe, the palace had to look reasonably intact, and it looked fairly well restored when we made our way to its stately portal.

We had made every effort to look like young professionals with a serious purpose, and we were treated as such throughout our tour. Prepared with a list of what we thought were informed questions, we got into conversations with the technical staff, the news announcers, the fellow who did the weather report, and the DJs with the beguiling voices. None of them were heartthrobs. All wore military uniforms and introduced themselves with their rank, usually private first class. As we had imagined, they had been drafted after they finished college and had been assigned to the radio station because they had been journalism students or music majors back home. They laughingly assured us that they were very lucky to have been given these assignments and that the U.S. military was not generally known for giving careful consideration to the preferences and special skills of new draftees.

Back out on the street after this momentous visit to the world of radio, Margret looked preoccupied and was uncharacteristically silent. In the course of what remained of the afternoon, she did talk about how the friendly and easygoing AFN staff had reminded her how much she missed her American family in Detroit and the life she had lived while being part of their family. She seemed particularly touched by their frequent comment that they were forgetting that she was white. She wanted to return to Detroit to spend another year with them, and always be part of their family, but she also said that she would miss her life in Germany if she moved to Detroit permanently and couldn't imagine living so far from her father and younger brother that visits would be rare because of the great distance and expense. She also mentioned her mother, with whom she had never gotten along, and added that her hope for a better future in that relationship was another reason why she would not want to leave Germany for good.

In contrast to Margret's lingering uncertainty about where she wanted to live as an adult, my decision was simple and firm. I wanted to leave Germany and go to America. I knew no one in America, but I had a deep conviction that if I worked hard enough in that land of immigrants, I could build a normal life there, something that I couldn't even imagine being able to do if I stayed in Germany. While the idea of living like the Americans I had observed during the years of growing up in Frankfurt pulled me forward, I felt a far stronger push to leave the country of my first language because of its unbearable history.

Margret and I never returned to the Höchst Castle, but it remained an unforgettable adventure for us, and I promptly wrote an article about it in the school newspaper, where it was read with less enthusiasm than I had expected. I had never considered the possibility that my fellow students might not share my intense interest in the American military radio station, and I was surprised, but not in the least discouraged. Margret and I had accepted the invitation from the DJ of the AFN jazz program to hear him play his tenor saxophone with a German jazz band on Saturday nights, and there, in a jazz club called the *Jazz Keller*, among the eighty or so people sitting on barstools or at tables, glasses of Coca-Cola and shot glasses filled to the brim with rum in front of them, were half a dozen boys from our school. They were just as surprised to see us there as we were to see them. This was not because we all knew that we were awfully young to be in a club where alcoholic beverages were served but because we had not given one another enough credit to be "sophisticated" enough to know anything about jazz.

Fans of modern jazz in the postwar reconstruction era prided themselves on their liberal, international attitude, which was tinged with more than a touch of nihilism and a cynical worldview. This attitude was shared by the people who were interested in modern art and existentialist philosophy—readers of Jean-Paul Sartre's book *Being and Nothingness* and Albert Camus's *The Stranger*, and the dark postwar literature and poetry. Modern jazz, along with edgy neo-expressionist art and the bleak, bitter, and often cynical works of postwar writers were thought to be the *domaine* of "intellectuals," who looked down on the consumers of mass entertainment. To discover fellow students, most of them smoking cigarettes and pouring the rum into their Cokes, all of us wearing the obligatory oversized black turtleneck sweaters, our pale skin and stringy hair quite at home in this smoke-filled cavern, created a bond which we acknowledged silently without ever referring to it when we saw one another in school.

There were two jazz clubs in Frankfurt at the time, the *Storyville* with its bawdy house, red-velvet New Orleans-style decor lending a touch of authenticity to the riotously jubilant Dixieland music played there; and the *Jazz Keller*, a dimly lit space in a basement at the bottom of a dozen steep stone steps below a nondescript office building, where atmospheric flickering candles on every table illuminated huge posters of Harlem street scenes and conjured the ghosts of the Apollo Theater. After initial visits to the *Storyville*, I found that the New Orleans exuberance did not resonate with me, and I defected to the Jazz Keller, where the music was influenced by Charlie Parker, Oscar Peterson, Miles Davis, and the compositions of Duke Ellington.

Jazz had a dark history in Germany. When it arrived in German cities in the 1920s, it quickly won an enthusiastic following among the crowd who wanted to dance to it. After 1933, the Nazi regime classified jazz music as one of the "degenerate" arts, whose creators were marginalized, driven into exile, or deported to concentration camps. Books were publicly burned, artworks were confiscated, and dancing to jazz music or playing in jam sessions was expressly forbidden.

Among the musicians who chose to defy the official ban of jazz were Emil Mangelsdorff and his younger brother, Albert. As members of the *Hot Club Frankfurt*, they had played in various obscure venues throughout the city, were harassed by the Gestapo and threatened with arrest a number of times, but stubbornly continued to perform their music in spite of the escalating threats. After the war, the Mangelsdorff brothers and their friends were among the first musicians in Frankfurt to come together in the ruins and start playing again, and by the time Margret and I arrived in the *Jazz Keller* at the invitation of our new friend, the DJ from the AFN, they had become prominent in the international jazz scene and regularly performed with American musicians who were in town while on tour through European cities. Members of famous visiting American bands would show up at the *Jazz Keller* around 11:00 p.m., after their official concert performances were over, and do jam sessions with the Mangelsdorff brothers and their friends. We were in awe of these musicians from America with their disarming informality, and we loved how the instruments of this spontaneously gathered group played at first in formation to find the pulse of the ensemble and adjust to one another's breathing rhythm and then started floating their improvised solos above the group's complex sets of staccatos and fluid runs. The beguiling music from Albert's trombone and Emil's alto saxophone effortlessly draped itself around the sounds from the visiting musicians, and the energy in the room built as the players took turns stepping forward and leaning into their solos. I knew that these Saturday night jam sessions could go on until dawn, but our student contingent was never able to stay that long because none of us had a car, and the last streetcar home on Saturday nights ran at 2:00 a.m.

On a trip to Frankfurt in 2019, I spent a day looking up familiar landmarks in this city of my youth, at first glance unrecognizable with its gleaming Manhattan-style skyscrapers, and I cringed at the memory of how I rode a streetcar in the early morning hours and walked the final leg of the way home because I had missed the last bus, uncertain whether I would find the master lock bolted shut from the inside of our apartment door or left open so that I could let myself in with my set of house and apartment keys. I knew that Vera was undecided whether she should allow me to spend Saturday nights at the *Jazz Keller*. On some nights, she must have felt more at peace with her decision to let me go because she left the dead bolt unlocked so I could let myself in when I returned, but on other Saturday nights, she must have felt so conflicted about having given in to my pressure that she expressed her disapproval of my late nights by placing the dead bolt in the locked position, which meant that I would spend the rest of the night outside the apartment door sitting on the floor, dozing. I understood Vera's dilemma and accepted the risk that I would at times be locked out, but there was never any question in my mind that the discomfort was a price worth paying to hear the live music. This tacit accommodation between Vera and me continued in the following years, when I would occasionally have opportunities to travel with friends to more distant cities to attend concerts by Ella Fitzgerald and Louis Armstrong and the famous big jazz bands of the day, as well as the emerging stars of the "West Coast Scene," Jerry Mulligan, Paul Desmond, and Chet Baker with their "ultra-cool" sound. With these memories crowding one another in my head as I walked through downtown Frankfurt more than sixty years later, I was stunned when I happened to come across a flyer announcing an upcoming musical event featuring one of my old idols, Emil Mangelsdorff, now ninety-four, who still gives local concerts in which he plays his saxophone and shares memories of his adolescence in Nazi Germany, when he and his late brother Albert and their friends risked their lives playing American jazz music.

35

Garden Dreaming

It was probably Vera's psychiatrist, Doctor Nehle, who thought that planting a garden would be a healing activity for Vera. This recommendation could actually be followed because the Römerstadt administrators had recognized the importance of providing garden space for the apartment dwellers and made available several fallow fields between the massive retaining wall running along the edge of the developed area and the Nidda River. These fields were divided into quarter-acre allotments, each with a tidy fence and a gate, accessible by dirt paths, and leased to Römerstadt apartment dwellers. By the time Vera became aware of this opportunity to have a garden, most of the allotments had been assigned, but there was one which no one wanted, and Vera took it. It was an oddly shaped piece of land, in the form of a crunched trapeze, and at least twice the size of the other allotments; it hugged the far side of the round bastion wall that enclosed the little park at the base of the apartment building, the notorious site of the neighborhood boys' illegal soccer practice.

There were two reasons why nobody had wanted Vera's allotment. It offered no privacy since it was in full view of anyone who stepped up to the wall to enjoy the panorama of the Nidda Valley some ten feet below, and the ground was said to be full of live machine gun ammunition and unexploded hand grenades. The explosives were presumably left over from the days when the American military had used the land below the wall as their motor pool and ammunition dump. The practical-minded army engineers had created instant access to the motor pool below by simply driving a tank through the wall and flattening out the rubble into a ramp that led to the service area with its fuel tanks and quonset toolsheds sitting on top of the compacted soil. By the time the fields of the Nidda Valley became garden allotments, the Americans and their war equipment were long gone, and the former motor pool had reverted to an unremarkable weed patch, but the jagged edges and twisted rebar of the broken concrete wall remained unrepaired for another ten years and functioned as our own local war memorial.

Vera approached her garden project with the idea of creating a green refuge, where plants could grow freely from the seeds that the wind had blown in and the birds had deposited. She bought a horticulture book and learned that the winter months, when trees have dropped their leaves and gone dormant, are the best time for transplanting young trees. I recall many trips on the streetcar to tree nurseries in distant parts of the city, from which we returned with tree saplings, their bare roots nestled in moist peat moss and bundled in burlap sacks. These spindly sticks with roots at one end came with instructions to immediately dig holes and plant the saplings before their root systems dried out.

A casual observer might not have noticed that there was a designing intelligence at work in the weed patch, where native shrubs and leafless little trees could be easily taken for spontaneous growth, until Vera was able to convince the administrators that her garden deserved the same kind of fence and gate that had been provided for all the other gardens. A fence and gate were indeed installed, which elevated the status of the weed patch and let the neighboring allotment holders hope that the derelict lot would soon be brought up to code. A generous observer might have noted that Vera's garden design suggested the possibility that there was someone at work with a tentative plan to rehabilitate this abused piece of earth. Curious neighbors asked Vera if any of the many holes she had gingerly dug in the rich river valley soil had yielded Roman artifacts or unexploded hand grenades, neither of which had ever surfaced, but Vera reported that she regularly came across spent rifle cartridges mixed in with live rounds of ammunition, which she dutifully delivered to the local police station for safe disposal.

With Frankfurt's mild climate and sufficient rain, a garden can do quite well on its own for weeks at a time. Vera might well have spent a rare sunny winter day planting more leafless little trees in her garden and then discovered budding blossoms or sprouting leaves on those trees when she ventured back to her garden one or two months later. Imported saplings and native volunteers thrived side by side, showing no signs of damage from the soil contamination predicted by naysayers for a plot of land with a motor pool history.

Vera's gardening was like her parenting. Propelled by strong nurturing impulses and a romantic imagination, she dreamed of family life with cheerful children playing in a well-appointed parklike garden with flowering meadows and beds of strawberry plants close to the ground, and apples and cherries hanging from tree branches above. Grapevines would climb on wire netting and cover the bare concrete wall, shade trees were to shelter the busily engaged family against the intrusive passers-by looking down from above, and a thorny hedge of blackberry bushes was to get support from the fence until it reached its mature height, at which point it was sure to dwarf the fence and then claim more and more space on either side of the fence for its mission as a formidable bulwark against the outside world.

Not only the hedge was allowed to seek the full extent of its growth potential. Every plant was invited to bring its gifts and test its capacity for coexisting with other plants thought to be incompatible. Pine trees and fruit trees shared cramped quarters, until the pines had a growth spurt and stole so much sunlight that the brave little fruit trees started to look like they had rickets. One cherry tree held its own against its neighboring pine, taking advantage of a tilt in the pine's trunk which during the summer funneled enough direct sunlight to the cherry-laden canopy. Plants invented new ways of accommodating themselves to ever-changing microenvironments as some plants died and others multiplied, and there were always the birds, attracted by the cherries, dropping their deposits of seeds from other parts of the neighborhood and contributing to the variety of what grew in such close harmony.

During the early years of the garden, Vera had suffered several health crises, and the plantings, spontaneous or by design, had to largely fend for themselves, which they did well enough so that the casual observer could no longer have any doubt that this was somebody's garden project. Critical minds could question the competence of the gardener and find fault with letting plants do whatever they wanted or wasting rich river valley soil on "useless plants" instead of the cultivation of spinach, carrots, and peas; that bees and many other "useful" insects were attracted to the wildflowers and volunteer shrubs escaped the critics' notice. There was probably quite a bit of talk about the absentee gardener's identity, with speculation that it might be "the woman who plays the piano all day," but the disapproving gossips had to admit that on the plus side, there were the enormous quantities of delicious blackberries every summer, which were eagerly harvested by neighboring gardeners who felt entitled to this bounty because the hedge was in the public domain as long as its invasive runners grew right next to the main path leading to all the other gardens.

Once the trees had grown canopies thick enough to form a protective visual barrier and provide privacy to the sitting area under the cherry tree, Vera began to go to her garden more often. With her soft pianist's hands, which she anxiously protected against possible injuries by avoiding house cleaning chemicals, she planted tulip and crocus bulbs for early spring color, fertilized the fruit trees, and dreamed that this garden could become a summer idyll where we would all gather to spend contented Sunday afternoons. She invited, summoned, urged, nagged, hinted, cajoled, bribed, and pleaded, but the response was lukewarm at best. Harry rolled out his story of how he had walked all the way to Sebastopol on the Crimean peninsula and that this was enough physical activity for a lifetime. Stefan showed some interest in horticulture for a brief moment after he returned from a class trip to the Taunus Mountains with a spruce sapling in his backpack. He planted it in the garden and watered it for a while, until it showed signs of having made itself at home among the lowlanders. He considered it his pet and taught it early self-sufficiency. He, like René, groaned when Vera asked them to carry lawn chairs, folding tables, and buckets full of tools from the apartment down to the garden and to go back up to the apartment to get the baskets with necessary items for making afternoon tea on a small camp stove. Then at the first opportunity, they headed off in the direction of the nearest soccer game, which left me—not yet the devoted gardener I would become in later years—unenthusiastically agreeing to help with the digging, pruning, tilling, turning of the compost pile, and the watering on hot summer days, activities that felt like annoying chores at the time but left a rich archive of muscle memory in the palms of my hands, the tilt of my wrists, and the grip of my fingers, dormant memories that sprang to life many years later, when I bought a small house on a large empty lot in Southern California.

In a box of fading family photos and letters, pictures of Vera's garden trace the development of her plantings. In one picture, Vera is standing next to a waist-high dahlia covered with large burgundy blooms fit for a wedding banquet's centerpiece. In other photos, the flowers and blossoming trees are the sole focus of the photographer, presumably Vera herself. She had tried to capture the contrast between different foliage growing next to one another; she had also studied the different gradations of green in deep shade, and one summer, she must have had great success with roses, judging from the close-ups of various blossoms, mostly yellow tea roses. There were also years when the grapes produced abundant fruit, and when the most successful of the cherry trees was so tall now that picking the cherries would require climbing a ladder, the cherry abundance was officially deeded to the birds, who repaid Vera by advertising her open house to all their friends from the entire Nidda Valley; this filled the garden with a "festive atmosphere of joyous celebration" and gave Vera—as she wrote me in one of her many garden updates—far more pleasure than if she had eaten the cherries herself.

By the time Vera, in her midseventies and in failing health, no longer had the strength to go down to her garden, it had become completely self-sufficient as a pocket nature preserve. Harvesting the cherries, berries, and grapes, feasting on the insects and spiders, and nesting in the hedges and the pines, generations of birds treated the garden as their home. It was, of course, a thorn in the side of the utility gardeners, who couldn't fathom the beauty in an unconstrained natural setting and wanted to see this jungle cleared and the land put to good use. However, the allotment administrators must have believed that a lease is a lease, and as long as the annual fee arrives on time, the gardener's design is to be respected.

At a much later time in my life, after my own garden in California had grown into a forest with a canopy so impenetrable that it shows up on Google as a solid green rectangle, I developed a better eye for recognizing in the tiniest creatures and the most majestic trees how the cycle of generating life and then declining toward death goes on all around us and reveals itself to the interested observer with such power that only poetry can stand up to it:

> In daylight, a walk through the garden
> follows a network of paths, defined
> by their clearly visible borders.
>
> At night, it's a whole different story:
> spiders have spun their webs across the paths
> according to their own designs,
> joining bushes, formerly standing alone,
> to newly neighbored shrubs.
> Other webs suspend from higher branches,
> at different angles:
> great wheels, wafting curtains,
> beaded tapestries, and hanging bridges.
>
> Also: random masterpieces casually tossed off
> by distracted weavers, precariously hung,
> prone to dropped stitches and slipped anchors.
>
> Or: tiny wonders of perfection,
> precision crafted to strict standards of
> arachnid engineering.
> This riot of nocturnal extravagance brings
> all foot traffic to a halt
> while the silent weavers rule.

THE FRANKFURT KITCHEN

The weavers are a motley crowd.
Some have finished their weaving for the night
and sit unmoving in the centers of their world,
two eyes glinting in a flashlight's beam,
while procrastinators hustle to catch up,
hooking their last stitches, tying their final knots.

If visitors were there to view this gallery,
they might come upon Spider-Woman as
she awakens to a sudden purpose,
stretches her limbs, tests her joints,
angles across her tightrope grid, reaches
its periphery, and stops to meet her guest, who,
accepting his mission,
gingerly lowers himself down a single thread
into the eight waiting arms.

What happens next would take an observer's
breath away:
A courtly touch opening a dainty minuet,
then a queasy crescendo
bursting into a mad percussion of skeletons
rattling,
leaping, arching, pounding, grasping, clutching,
throttling one another in a menacing embrace,
a rush of dread and desire, death threat, and
ecstasy,
with assigned roles of winner and loser.

What the visitor would see next is how
Spider-Woman,
her purpose done,
struts back to her hub, while her guest, dazed,
staggers on an uneasy course toward safety,
probably never to be seen again.

Even after Vera's death, someone continued to hold a protective hand over the bird paradise, and it was a decade or more before some heavy equipment arrived to remove the fence and the berry thicket, clear much of the tangled undergrowth, and take out dead fruit trees and rusted garden tools. Vera's garden was now a public park, and Stefan's spruce stood out as a landmark, far taller than anything else in this habitat.

On more recent visits to the garden, I have noticed that conventional approaches to maintaining Vera's public park are encroaching. The soft, nutrient-rich natural ground cover created by years of falling leaves has been replaced by a bristly, tidy lawn, and more and more of the original trees and shrubs, including the big cherry tree, are gone as the site increasingly resembles the professional landscaping esthetic favored by developers of commercial buildings and office parks.

36

The Salzburg Music Festival

While most of my memories seem to be stored in the format of stories with a beginning and an end, other memories flash across my mental screen in a brief exposure before they sink back into the muddy bottom of my mind's reservoir of images. Maybe these brief flashes would be best brought to life through the creations of a caricature artist, whose skills I regrettably do not possess.

A sequence of eight caricatures would tell the story of a summer vacation in the Austrian Alps. In the first drawing, Vera and her children are obviously going on a trip, approaching the main portal of a large railway station. Vera, in a smart travel outfit and wearing a jaunty hat, her purse slung over her right arm and the handle of a closed umbrella in her left hand, is about to enter the station through one of its massive doors as she beckons for us to follow. My brothers and I are standing some thirty feet away, looking at the enormous amount of our luggage which we have just set down for a moment to rest but are obviously expected to carry to our train. We are laughing hysterically at the preposterousness of all this weight but reach down anyway and grab the handles of the suitcases, sweat pouring in big beads from our heads, knees buckling, backs bent, the bubbles floating above our heads showing pictures of footmen in white wigs, yellow leggings, and pointy shoes following an Imperial Highness on her journey to the summer palace.

In the second drawing, we see a pretty little chalet on a narrow country road in an alpine valley, picturesque mountains in the background, a road sign saying "Salzburg 20 km." Standing on the second-story balcony of the chalet, an old man and an old woman are watching my brothers play soccer on the lawn in front of the chalet. The man says to the woman, "I told you this was a bad idea. They have kids, they are here all the time, they aren't just sleeping here and gone all day, they are going to tear up the house and the garden. I knew it! And where is the father? She said her husband would come a few days later, when the music festival in Salzburg starts. Where is he? I told you this was a bad idea!"

Drawing number 3 shows how a mailman has just delivered a telegram to the woman who answered the door. It's Vera. She reads the telegram in the open doorway, then says to the girl standing next to her, me, "Your father says that he won't be able to come."

In drawing number 4, we see the old couple, Vera, and me, sitting at a rustic kitchen table. Vera's speech bubble reads, "My husband is unable to get away, so we have to return home." The old people look skeptical. Number 5 shows us at the same table. The old man looks like he is at the end of his wits. "We have been sitting here for almost an hour reminding you that you signed a contract for the full six weeks, so you can't just leave after two weeks without paying for the remaining four weeks." Number 6 shows the same scene, but the speech bubble floating near the old woman's smiling face says, "Young lady, that was very smart of you to suggest that your mother find other tenants to take over your contract. We will agree to that, and we think you will be a fine lawyer someday."

In the seventh drawing, Vera and her children are gathered on a platform in the Salzburg train station. A train full of merry vacationers has just arrived from Frankfurt. An elegant man and a slender woman in a fur jacket holding a small poodle in her arms are greeting Vera, while my brothers and I are huddled around our enormous pile of luggage, with a soccer ball in a net slung over Stefan's shoulder; the bubble reads, "Wonderful to meet you. We were so excited to see your ad in the Frankfurt newspaper. We had just about given up on our plans to come for the Salzburg music festival."

In the final frame, Vera turns to the waiting train on the other side of the platform. A sign says, "Train to Frankfurt departing in four minutes." Vera beckons for us to hurry up and bring the suitcases over so that we can all board the train. The bubble hovering over our heads shows three bone-tired pack mules.

37

The Book Fair

I don't remember my sixteenth birthday, or my fifteenth, for that matter, but as I headed into my seventeenth year, I felt that something was different about me, although I would have been unable to say what it was. If someone had pointed out my growing restlessness and my lack of interest in school as signs that I was changing, I would have argued heatedly that this had nothing to do with change in me and everything to do with the fact that my parents were in the process of separating and that I did not expect them to be able to support me through years of university studies, a prospect that did not fit into my plans anyway.

I must have had a vague sense that I was outgrowing my role at home since I had less and less patience for the family dramas that I had always tried to prevent from happening when I saw them coming, or mediate and smooth out when they happened anyway. I was now getting tired of cringing every time I replayed in my mind so many embarrassing moments, like the time when we were all leaving for a rare family outing, Harry, the boys, and I sitting downstairs in the car waiting for Vera while the engine is running to warm up on this snowy winter evening. We wait and wait while the steam from our breaths and the freezing cold outside conspire to turn the car windows into milk glass, which suddenly throbs raspberry red when a police car with its flashing emergency lights pulls up next to us and the officers run toward our building.

It turned out that Vera, up in the apartment, couldn't find what she was searching for and had leaned out of our kitchen window, shouting "Hallo! Hallo!" to get our attention and, with no response from us, had persisted in her shouts until a concerned neighbor called the police to report that he had heard cries for help from the third floor of the apartment building up the street.

What was keeping me busy now at seventeen was my search for opportunities that could lead to more substantial work than my tutoring job persuading fifth-graders that Latin grammar was worth learning and that, yes, the inconsistencies of English pronunciation and spelling were infuriating, but they could be learned with enough practice. In addition to trying out the role of a teacher, I tested myself as a translator of unintelligible recipes for cooking Indian dishes, instructions for knitting socks and gloves, and other domestic activities for the weekend edition of a local newspaper. Twice now I had been hired, probably after Harry had called in some favors, by an American publishing company to work in their booth at the annual Frankfurt International Book Fair. The book fair is a defining event in the official calendar of the city of Frankfurt and dates back to the fifteenth century and the days after Johannes Gutenberg had invented the movable-type printing press. Gutenberg's massive wooden contraption was clearly inspired by the wine presses that he had seen in the wineries along the Rhine River near his hometown of Mainz, where Harry grew up. Over the centuries, this book fair became the place where every year in October, publishers, booksellers, authors, agents, translators, and illustrators come together to showcase their new works and celebrate the written and printed word. In the nineteenth and early twentieth centuries, the Frankfurt Book Fair had been overtaken by the Leipzig Book Fair in eastern Germany, and both fairs were suspended during World War II and the immediate postwar years. They resumed in 1949, and Frankfurt's book fair returned to its predominant position, while Leipzig suffered from its location behind the *Iron Curtain* in the Russian-controlled East Germany. The Frankfurt Book Fair has grown with each year; until today, it is the largest trade fair for books in the world, taking over the vast spaces of the convention center facilities and adjoining exhibition halls. Unsuspecting tourists who come to Frankfurt in early October find that there will be no hotel rooms for them within a thirty-mile radius of the city while the book fair is in progress.

The people who, over the centuries, wrote, printed, bound, sold, and bought books chose Frankfurt for their annual gathering for the same reason that the city was sought out by many other trade associations as the site for their fairs: it was easily reached at its location not far from the Main River's confluence with the Rhine. Both rivers were easily navigable and historically important transportation routes—the Rhine to the north and the south, and the Main to the east, reaching deep into the regions of Franconia and Thuringia with their cities, universities, and religious centers of learning.

Frankfurt's origins on the old Roman Road from Mainz to Nida, the city beneath the Römerstadt, obviously date back to Roman times, and sections of first century AD stone walls and other structures and artifacts have been unearthed on the low hill near the southern bank of the Main, where Frankfurt's cathedral would be built a thousand years later. In addition to its geographical location, Frankfurt's political status promoted commercial development. It was a Free Imperial City, which meant that for much of its history, it was subject to no local prince, had an imperial charter to govern itself, and answered directly to the emperor, to whom it paid exorbitant taxes for the privilege. Frankfurt's inhabitants thought of themselves not as subjects but citizens who valued collective responsibility for the well-being of their city, along with an attitude of openness toward new ideas and the people who bring the ideas from all over the world. The city's architecture reflected the pride of well-to-do burghers who enjoyed finely built civic structures but rejected the excesses of monarchical grandiosity. With its history of centuries-old self-governance, Frankfurt was a natural site for the first national assembly to create a democratic constitution in the *Paulskirche* in 1848, a chapter in history which Frankfurt schoolchildren are urged to study diligently and repeatedly.

To work at the book fair was clearly a desirable assignment. I could put my English to good use and learn from the publishing company's American staff how to answer the basic questions of the hundreds of international visitors who would pass the company's exhibit every day. Of course, the staff members also talked about their lives in New York City, where they worked, and their homes in

Westchester County or on Long Island, the sports that their children were involved in, and the New York Yankees games they were missing while they were in Frankfurt. My decision not to go to school for an entire week because of my job at the book fair seemed perfectly reasonable to me because here was my chance to get to know real American civilians and hear what they were thinking and talking about—in contrast to the American military and their families, who were a familiar part of our everyday environment. I felt at home in the realm of book publishing. I had loved books all my life, holding them and turning their pages before I had learned to read, and once I could read, I inhabited the worlds they opened up for me, whether it was the alpine meadows of Heidi's Swiss childhood, Greek islands and Homeric battles, or the landscapes of the Wild West. Every time I finished a book, it became a document in the history of my developing thoughts and ideas, and I felt bonded with it as though it had become a part of me. I didn't notice the contradiction between my love of books as the repositories of scholarship and literature and my firm plans to leave school at eighteen, with or without the Abitur exam, and emigrate to America, where I would work on any job I could find and follow whatever practical work opportunity opened up before me there.

The high point of the book fair was the annual ceremony in which the Peace Prize of the Booksellers' Association was awarded. In 1957, my first year of working at the book fair, I was invited to join my American employers at the award ceremony. The recipient of that year's award was Thornton Wilder, whose play *Our Town* was familiar to me from its repeated performances at the American playhouse by the amateur theater group made up of U.S. military dependents. The playhouse was a plain one-story cement structure not far from the Römerstadt, its performances were advertised on the AFN, and the cast warmly welcomed the small audience of military families and the handful of Germans, including me, who showed up. I remember *Grover's Corners*, New Hampshire, where George and Emily grew up, fell in love, and got married, and I imagine that the portrayal of this small American town with its down-to-earth, lower-middle-class families who worked hard, behaved honorably, and treated one another with kindness helped shape my idealized view of life in America.

With gratitude for the generosity of my employers, I found that my ticket to the elaborate award ceremony with several prominent speakers and a string quartet was for a seat in the third row of the large hall. When the audience had settled in, a group of dignitaries entered the hall to warm applause and made its way up the main aisle to the first row, where seats had been reserved for them. I recognized Thornton Wilder from his photo on the posters, but in a split second, my attention was diverted to the man next to him, and I knew before I could believe it that this was Albert Schweitzer.

In a Germany where shame for its immense atrocities was never far from the public discourse, the idea of being proud of anyone or anything German seemed like a foreign concept. One exception was Albert Schweitzer, who was widely admired, loved, and indeed revered for his humanitarian actions, his philosophy of *reverence for life,* and perhaps also for simply giving Germans someone to be proud of.

Had Schweitzer been born five years before his actual birthdate, January 14, 1875, he would have been born as a French citizen, since his village of Kaysersberg in Alsace was a part of France until the Prussians won their war with France in 1871 and annexed Alsace. Although Schweitzer lived his life as a German citizen, even when Alsace was returned to France after World War I, his identity transcended national borders, and he was a European long before the European Union existed.

Schweitzer's life had two parts. Until the age of thirty, he was a scholar of theology who preached a very liberal interpretation of the gospel. He was also a philosophy lecturer at the University of Strasburg, an eminent organist, and author of the—at the time—definitive book on the music of Johann Sebastian Bach. At thirty, Schweitzer embarked on the second part of his life when he entered medical school to become a surgeon and specialist in tropical diseases so that he could serve as a medical missionary in Africa.

In letters to family and friends, Schweitzer explained that he had made this decision as a way of atoning for the sins of Europeans who had invaded Africa, enslaved its people, colonized their lands, exploited their resources, and killed untold numbers of them by infecting them with diseases against which the Africans had no immunity. To raise money for his project of building a hospital in Africa where he could provide medical treatment to the local population, Schweitzer had gone on lecture and organ recital tours throughout Europe. He entered an agreement with the Paris Missionary Society, which allowed him to build his hospital on grounds adjacent to their mission in Lambarene on the banks of the Ogowe River in French Equatorial Africa—today's Gabon—but only on the condition that he restrict his activities to treating the sick and refrain from spreading his liberal Christian views.

Schweitzer's biography was well-known and had made him a near-mythical figure so that his sudden appearance with Thornton Wilder inevitably overshadowed the festivities. Larger than life yet deeply humble in his demeanor, he instantly commanded the attention of everyone in the hall. He was still of strong build but slightly stooped at eighty-two, in a rumpled black suit and white shirt, his head sculpted as if from a massive block of hardwood, his dramatic mustache completely covering his mouth, and his thick white hair brushed back, parting and curling forward until the tips framed his temples. He had apparently injured his left hand because it was wrapped in several layers of a linen bandage that looked as though it had been white some days ago and had remained unchanged because the needs of others were of greater priority. The end of the bandage had obviously been secured by being tucked in between some of its layers but was coming loose and dangled from the injured hand.

It turned out that Thornton Wilder and Albert Schweitzer were old friends, and Schweitzer, who had been the recipient of the Peace Prize in 1951, and then received the Nobel Peace Prize in the following year, had agreed to be Wilder's guest for this occasion. For me, seated two rows behind him to his left, with a full view of his profile, the ceremony itself receded from my awareness as I simply focused on the experience of being in Schweitzer's presence. I felt no impulse to approach him in any way; it was enough to be exactly where I was for as long as the ceremony lasted, and when it ended, and all the dignitaries from the first row had filed out of the hall, I quietly left with a feeling that resembled what I imagine a state of grace to be. I do remember that the image of Schweitzer's bandaged hand conjured for me the aura of the charismatic jungle doctor. The humility of this hand has remained etched in my mind as the emblematic antithesis of the arrogant and life-destroying evil of Hitler's Germany.

38

The Three Kings

While my days were flying by as I juggled my various interests and responsibilities, it became clear that Harry had traded in his status of "being seldom home" for the one of "not living here anymore." Vera met this new reality with a mix of despondency, anger, and denial. My brothers claim that they have no memory of the family dynamics during that time, and maybe this is due to the fact that Vera was able to carry on without acknowledging that a big change was taking place within our family in that Harry had essentially moved out. Her stony facade may have helped her go through the motions of holding a household together, but I saw the anger and the pain when I would find her crying in the music room late at night. Overwhelmed by the turbulence of her emotions, she distilled them all into the one question which she repeated to me not just during the immediate crisis but in the years that followed: "How could he leave me like this, when I stood by him during the Nazi years?"

I had learned long ago that the most helpful thing I could do when Vera fell into despair was to listen to her and say nothing for a while, and when it looked like she was now open to hearing a response, I offered some observations that usually included practical ideas on how to go forward. In that spirit, I asked her if she and Harry had talked about their separation, and I was stunned to hear that they had not. With the false sense of omnipotence which often afflicts precocious firstborns who have had early responsibilities, I prescribed immediate communication for this couple—my parents—who knew how to talk with each other at great length about music and politics and world affairs but couldn't find words to talk about their relationship. I urged Vera to call Harry on the phone and arrange for a place where they could meet and talk about what had happened to their relationship, and when she hid behind one excuse after another, I said that if she didn't do this, I would. Unbelievably, she took me up on my offer, and the next morning, I was on a train to Cologne to meet with Harry.

Cologne is the city to which Harry's father, Willy Saarbach, had moved the family business in 1912 after the death of his father, August Saarbach. Willy's younger brother, Max, had died as a teenager in 1910 of meningitis, and when the youngest brother, Ernst, took his life in 1923, Willy was left as his father's only male heir. Willy's three sisters were married and reportedly showed no interest in the business, leaving Willy as the only family member to take over the firm. It seems that Willy ran the company with great skill because it grew into one of Germany's most prominent distributors of foreign newspapers and magazines.

I had been in Cologne before, the last time about a year earlier, on the occasion of Willy's seventieth birthday, an elaborate affair in a gilded hotel ballroom, where Willy was awarded the *Bundesverdienstkreuz, (a* federal prize to honor outstanding accomplishment) by a government official who arrived to conduct the award ceremony. Willy and Fredel were not pleased to see us, assigned us to a table at the back of the room, as far as possible from the podium and flower arrangement that had been set up on a small stage for the moment when the medal would be awarded and the congratulatory speeches would be given.

I was relieved to find that our table in the rear made us nearly invisible, but Harry and Vera were offended, and Harry seemed hurt, maybe only in his pride, or perhaps in a deeper place. We had traveled the four hours to Cologne in Harry's old Opel, and as he searched for a place to park, he joked about the rusty Opel looking like a poor relative among the shiny limousines in the hotel parking lot and laughed at the quizzical looks we got from the hotel's valets. Harry seemed to enjoy his defiant gesture of showing up at his father's gala in an embarrassing vehicle, but being seated at the back of the room did not amuse him. In all, Willy's birthday extravaganza was a thoroughly distasteful experience, and it left me wondering not so much about the reason for Willy's and Fredel's coldness toward us but why Harry and Vera, who were seldom together anymore, would bother to subject themselves to such an event. It never occurred to me to ask why Harry was not working in the family business even though it had his name on it or why my brothers and I were never invited to visit our grandfather in his stately home in Cologne; it was clear that Harry's relationship with his father and stepmother was poisoned, probably by old secrets too shocking to say out loud.

As an antidote to the negative association between the city of Cologne and my unpleasant grandfather, I heard a curious story years later that the bones of the three kings of biblical fame were housed in the colossal Gothic cathedral in Cologne. I found the story bizarre, exotic, and completely unbelievable, a figment of a pious soul's imagination. The idea that the biblical three kings followed the bright star through the deserts of the Middle East in their search for Bethlehem, where they wanted to present their gifts to the newborn king, and then ended up in the cold, drizzling rain of Cologne struck me as utterly hilarious. However, the story turns out to be based on a historical account of how the Roman emperor Constantine took the bones of the three kings, or what was in the fourth century AD believed to be their bones, to Italy and gave them to the bishop in Milan. There they stayed for eight hundred years, until the celebrity emperor Frederick Barbarossa took them away from the bishop of Milan and gave them to the archbishop of Cologne. There, the bones were at last properly stored in a gilded vault, for which a new cathedral was now needed. It was built over the next six hundred years and became the largest Gothic church in northern Europe. True or not, this story is what comes to mind when I think about Cologne now, and it wipes away the old unpleasantness that for years crept like mildew over my memories of the city.

After arriving at the train station in downtown Cologne near the cathedral, I had no trouble finding Harry's hotel. When I knocked on the door of his room, he opened instantly, as though he had been waiting on the other side, and gave me a hug that felt like the desperate grip of a drowning man. I was still in my city-navigating/problem-solving travel mode, and I remember thinking that somebody had to steer this listing boat, so I would need to keep a clear head.

What an observer of this scene would have witnessed was a father in a state of emotional upheaval explaining himself to his levelheaded, faintly skeptical daughter. What the father wanted his daughter to understand was that his painful decision to leave his family was not selfish, arbitrary, and impulsive but driven by the realization that his early emotional connection with his wife, based on their passionate engagement with music, was not enough to counterbalance the chronic, hurtful conflict brought on by their incompatible personalities.

In Harry's explanations, Paddy's name never came up, but it was clear that Harry had found in Paddy someone more compatible and was torn between her and Vera. I wondered what Paddy must be like to have thrown Harry into this turmoil, but I didn't ask. What Harry did talk about with unexpected openness was his lifelong fear of conflict and avoidance of controversy at all cost, his history of covering up unhealed wounds from old insults, his yearning to feel understood, and, what shocked me most, his deep sense of failure. He hinted at having caused a great deal of pain to others as well and was hoping for eventual reconciliation. I felt that it was not the right time to ask about details or to mention his past infidelities. I merely tried to hold my own in this heady conversation, pretending to know what I was talking about, although I had not experienced these tortures myself and was determined to make sure that I never would. After a long time of deep soul-searching, with Harry's tumultuous inner struggle reflected in waves of heaving and crashing emotions, the conversation eased toward more practical matters and took on the tone of the negotiations mediated in divorce proceedings, where the parties have basically accepted the inevitability of the dissolution and are working out practical details.

Harry seemed genuinely touched that I had come, and we parted on cordial terms. Back on the platform waiting for the train to Frankfurt, and reliving what seemed like the aching lyricism, the broad sweep, and the nervous rush of a Mahler symphony, I started to sort out what had been accomplished by my trip, and it was obvious to me that I had been able to obtain some clarity about my relationship with my father but had completely failed in the stated purpose of the trip, which was to clarify Vera's relationship with her husband. My first task after getting home would therefore have to be to explain to Vera that I had been unable to deliver what I had promised. I would be able to tell her, however, that the trip was not a waste of time because I had come away from the meeting with Harry convinced that the best course of action was to have an amicable divorce.

As I boarded the train for the return trip to Frankfurt, I was preoccupied with the problem of how to formulate my thoughts about all this in such a way that Vera would quickly see the wisdom of ending her tortured marriage. Absentmindedly, I chose a six-passenger compartment and took a window seat opposite the only other occupant of the compartment, an unremarkable-looking man maybe in his midthirties, his business suit and briefcase suggesting a respectable person traveling for a legitimate purpose. I remember writing notes to help me remember the main arguments I wanted to present to Vera when I noticed that the man had changed seats and was now sitting next to me, looking at my writing and urging me to put my papers away so we could talk. I must have looked startled, and I was certainly at a loss of what to say, especially after he started leaning into me and groping me. I was frightened, jumped up out of my seat, grabbed my bag, and tried to reach the compartment door, but he was closer to it and stood in front of it to block my exit. Now I was terrified, and I wanted to scream, but something held me back as I suddenly felt an anger rising in me which momentarily pushed the fear aside. I knew that if this man raped me, I would be blamed for having put myself into this situation, traveling alone, choosing a compartment with only one man in it, like a woman seeking an adventure. In my rage, I looked at him and said that he couldn't possibly expect me to be interested in whatever he had in mind since I had just spent the day with my father who had a terminal illness and whom I may never see again.

To my astonishment, the man's face turned red, not in rage but in shame as he stepped aside and mumbled an apology. I remember hearing words like, "I didn't know. I'm so sorry. I understand," and I was out the door, away from that compartment, hurrying down the corridor and through the connecting doors into the next railroad car, which had open seating and was almost fully occupied, leaving few single seats and no chance for the man in the suit to sit next to me again. Looking back at that incident, I realize that some progress has been made since the 1950s, when such behavior was still seen as part of what women traveling alone had to accept from men who thought they were entitled to actions which we today call sexual assault and treat as a crime.

39

The Supreme Allied Commander

It was fitting to be an adolescent searching for an identity in the West Germany of the late 1950s, because the whole population seemed to be in the throes of trying to decide who they were going to be as the new Germans and what they were going to do with their ghastly inheritance from the Nazi empire. What they all knew, and generally accepted, was that their Germany was integrated into the cultural sphere of "The West," which was dominated by the United States. Dwight D. Eisenhower, the general who, as supreme commander of the Allied Forces in Western Europe had led the legendary invasion of Nazi-occupied Europe on D-Day, June 6, 1944, when I was a three-year-old and living in Marschwitz, was in his second term as president of the United States. He had been elected in 1952, after guiding NATO through its early years of formulating its mission, and he was now leading the United States through a period of astonishing prosperity and growth, with giant public works projects like the interstate highway system, the strengthening of social security programs, and a proliferation of scientific research from agriculture to robotics. He had ended the Korean War with an armistice agreement, which was intended to lead to peace negotiations at some point, but even though those negotiations were going nowhere, President Eisenhower's image as the peace-seeking "leader of the free world" smiled at us with engaging benevolence from the walls of American consulate lobbies, branch offices of the major American banks, cultural foundations like the ubiquitous *America Haus*, science and technology exhibits that traveled from city to city, and sports extravaganzas like the *Harlem Globetrotters, or Holiday on Ice.* President Eisenhower embodied stability and steady progress toward a better world for the children and adolescents of my generation, and when he retired from public life at the end of his second term, we were as disoriented as subjects in a monarchy when the only king they have ever known dies.

If one is willing to downplay the chronic anxiety caused by the Cold War with the Soviet Union and overlook the mean-spirited attacks and paranoia unleashed by Senator Joe McCarthy's campaign against alleged communists in the U.S. government and other institutions, including the Hollywood movie industry, the case could be made that the Eisenhower years were the era of American greatness—for white men. Nostalgic whispers can still be overheard to this day that what made the fifties great was that "women and negroes knew their place." For women, their place was in the home, where they deferred to their husbands and could hold checking accounts and take out loans only with the husband's consent. Black people were expected to defer to whites and were excluded from educational and professional opportunities, confined to segregated housing and schools, banned from many restaurants, hotels, and theaters, directed to separate public restrooms and water fountains, and were at risk of being lynched by a jeering mob if perceived as trespassing on white privilege. Similar injustices were suffered by people of Hispanic and Asian ethnicity.

These inequalities could be overlooked by an idealistic young person on the other side of the Atlantic, going through the motions of attending school and meeting the responsibilities of daily family life that were placed in front of her. At school, I mingled with fellow students who were talking about attending the university in the next year to become lawyers, scientists, or politicians, while I nurtured a vision of a completely different life, which would begin with my leaving the country.

The only person with whom I talked about moving to America was Margret. I missed her when she had not come to school for several days, and when she still had not returned after two more weeks, I called her home phone number, the only means of communication before the age of the personal cell phone. Her mother answered and told me in a sarcastic tone that Margret was sick and that I should call back another time.

A week later, when I called again, Margret's mother coldly agreed to let me come over for a visit. Margret was in her room, sitting up in her bed, her face pale and drawn, and she seemed thinner. She offered a weaker version of her characteristic contagiously cheerful grin and joked about her new status as a bedridden person who was seeing the world in a new way, thanks to her horizontal perspective. The joking didn't last long, however, and I noticed that she was fighting back tears. From sentence fragments stifled by sobs, I learned that she had been pregnant and had found an illegal and incompetent practitioner who had performed an abortion that resulted in severe hemorrhaging. She was hospitalized for several days after receiving emergency transfusions, and she had still not recovered completely from the blood loss and subsequent surgery. She didn't know yet at that moment that the procedure which terminated her pregnancy also injured her reproductive organs in such a way that she would not be able to have children in the future. I was shocked and bewildered to hear all this and found myself transported back to the day when I came home from school to find an emergency medical team carrying Vera in her bloody blanket on a gurney down the stairs to the waiting ambulance.

Weeks later, Margret and I were sitting in a café, her first time out of the house after her ordeal, and she explained why she had determined that she had no choice but to terminate her pregnancy. She had never felt safe to tell anyone, including me, that she was in love with a Black man, an Army sergeant who was stationed near Frankfurt. She said that he loved her too, and they wanted to marry, but he was afraid to submit his request to marry a German woman to his commanding officer because he had seen other Black soldiers being harassed for dating German women. They had talked about waiting for the end of his enlistment period, when he could get out of the military, and they would live in Germany somehow, in spite of his poor job prospects there. They had weighed the possibility of living in the United States, but moving to his home state of Mississippi was out of the question due to the violent rejection of interracial marriage that they would face there. They considered moving to Los Angeles or New York City, where they were more likely to be accepted, and of course, there was Margret's American hometown of Detroit to think about, but all these plans overlooked the fact that the man she loved was still in the Army, which he had thought of as his career. In the midst of all these deliberations, Margret had found herself pregnant and was certain that her parents would not welcome a biracial grandchild. In telling me all this, she was clearly reliving the wrenching emotional conflict brought on by her pregnancy, and there was no doubt that her decision to end the pregnancy was agonizing: "In the end, I simply could not bring a baby into the world knowing that it would be rejected, pushed away, belong nowhere because its parents' skin was not of the same color."

To prove her point, Margret described her parents' reaction to her abortion. Her father, generally a kind and generous man, avoided the odious topic and deferred to her mother, who had to deliberate for a whole day and then agreed only reluctantly to let Margret back in the house, under the condition of complete isolation from Margret's friends, and especially the Black boyfriend. I had obviously received an exemption, but the ban against the boyfriend remained in place indefinitely. The parents also informed Margret that her "carefree school days" were over, that she needed to find a job to begin supporting herself, and in view of her approaching eighteenth birthday, plan to pay them rent. Margret appeased her parents by telling them that she would comply with their conditions, but she had no intention of giving up the man she loved. Thus began a carefully orchestrated sequence of ruses and deceptions in which I offered to play a part as well and which would bring on a fateful turn in my own life.

Margret's boyfriend, Carlton, had a friend, Byron, who was white. The two men had met in basic training years ago, had gotten along well, and now found themselves stationed together in the same barracks near Frankfurt. When Carlton told his friend about his situation, Byron offered to stand in for Carlton and arrange dates with Margret, pick her up at her home, and introduce himself to her parents as her date. To add a layer of authenticity to this arrangement, and in a gesture of solidarity with my friend, I agreed to be available for a double date, so Byron brought another white friend along as a date for me. The three of us picked up Margret at her home. In the course of the evening, Margret would disappear so that she could be with Carlton, who was waiting for her nearby. The terrible experience of her abortion and his inability to be with her during this ordeal had strengthened their bond even more, and they were wearing simple gold wedding bands as personal tokens of commitment to each other. As soon as Margret left, Byron excused himself as well as he had a different agenda for his visits to Frankfurt, and this left me with my blind date, a polite, studious-looking young man named James whom I could not imagine in a military uniform. James introduced himself as a Midwesterner from North Platte, Nebraska and in the course of our conversation mentioned that he had been drafted after he had recovered from the serious illness that had forced him to quit law school at Georgetown University in Washington, DC.

In the course of several more dates, I got to know James as a serious, dependable person with an English major's knowledge of literature and poetry, a devout Catholic who had graduated from Notre Dame University in South Bend, Indiana, and a man who felt completely out of place in the military. He was the proud descendant of his Scottish and English ancestors, from whom he had inherited blond hair, pale-blue eyes, and fair skin, which burned easily on a sunny day. He had been assigned to a clerical job in his unit and was spending his days performing repetitive tasks and dreaming of traveling, and hopefully settling, in Europe after his discharge. His great-great-grandparents had arrived in America in the mid-nineteenth century and had settled in the Midwest where, like so many other early immigrants, they put down deep roots, which lent them a proprietary tone when they talked about their hometowns and the land around them. James's father and grandfather were attorneys and alumni of the same schools which James, the family's only male heir, later attended himself.

The story of how James's ancestors settled in the broad Platte Valley of western Nebraska, where the river has room to lounge in a bed one mile wide and two feet deep without ever having to carve itself a canyon, could have been written by the novelist Willa Cather, whose books about the settlement of the prairie I had not yet read when I listened to James's descriptions of life in the Nebraska of his great-grandparents. The Americans I had met so far were usually from urban areas, specifically the cities in the northeast, and every once in a while, someone was from California. The sound of the word *Nebraska* and the lore of the prairie held a special fascination for Germans, and certainly for me, as the site where the near-mythical events took place that transformed the land from hunting grounds of the native warriors to the vast fields of grain which feed the world.

Growing up with Harry and Vera as my parents, and observing how Vera suffered from Harry's infidelities, I developed at a very early age a conflicted attitude toward men and knew that I didn't want Vera's life. I do remember early moments of gratification when I would hear my father, Harry, say that he was proud of me, but there were so many times when he was absent or distracted and uninterested that I eventually came to think of him as unreliable, both as my father and Vera's husband. As a consequence, I determined at a young age that I would prevent repeated disappointment by training myself to expect nothing from him and from men in general. I must have formed a very skeptical view of men as persons one must guard against, keep at bay, never depend on, certainly never fall in love with, which left little room in my imagination for the romantic ideas commonly attributed to young women. I was not immune to the heady excitement of going on dates with young men who were rebellious and had original ideas, read contemporary French poetry, and knew about the latest Italian films before they were even released. However, I was always grateful when my lack of interest in deepening a relationship with a potential boyfriend was accepted without protest, pestering, or pressure.

40

Nuns and Lions

Although a lot of my time and attention were now taken up by matters that were outside the scope of my family life, I still went home every evening, was relieved when Vera had felt well enough to have cooked dinner, told my brothers yet again that I wished they would turn down the volume on the TV, and cleaned up the kitchen after we had finished eating. Often I came home early enough to stop on the second floor and look in on Antoinette because she seldom came upstairs anymore after my brothers and I were old enough to be at home without supervision.

Antoinette always greeted me excitedly as though I had been on a long trip and was now safely back home. She would steer me into her tidy room, which looked like a conventional living room with a sofa, two upholstered chairs and a table between them, a large antique wardrobe—probably purchased by Vera at one of the American furniture auctions—against one wall, two more wooden chairs, and a small desk with her beloved radio on the adjoining wall beneath the window, with a view of the gardens below. I knew that this room changed its function every night with the conversion of the sofa into a bed, but I don't remember ever seeing Antoinette activate the mechanism which flattened the sofa into a bed, nor did I ever see her in nightclothes.

With the exception of a few trips to France over the years to visit her sister Jeanne and her brother-in-law Henri, Antoinette was always home, waiting. She seemed practiced in it, as though she had studied waiting in her childhood convent as a devotional art form. She waited while making no demands, voicing no complaints, displaying no impatience; she didn't try to distract herself while waiting, she showed no signs of boredom, and she engaged in the act of waiting as if it were in itself a purposeful activity.

The continuity of Antoinette's quietly immutable existence was underscored by her unchanging appearance; she always dressed in the same style of straight, tailored dark-gray skirts of mid-calf length, which rode up to just below her knees when she sat down and revealed slender legs and ankles in nylon stockings, and small feet in leather pumps. The dark skirts were always paired with white blouses fastened at the collar with her exquisitely beautiful mother-of-pearl cameo brooch displaying the profile of a regal lady. It was probably my imagination which suggested that the profile could be that of her mother because I have no memory of Antoinette ever saying so. Also always present was her amethyst ring on her left hand, and her fine white hair was tied in the same little knot at the base of her delicate neck. This porcelain quality of Antoinette's aura was heightened by the faintly visible pulse that throbbed in her alabaster temples whenever she was agitated.

Antoinette inhabited her room in the way in which a bird inhabits a hollow in a tree; it was her refuge, and it was her perch, from which she could view her world and, by way of her radio, listen to what was going on in the country of her birth. She kept up with the local Frankfurt news and the weather forecast, but what she most wanted to know about was the news from France, with its unending political turmoil, frequent calls for new elections, and installation of one weak government after another, until her idol, General Charles de Gaulle, finally became president in 1959, the year in which I turned eighteen. Antoinette had adored de Gaulle ever since he fled to London on June 18, 1940, days after Hitler invaded France; her eyes would well up when she told me the story of how de Gaulle—as de facto head of the legitimate French government in exile—broadcast appeals from London to his countrymen across the English Channel to fight the Nazis and their French collaborators and how he agitated, provoked, and annoyed Churchill and Roosevelt with his relentless quest to have France, by which he meant himself, seated at the table where the Allies plotted the course of the war. When

Antoinette talked about the day when General Charles de Gaulle, taller than anyone else around him, entered Paris after the Allied forces had liberated the city, her voice and the expression on her face were those of a person whose home was in France and nowhere else.

Antoinette's heart was big enough for two idols. Next to Charles de Gaulle, she also loved Marshal Philippe Pétain, a great general from the First World War, who took over the French government and signed the infamous armistice with the Nazi regime after it had invaded France and swept its ineffective military aside on its triumphant march to Paris. With the Nazi military in full control of Paris, Pétain chose to accept the top post in a collaborating puppet government, and it had been calculated that his decision saved tens or maybe hundreds of thousands of French lives, but his role as Hitler's accomplice in the murder of seventy-five thousand French Jews cost his country its honor.

Antoinette was meek and easily intimidated and never spoke up for herself, but she firmly held on to her two heroes and ignored anyone's attempt to persuade her that these two men represented irreconcilable points of view and courses of action. She adored them both, and together they personified for her the France she loved.

I have no memory of ever seeing Antoinette downstairs on the street, but she must have gone to the grocery store on weekday mornings when I was in school because she cooked for herself every day in the apartment's shared kitchen, which was of course a carbon copy of ours on the third floor, and she never ran out of the Valerian medicine that she bought at the pharmacy and took daily for her chronic anxiety. In the fall and winter, she always had apples in a ceramic bowl on her table. She knew that I loved the small fragrant Winesap apples that are harvested in late fall and stored through the winter in dark, peat-filled bins to last till early spring, and she bought those whenever she could find them in the store.

Our conversations usually started with Antoinette's questions about my day at school, unless there were special topics which I had mentioned to her on a previous visit. She would also ask how things were going with James, whom she had met; she said that she found him well-mannered and likable and a good choice as a boyfriend. We would sit and talk, and if I had nothing left to talk about and there was time, she would tell me stories about growing up with many other girls in her convent, where some of the nuns ran a tight ship like stern mothers, who insisted on proper bathing etiquette, which required that the girls put on their long white linen bathing gowns before they got into the bathtub, and threatened long hours of extra homework or scrubbing floors for any girl caught sleeping in someone else's bed. Some nuns had a sense of humor; others acted more like kindhearted, affectionate grandmothers; and very young nuns could be bossy like older sisters; the oldest nuns were best avoided because some of them could be mean. I was intrigued by Antoinette's descriptions of life in a convent, where the girls wore uniforms and the nuns all wore identical habits with the elaborate headgear and the routines of each day unspooled according to a rhythm that may not have changed much over a hundred years. I felt such a sense of wonder at the way Antoinette grew up that I didn't even notice that she never once mentioned her mother, who apparently prevailed on her lover, a kind and generous man, to travel on her behalf several times a year to the convent to visit her secret child. There is no proof that Antoinette was deeply hurt by her mother's indifference toward her, but I have no doubt that the stigma of her illegitimate birth had a profound and lifelong effect on her emotional development and sense of self-worth.

Antoinette's stories were always about her childhood and youth in France and never about her adult life in London, and later in Mainz, where she had raised her only child, my father, Harry, as a single mother after her divorce from Willy, whom she also never mentioned. She knew that Harry had recently moved out of the apartment upstairs and was not likely to come back to visit her, but she never talked about that either; she was not close to her daughter-in-law, Vera, and her only communication with her two grandsons consisted of the noise she heard in the staircase outside her apartment door when Stefan and René stormed up or down the staircase, skipping two or three steps and landing hard on the wooden planks. She had no friends in the neighborhood, in spite of having lived there for ten years, the same ten years in which I had grown up there and which seemed like an eternity to me. I knew that Antoinette's relationship with Käte was distant—not strained or conflicted but essentially nonexistent—even though both women lived in adjoining buildings and saw each other at our apartment for Christmas and other family gatherings, where Käte's presence dominated with its riveting authority. Antoinette was on superficially friendly terms with Bragge and his wife, the principal tenants of the apartment, and they connected her to the immediate, practical affairs of the neighborhood, such as the seasonal changes in the garbage pickup schedule. The larger world, however, came to Antoinette through her radio, which let her know all the important things that were going on in France.

I thought for a long time that Antoinette's isolation was a consequence of her language difficulty, but she was actually quite fluent in German, although she spoke with a strong French accent. I knew that she was by nature timid and insecure, although her history of being a sought-out bridge player in her earlier life in Mainz would indicate that when she felt accepted in a familiar environment, Antoinette could be charming and maybe even outgoing. Her enduring graceful appearance and elegant bearing suggested as much, but whenever I came up with ideas on how she might meet new people, Antoinette waved off any further discussion of the subject.

I don't think I ever wanted to notice how small Antoinette's life was and that there was no one in whose life she played an essential part. I could see that whatever was in this one room was all that Antoinette had, that almost nothing had been added to the contents of the room over the years, except a few books and magazines in French, and that she never went to a concert or any other type of social event. She did go to a movie theater once, to which I can testify because I was there too. This rare event occurred when Harry unexpectedly came downstairs one day and rang her doorbell, and I went to see who it was. He asked us if we wanted to go to a movie with him, and without asking what the movie was, we agreed. This was all so unusual that I felt we were about to embark on a rare adventure as we got into Harry's car, Antoinette in the passenger seat and me in the back. Harry drove us to a movie theater in downtown Frankfurt, not far from the Jazz Keller, which I would discover some time later, and he bought three tickets for the American movie *Battle Cry*, which had just opened in Frankfurt. It was causing a sensation with its wide *Cinemascope* format and lineup of Hollywood stars: Van Heflin, Aldo Ray, Tab Hunter, and Anne Francis. Antoinette and I were quickly overwhelmed by the photogenic muscle strength and rugged looks of all those Marines fighting in World War II scenes, which we didn't recognize as the World War II that we knew. The heroic action on the vast screen was accompanied by a deafening soundtrack, and I felt an overpowering sense of awe and at the same time a curious detachment from this outsize martial spectacle. Afterward, on our way home in the car, it became clear that Harry had paid little attention to the movie; later, it turned out that he and Vera had argued earlier that day and he had walked out, and on the spur of the moment had invited us to the movie as coconspirators in his escape.

Antoinette never said what she thought of *Battle Cry*, as though it was so far removed from her world that she could not find a place for it in her mental inventory. She looked relieved to be back safely in her quiet room, where she waited with shy hope for someone to visit her, waited for the news and other favorite radio programs with songs by Edith Piaf and Maurice Chevalier to come on, waited to be needed upstairs, waited for letters from her half-sister Jeanne, and waited for me to stop on my way to the third floor. This is how as a child she must have waited for visits from her mother who never came. She waited almost as if waiting was an activity with its own inherent merit. There were no open books or solitaire cards on the table to suggest that she had tried to entertain herself while waiting, and I don't remember that she ever complained of boredom. Looking back, I wonder if this skill of attentive waiting, which requires the embracing of submission, acceptance, and surrender of the self, was taught by the nuns who had raised Antoinette from infancy; maybe in their convent, patient waiting was practiced as a form of religious devotion.

There were rare moments when Antoinette's stoicism wore thin, and she admitted to feeling lonely or abandoned; her plaintive refrain of "I'm just a poor creature" sounded even more forlorn in her French accent. I knew how to steer our conversations away from such painful phrases and utilized my arsenal of consoling, reassuring, encouraging and cheery platitudes to get her to look at the bright side of things and laugh about funny neighborhood stories. I urged her to take Vera's occasional incivility in stride, and I teased her how lucky she was that—unlike me—she didn't have to put up with Stefan and René, their relentless teasing, their noise, and their messes. My rendition of life with my brothers could bring on some needed laughter about their latest outrages, at which point I made some mocking comment about the disasters I would surely find in a few minutes when I got upstairs.

With the intention of adding some color to Antoinette's life, I once invited her to join me and James for a trip to the Frankfurt Zoo. I wanted to see the new reptile house that had recently been opened. The zoo had been completely destroyed in the last air raids over Frankfurt in early 1945, and when the American military entered the city shortly afterward, they found only twenty animals still alive. Even before the German capitulation was formally declared on May 8, 1945, the newly installed American military government searched for a new zoo director and found Dr. Bernhard Grzimek, who had just turned down the post of Frankfurt's first postwar police chief but was interested in the position at the zoo.

Germans in the postwar era were used to the absurdities created by regime changes and political realignments, redrawn borders, and the vicissitudes of victory and defeat, and for them, Dr. Grzimek's biography captured the essence of this upside-down world and made him a well-known figure not only in the Frankfurt region but throughout West Germany. He was born in Silesia, now a part of Poland, not far from the *Marschwitz* of my early childhood, and was five years old when the First World War began. He received a doctorate in veterinary medicine 1933, right after Hitler had come to power, and was drafted into the *Wehrmacht* during World War II as a military veterinarian. In January 1945, when Vera, Stefan, and I were fleeing from the Red Army advancing on Berlin, Grzimek's apartment in Berlin was raided by the Gestapo because someone had denounced him for smuggling food to a Jewish family hiding nearby and waiting for liberation by the Red Army. In 1947, two years into his tenure as zoo director in Frankfurt, Grzimek became the target of a whisper campaign accusing him of having been a member of the Nazi Party, and he was suspended from his post and detained in a *denazification* camp, until an American military investigation found him innocent of the charges and a victim of a smear campaign originating in the office of a rival zoo director in the city of Munich.

Bernhard Grzimek was reinstated as head of the Frankfurt Zoo and went on to become a much admired trailblazer in the early environmental and conservation movement, leading many research projects for the study of the natural habitats of zoo animals so that enclosures could be created that resembled their native environment as much as possible. During Dr. Grzimek's thirty-year tenure, which ended long after I left Germany, the Frankfurt Zoo became a state-of-the-art institution, and his visionary work in the establishment of protected habitats for Africa's endangered wildlife has been recognized worldwide. In his book *The Serengeti Must Not Die*, published around the time of my zoo visit, he writes with startling prescience about the urgent need for establishing national parks, such as *Serengeti National Park* in Tanzania, which he helped to establish:

> Large cities continue to proliferate. In the coming decades and centuries, men will not travel to view marvels of engineering, but they will leave the dusty towns in order to behold the last places on earth where God's creatures are peacefully living. Countries which have preserved such places will be envied by other nations and visited by streams of tourists. There is a difference between wild animals living a natural life and famous buildings. Palaces can be rebuilt if they are destroyed in wartime, but once the wild animals of the Serengeti are exterminated, no power on earth can bring them back.

At first, Antoinette begged off and said that she did not feel up to going to the zoo and that we should go without her. I went upstairs to change and get ready, but just as I passed her apartment door on the way down the staircase, there she was in the doorway, in her coat, a hat on her head, timidly explaining that she had changed her mind and wanted to join us. We met James, who was waiting for us downstairs in his car. Antoinette actually seemed to look forward to seeing the zoo and, once there, valiantly strode down the paths between the many outdoor exhibits, past the new reptile house, where too long a line of people were waiting to be admitted, commented on the whimsical appearance of the warthogs plowing the soil in their compound, and admired the miniature savanna with the giraffes, zebras, wildebeests, impalas, and gazelles. There was also the monkeys' jungle gym; the long, narrow fenced run for a sullen cheetah; a small yard with a shade structure for a pair of spotted hyenas; and the adjoining small tree-shaded arena for a family of snoozing wolves. The high point of the outdoor exhibits was the prominently positioned concrete tarmac behind a deep moat where two elephants monopolized the attention of the visitors, who had already bought little bags of peanuts at the zoo entrance so they could feed the ear-venting giants when they stretched out their trunks across the moat and fluttered their pink, moist nostrils in hopes of more peanuts. Zoos in the 1950s did not have the necessary resources nor, I suspect, the proper understanding of animal behavior and knowledge of the animals' needs, to build the expansive habitats found in modern animal parks. The close confinement of the animals was not lost on Antoinette, and when she approached an exhibit and leaned in closer to catch the occupant's gaze, it seemed that she was discovering an affinity with the creature as it quietly endured its captivity.

As we approached the gray stucco building that housed the big cats, Antoinette became visibly alarmed, but she let us reassure her that there was nothing to fear. She had walked for more than an hour and was happy to find a bench where she could rest before the main attraction of the afternoon, which was the feeding of the lions. Her bench was situated along the back wall of an indoor viewing area, which was separated from three large concrete cells by massive steel pipes. Each of the cells had an opening like a large dog door that connected it to its outdoor compound not visible from the viewing area because the doors were shut. As the feeding time approached, a zoo worker appeared with a cart of large meat chunks, reached between the steel pipes into each cell, and deposited several of these chunks. What the visitors could not see was that outside, in front of those doors, three hungry lions had been pacing, waiting for these doors to open, and when the man with the cart pulled a heavy iron lever and raised the doors, the cats leaped simultaneously, each through their own door, into their separate cells with a murderous roar, and set about devouring the meat one chunk at a time, slowing for the final chunk as they stretched out on the concrete floor and savored the last bites.

When I turned to Antoinette on the bench behind me, I found her face white as a sheet, her eyes closed, with her trembling hands over her ears. I immediately realized that this spectacle we had come across by chance had frightened her; in a savanna ruled by roaring lions, Antoinette was clearly a terrified gazelle. She shuddered for a while longer but was calmer by the time we returned home. She assured me that there was nothing to apologize for, but it was clear that the experience had triggered in her an elemental fear, and our outing never became the funny story that such experiences can often turn into in hindsight.

I loved Antoinette, and I felt growing guilt and pain because I knew that with each step in planning my new life, I would move closer to the day when I would leave her behind, just as her son had left her behind. I did the same thing that he had probably done; I walled off the pain that comes with knowing that I was soon going to have to say a goodbye, which would likely be a final one.

41

Rotterdam

In the movie that I might have wanted to make of my life, I would now reach a point at which a montage of short scenes chronicles my path from leaving school to distancing myself from family life and becoming an emigrant. There would be isolated scenes in which I still sit in the Jazz Keller with friends from school. These scenes do not include Margret any more after she married Carlton and moved to a small town near his base, nor do they include James, who had said that he was uncomfortable and felt out of place in the smoke-filled basement milieu, which he must have experienced as dissolute and vaguely threatening. He clearly frowned on my musical taste and made disapproving comments about shadowy characters sitting in the semidarkness lit by flickering candles in red-tinted glasses on tiny tables with a growing number of Coca-Cola bottles and empty shot glasses, staring at the musicians on the small stage not twenty feet away and nodding in the nervous rhythm of the agitated music.

In one rather operatic scene, I have pneumonia and call James to cancel whatever plans we have for that weekend. The word *pneumonia* must have had an ominous ring to it and added a touch of high drama to his already romanticized notions about neurotic family life in old Europe, where things happened that were unthinkable back in his own deeply conservative family culture in Nebraska. Instead of staying away, he came anyway and looked relieved when he found me still alive.

Illness is a distinct theme in a number of scenes, and it is James's recurring bouts of severe gastrointestinal misery that dominate the action. In the last year of his military service, James had been assigned to a low-stress, rather monotonous position as an office clerk, and while he often complained about the boredom of the job, he was not subjected to any stress there. He counted the weeks, and then the days, when he would finally get his discharge papers from the Army, and his enviable life as an American civilian in a Europe where you could live on five dollars a day would begin. He bought a car, studied employment opportunities, followed some leads in other cities, talked to American civilians who were selling *Encyclopedias Americanas* and Oxford dictionaries to American military families, but his efforts were often frustrated by attacks of stomach pain. He had been diagnosed in college with stomach ulcers, which were given to bleeding when stress levels increased.

The dialogue in these scenes would have been short and rather dry. I knew from the years of caring for Vera how to respond to a person with chronic medical problems, and I felt capable of taking on the challenge of a committed relationship with a person whose health problems might become worse with time. What James offered me, in turn, was emotional stability and a sense of normalcy, which translated into feeling safe with him in a way that I never had while growing up. I had a nebulous sense of who I was or, perhaps better said, who I was not, but I would have been unable to say who I thought I was. What I did know, and could articulate, was the role I had played in my family: the firstborn child, the older sister, Vera's faithful companion, keeping chaos at bay in the kitchen, smoothing over conflict, keeping things going when they threatened to fall apart. I knew that I needed a new role, and the role that would come with marrying James seemed a rational, well-considered next step.

What we were able to discuss in practical terms was the fact that our circumstances were different, but James and I were both at loose ends at this point in our lives, and we became allies in our search for the next chapter. He had obviously made an effort to find a job in Germany so that he could say to himself that he had really tried, but in the end, the only option that made any sense was his return to the United States. He was adamant that he did not want to return to Nebraska, so we came up with New York, which was exotic enough for him to feel that he had in fact found a whole new culture and way of life for himself, almost as good as living in Europe, and New York was where I had always imagined I would live, at least in the beginning, because from all I had read, that was where all immigrants have always first landed and gotten their start.

In another scene, we talk in a matter-of-fact tone about getting married, and our problem is not how to arrange for a festive wedding but how to explain to Vera that we have no interest in a ceremony and guests and that her special preparations are therefore unnecessary. We agree that the most practical way to get married is to go to the city hall and sign the paperwork like rational, no-nonsense people who rent a house together and make a plan for how to divide the available space equitably to meet each occupant's needs.

Looking back, I remember that I was intensely aware of taking on a responsibility for which I felt well prepared, and he probably did the same; I was convinced that our compatibility of strengths and needs formed a sound basis for something as difficult and momentous as building a life together.

I did not succeed in persuading Vera that special wedding preparations were unnecessary and indeed unwanted. She saw the wedding as an occasion to have the chairs around our dining table repaired and reupholstered with matching material, a project that she had talked about for several years. She agreed to give up the idea of inviting guests because that would cause a lot of extra work, but she wanted six matching, newly refurbished chairs to surround our oval dining table for the nice lunch or dinner that she envisioned. If Käte and Antoinette were to be present at the small affair, and maybe one or two other people, which was likely, we would have to bring in additional, nonmatching chairs, but the central set of six refurbished chairs was what mattered. This meant that James and I would be ferrying chairs in his car, two at a time, to an upholstery shop, a plan to which I was immediately opposed on the grounds that the condition of the chairs didn't matter, and no one would care what the chairs looked like since we were all used to them the way they were. Our argument moved from the dining room to the kitchen because a tea kettle was whistling and needed to be turned off, and it continued in the kitchen, following a winding path through several conceptual

analyses of the idea of marriage and levels of significance of the institution as such, until I finally, in a fit of exasperation, blurted out, "It's
my wedding, not yours, and I can…"

I don't remember how I finished the sentence, or if I did, because
I suddenly felt a stinging pain on the left side of my head, and it took
me a few moments before the shock wore off enough that I realized
that Vera had slapped me in my face. I was too stunned to feel anything else, and it is that stunned feeling which I can call up to this
day. Even then, and certainly in the long years since then, I understood that Vera had, in that split second, lost control over all her
accumulated rage at being abandoned by Harry and now abandoned
by me, without being able to do a thing about it. Vera didn't say a
word, walked out of the kitchen without her tea, and was probably
equally shocked by her action, although she never acknowledged it.
She didn't talk to me for days, and the best way to leave this unbearable situation behind me was to go on a trip with James. When I got
back, I sought her out and told her that this silence campaign should
be ended because I would be gone in a few months, and the remaining time was too important to be wasted like this. She didn't respond
immediately, but a short time later, we were on speaking terms again.
James and I got married in a civil ceremony at city hall, Vera was the
witness and took us to lunch in a nice restaurant, and the chairs were
never mentioned again.

This painful incident would cast a long shadow into the
future. Fifteen years later, on one of her visits to California, Vera
and I were sitting at the table in my cheerfully mismatched sage-
green, plum-purple, cranberry-red, and egg yolk-yellow kitchen,
and we talked about my years of growing up in Frankfurt, how she
had taught me how to sew clothes and cook a meal, and how I had
always complained about the rigid kitchen design in which there
was no space for creative variations in the fixed template. Suddenly,
Vera started to talk about how much she had always disliked my
friend Margret, and I was astounded to hear her say that she blamed
Margret for influencing me to "run away from Germany and capitu-
late to the materialistic way of life in America." I felt a rush of anger,
partly because of this attack against my friend and partly because I

was outraged that anybody, and especially my mother, would take me for a person who is incapable of making her own decisions and needs the guidance of others to help her figure out what she should do. A third factor which contributed to my anger was the realization that Vera had obviously not paid any attention to all the signals from me throughout my adolescence, announcing that I was unable to see my future built on the ruins of the Nazi extermination machine. I felt the heat in my face as I defended Margret and went on to explain "my true reason" for leaving Germany: that I had run away from her. I saw immediately the pain that I had inflicted, but I was unable to lead the confrontation away from the cliff, and we both went over the edge, survived the fall, got up, dusted ourselves off, and went on with our lives for another ten years.

In the next scene, I am on one of my visits to Frankfurt, and Vera and I are in the kitchen discussing what to cook for dinner. I remind her that I don't eat meat, and she exclaims with a tone of false innocence: "Ah, just like Adolf Hitler! He didn't eat meat either." While I am still sorting out my reaction to this odd remark, I hear her commenting on my hair, which, she says, reminds her of Eva Braun, Hitler's secret wife. At this point, I gather my wits and call up the skills which I have learned since our last disastrous attempt at truth telling and say to her that we need to sit down and talk about why she is so angry at me. It works, and Vera is able to look me in the eye and tell me that she has never stopped being angry at me for abandoning her and going to America all those years ago. I tell her that I understand her anger and had known before I left that this would cause pain but that I had felt so powerfully that I needed a new world in which to build my life that I had no choice but to leave. Vera reveals that in the months before my departure, she spent many hours with Käte, seeking her advice on whether she should allow me to leave, and that Käte told her not to try to stop me because that would create a rift which would be harder to bridge than the whole Atlantic Ocean. We talk for a long time about the war and the Holocaust, mass displacement and emigration, and the tragedies that are brought on by these catastrophes, and finally the terrible cycle of unresolved reciprocal injury starts to heal.

The chronicle of my departure contains a few more scenes. There is my visit with Käte, in which I tell her about finally receiving my German passport in the mail, taking it to the American consulate to receive appropriate immigration visa documents, certified copies of which must in turn be presented to the Holland America Line when making reservations for the Atlantic Ocean crossing voyage to New York.

Lately, I had not seen Käte as often as in the past, although we lived so close. This was in part due to her rule that visitors needed to make an appointment because she disliked surprise visits. Käte did not like to be kept waiting, and visitors were expected to show up on time. In the past, there had been occasional uncomfortable moments when she expected me at a certain hour, and I was still rushing around our apartment trying to get something done at the last minute before heading next door; the phone would ring three minutes after the hour, and she would be questioning why I was late. Since I was not home as much now as before, this appointment process became an obstacle to the spontaneous visits that would have fit more easily into my day. Also, I dreaded having to explain to Käte that I was thinking of leaving school without the graduation exams. I had once mentioned to her that I had found myself standing in a packed streetcar one day on my way home from school asking myself why I am even going to school at all, for what purpose? She looked troubled when I said that, and I quickly changed the subject and did not bring up school again.

As I now tell Käte all about the intricacies of my travel preparations and show her a brochure describing the *Maasdam*, a midsize ship for a few hundred passengers and a first-class section for twelve, she laughs and describes the much larger ocean liner that she took years earlier on her own voyage to Canada to visit her friend in Vancouver. We are now in safe waters, away from potentially difficult topics, talking about what to do against seasickness, what kind of weather to expect in November, and how much colder it is on deck when the wind blows hard. Woven into our conversation are wistful comments by Käte hinting at her own dreams in years past of exploring new countries and possibly settling in a new world of her own. I sense in her voice an undertone of deep sadness, and it dawns on me that she will miss me and would have preferred that I stay, but that she generously lets me go on a path that she would have liked to have gone herself.

In that same scene, Käte reaches into her packed wall-to-wall bookshelf and hands me the book on the founders of the world's major religions, the *Sons of God*, which I had marveled at as a child, when I believed what I had been told that there was only one *Son of God*. Looking back on my eleven years of growing up in Frankfurt, one way of measuring my growth during that span of years might be my emerging understanding of what the author must have wanted to express by choosing this title. Käte wants me to take the book with me to America, and I have it to this day.

As the date of my leaving draws closer, the montage of scenes becomes choppier and the images rush by in a cascade of flashbacks: Vera and I are climbing three flights of stairs to a small attic apartment where we meet a tiny, wiry old man who tells us in a Slavic accent that the portable electric sewing machine which he advertised in the paper a few days ago is still available. He invites us into his cramped workroom and tells us about his life as a tailor in a small town in Eastern Poland before and during the war and his escape from communist rule to Western Germany sometime in the late 1940s, where he was able to find customers for his individually cut, sewn, and fitted men's suits and fine wool winter coats. He describes for us how he has done his life's work on a beautiful black-and-silver Singer sewing machine, which was powered by a foot pedal for decades. To prepare for his escape to the West, he shows us how he detached the machine from its workbench with its flywheel and pedal-driven belt and mounted a small electric motor at the rear of the machine, with a power cord leading to a small floor pedal. He cradled his machine in a wooden case so that he could carry it across borders like a suitcase, and when he reached Frankfurt, it provided him with a living for another decade, until now, when he feels too old to go on and wants to see his beloved machine in the hands of people whom he likes. He must have formed a favorable impression of us because he agrees to sell the machine to Vera, who tells him that she is buying it for me, her daughter, so that when I go to America, I can sew my own clothes and window curtains. The tailor is overjoyed that his machine is going to America, a place where he had always wanted to go himself.

In quick succession, there are short takes of Vera and me finding, through another newspaper ad, an authentic steamer trunk from the days when transatlantic travel meant one to two weeks at sea, requiring enormous amounts of luggage for a well-turned-out appearance for dinner every evening. The steamer trunk sits in my room with its lid open, while I decide which things to take for my new life and which things to leave behind. Antoinette brings me two plaid blankets, which go in the bottom, covered by a layer of books, Käte's gift among them, followed by clothes, shoes, and other things which seem like they must come along on one day and look superfluous on the next. Finally, my choices cannot be reversed anymore because a delivery truck arrives to pick up the heavy trunk for advance shipping to the Holland America Line Pier in Rotterdam, and I will not see it again until my arrival in New York.

On the day of departure, Harry shows up in his car. I don't remember if I was surprised or not. He has come from Paris to take James and me to Rotterdam. Vera is accompanying us as well. Harry and Vera are in the front seats; James and I sit in the back. Rotterdam is three hundred miles away, and the *Maasdam* departs in the late afternoon, so the time for goodbyes is short. As we leave, Antoinette is on the landing of the staircase in front of her apartment door, pale and unable to speak, trying not to cry, and I see Käte standing there as well. She has come over to see me off, and when I look at her face, I realize that I have never seen her cry, and now tears are welling up in her eyes, which she is swallowing hard to force back. I don't remember saying goodbye to Stefan and René. I know that I will be overcome by my own feelings if I let the heaviness of the moment sink in, so I numb myself; give hugs; promise to write; walk down the stairs with my sewing machine case in one hand and my travel bag in the other, out the front door, into Harry's car, with James sitting next to me; and we are off. I remember absolutely nothing about the drive to Rotterdam, until we arrive at the Holland America Pier, and there is the *Maasdam,* not immense like the famous *Queen Mary* but daunting nevertheless, when you stand right next to it and are about to board it. The boarding process is a protracted ritual involving the checking of many travel documents. A few close family members are allowed to accompany ticketed passengers on board, but the time for last-minute excited small talk on the large forward deck runs out fast, and soon the public announcement system asks the visitors to leave the ship. I do not try to imagine what Harry and Vera might be feeling at this moment, but I do my best to project confidence and optimism with my levelheaded assurances. I instruct them to stand in a certain spot near the main entrance doors to the terminal building so that I can find them in the small crowd when I get to the upper deck to wave goodbye. I see them wave as the dock workers go through the final maneuvers of disconnecting giant hoses and unfurling the heavy cables which had secured the hull to the bollards; the ship's horn blows from the direction of the bridge, and all of a sudden, there is a moat of dark water between the ship's hull and the pier, and a slight shudder goes through the ship as the passengers jostle for a final glimpse of the people they are leaving behind.

I don't know how Vera got home. I want to believe that Harry drove her home to Frankfurt before hurrying from there to get back to Paris in time for the birth of his new baby daughter, the second of his three children with Paddy. It was November 9, 1960, the eve of the twenty-second anniversary of *Kristallnacht,* the "Night of the Broken Glass," which had signaled to all who were paying attention at the time that the campaign of attacking Jewish lives and property throughout Germany and Austria was now official policy and would henceforth be conducted with unimaginable cruelty in all territories under Nazi control, until the "final solution" to the "Jewish question" was accomplished.

POSTSCRIPT

November crossings of the Atlantic are notoriously rough, and this voyage was no exception. The *Maasdam*'s itinerary called for a quick trip across the English Channel to the Irish port of Cobh, where a few passengers were waiting, along with a harbor pilot to guide the *Maasdam* safely back out to sea. By the time the tricky coastal waters had been navigated, a predicted powerful storm was arriving early, and it was too dangerous for the pilot to leave the ship. He had obviously been in this situation before and headed straight for the bar, where he sat drinking for the next fourteen days, the first seven of which saw the *Maasdam* shovel and plow its way through the crashing waves at about the same speed with which the storm pushed it back toward Ireland. The second week of the passage was calmer, but my seasickness never went away completely.

Our companions in the ordeal were mostly Dutch families who had been expelled from what they thought for generations was their homeland in the Dutch East Indies when the native population rose up against their colonial overlords after the end of World War II and proclaimed their independent nation of Indonesia. The expelled colonials had found themselves unwelcome back in Holland and were now continuing their migration in search of a new homeland, which they hoped to find in the United States or in Canada. There were a few bored first-class passengers returning home to New York and Connecticut who came downstairs to socialize and ask if anyone knew the results of the American elections held a few days earlier. They had voted for Richard Nixon, but if they were upset by John Kennedy's victory, as announced in a special bulletin from the captain, they didn't show it.

As the *Maasdam* made its way across the Atlantic and was now closer to the American coast than to Europe, I allowed myself for the first time to give some thought to the reality that I was pregnant. I had decided to leave this fact unmentioned during the weeks leading up to my departure since I was certain that it would have added yet another emotional layer to the already intense feelings with which my family watched me get ready to leave. Now that I was closer to my future than to my past, it seemed appropriate to begin to acknowledge that I would have a child to take care of by the end of the long New York winter, which was starting soon. I was unclear about the details of how all this would come about but felt unshakably confident that everything would work out.

The *Maasdam* entered New York Harbor a week late, just in time for Thanksgiving. It was a foggy late November morning shortly after sunrise, and those travelers who had awakened early to catch a first glimpse of the Manhattan skyline and now stood shivering in the cold wind on the upper deck were rewarded with the view of the Statue of Liberty, a distant ethereal greenish apparition hovering in the rosy morning mist over the white-capped waters of New York Harbor. Estimating the distance across the wide mouth of the harbor, a viewer could calculate that the statue had to be colossal, but at the moment when the *Maasdam* greeted it from afar, it looked like a fragile figurine hovering above the waves. It did not occur to me as an idealistic young immigrant that the iconic structure would within my lifetime be reconfigured by the United States Citizenship and Immigration Services from a beacon of hope for "the tired and the poor...yearning to breathe free" to an ornamental marker on the final approach to Fortress America.

ABOUT THE AUTHOR

Heidi Laird immigrated from Germany in 1960. She raised her two young children in Tucson, where she studied German literature, philosophy, and psychology at the University of Arizona. After obtaining graduate degrees at the University of California at Riverside, where her special focus was on the study of the authoritarian personality, she turned from teaching to clinical work as a psychologist. She recently retired after thirty years in private practice specializing in the treatment of childhood trauma. She lives in Southern California.

9 781649 529749